THE HULK WILL ALWAYS BE A PART OF DR. BRUCE BANNER, BUT BANNER WANTS TO BE REMEMBERED FOR HIS CONTRIBUTIONS TO SCIENCE AND NOT FOR TURNING INTO A BIG, GREEN FORCE OF RAGE AND DESTRUCTION. TO ACHIEVE THAT GOAL, BANNER HAS STRUCK A MUTUALLY BENEFICIAL DEAL WITH MARIA HILL, THE DIRECTOR OF S.H.I.E.L.D. SHE PROVIDES BANNER WITH A LAB, STAFF AND ALL OF THE RESOURCES HE NEEDS TO BETTER MANKIND, AND BANNER PROVIDES S.H.I.E.L.D. WITH THE HULK FOR ANY MISSIONS THAT MIGHT NEED EXTRA MUSCLE.

INDESTRUCTIBLE
HULK

GODS AND MONSTER

WITHDRAWN

VOLUME 02

INDESTRUCTIBLE HULK VOL. 2: GODS AND MONSTER. Contains material originally published in magazine form as INDESTRUCTIBLE HULK #6-10. First printing 2013. ISBN# 978-0-7851-6832-4. Published by MARVEL WORLDWIDE, INC., a subsidiary of MARVEL ENTERTAINMENT, LLC. OFFICE OF PUBLICATION: 135 West 50th Street, New York, NY 10020. Copyright © 2013 Marvel Characters, Inc. All rights reserved. All characters featured in this issue and the distinctive names and likenesses thereof, and all related indicia are trademarks of Marvel Characters, Inc. No similarity between any of the names, characters, persons, and/or institutions in this magazine with those of any living or dead person or institution is intended, and any such similarity which may exist is purely coincidental. **Printed in the U.S.A.** ALAN FINE, EVP - Office of the President, Marvel Worldwide, Inc. and EVP & CMO Marvel Characters B.V.; DAN BUCKLEY, Publisher & President - Print, Animation & Digital Divisions; JOE QUESADA, Chief Creative Officer; TOM BREVOORT, SVP of Publishing; DAVID BOGART, SVP of Operations & Procurement, Publishing; C.B. CEBULSKI, SVP of Creator & Content Development; DAVID GABRIEL, SVP of Print & Digital Publishing Sales; JIM O'KEEFE, VP of Operations & Logistics; DAN CARR, Executive Director of Publishing Technology; SUSAN CRESPI, Editorial Operations Manager; ALEX MORALES, Publishing Operations Manager; STAN LEE, Chairman Emeritus. For information regarding advertising in Marvel Comics or on Marvel.com, please contact Niza Disla, Director of Marvel Partnerships, at ndisla@marvel.com. For Marvel subscription inquiries, please call 800-217-9158. **Manufactured between 7/12/2013 and 8/26/2013 by R.R. DONNELLEY, INC., SALEM, VA, USA.**

10 9 8 7 6 5 4 3 2 1

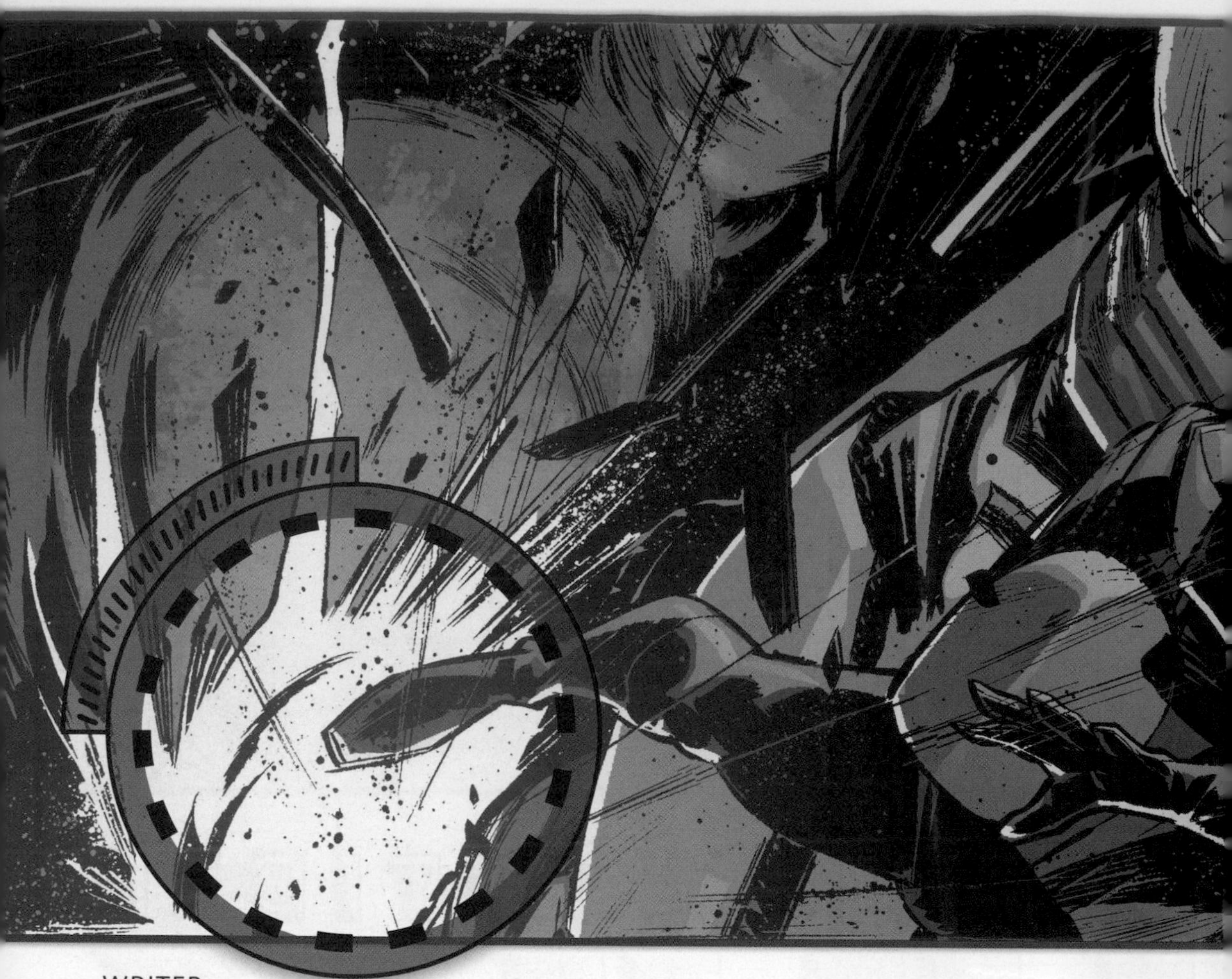

WRITER
MARK WAID
ARTISTS
WALTER SIMONSON (#6-8)
& **MATTEO SCALERA** (#9-10)
INK ASSISTS (#7-8) **BOB WIACEK**
COLOR ARTISTS
ANDRES MOSSA (#6-7), **JIM CHARALAMPIDIS** (#8)
& **VAL STAPLES** (#9-10)
LETTERER
CHRIS ELIOPOULOS
COVER ART
WALTER SIMONSON & **LAURA MARTIN** (#6-8)
& **PAOLO RIVERA** (#9-10)
ASSISTANT EDITOR
JON MOISAN
EDITOR
MARK PANI(

COLLECTION EDITOR
JENNIFER GRÜNWAL
ASSISTANT EDITORS
ALEX STARBUCK
NELSON RIBEIRO
EDITOR, SPECIAL PROJECTS
MARK D. BEAZLEY

DAVID GABRIEL

EDITOR IN CHIEF
AXEL ALONSO
CHIEF CREATIVE OFFICER
JOE QUESADA
PUBLISHER
DAN BUCKLEY
EXECUTIVE PRODUCER
ALAN FINE

PREVIOUSLY

WITH THE EARTH'S OCEANS OVERRUN BY SEA MONSTERS, S.H.I.E.L.D. SENT BRUCE TO GO GREEN, SUBMERGE AND SMASH. HOWEVER, THE ROGUE ATLANTEAN WARLORD ATTUMA WAS BEHIND THE MONSTER ATTACKS AND TRAPPED HULK AT THE BOTTOM OF THE OCEAN. NEAR DEATH, THE BIG GREEN GUY WAS RESCUED BY LEMURIAN REBELS, WHO REVEALED THAT ATTUMA PLANNED TO WIPE OUT ALL SURFACE LIFE ON EARTH. TEAMING UP WITH THE REBELS, HULK WAS ABLE TO HELP THEM TURN THE TIDE AND STOP ATTUMA.

NOW, HAVING LEFT LEMURIA WITH INVALUABLE TREASURES AND ALLIES, BRUCE CONTINUES TO LIVE UP TO HIS END OF THE DEAL WITH S.H.I.E.L.D.

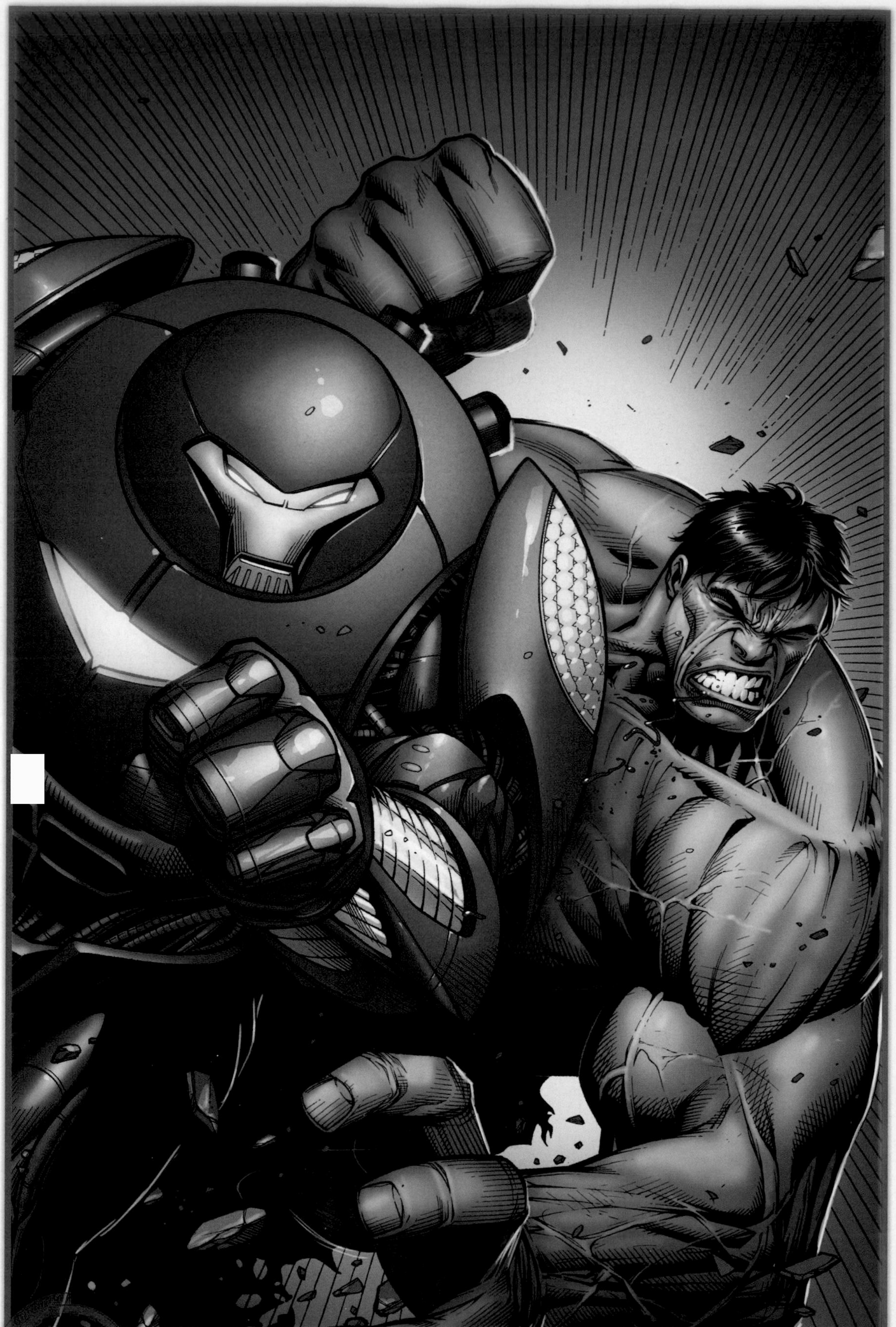

MANY ARMORS OF IRON MAN VARIANT BY DALE KEOWN

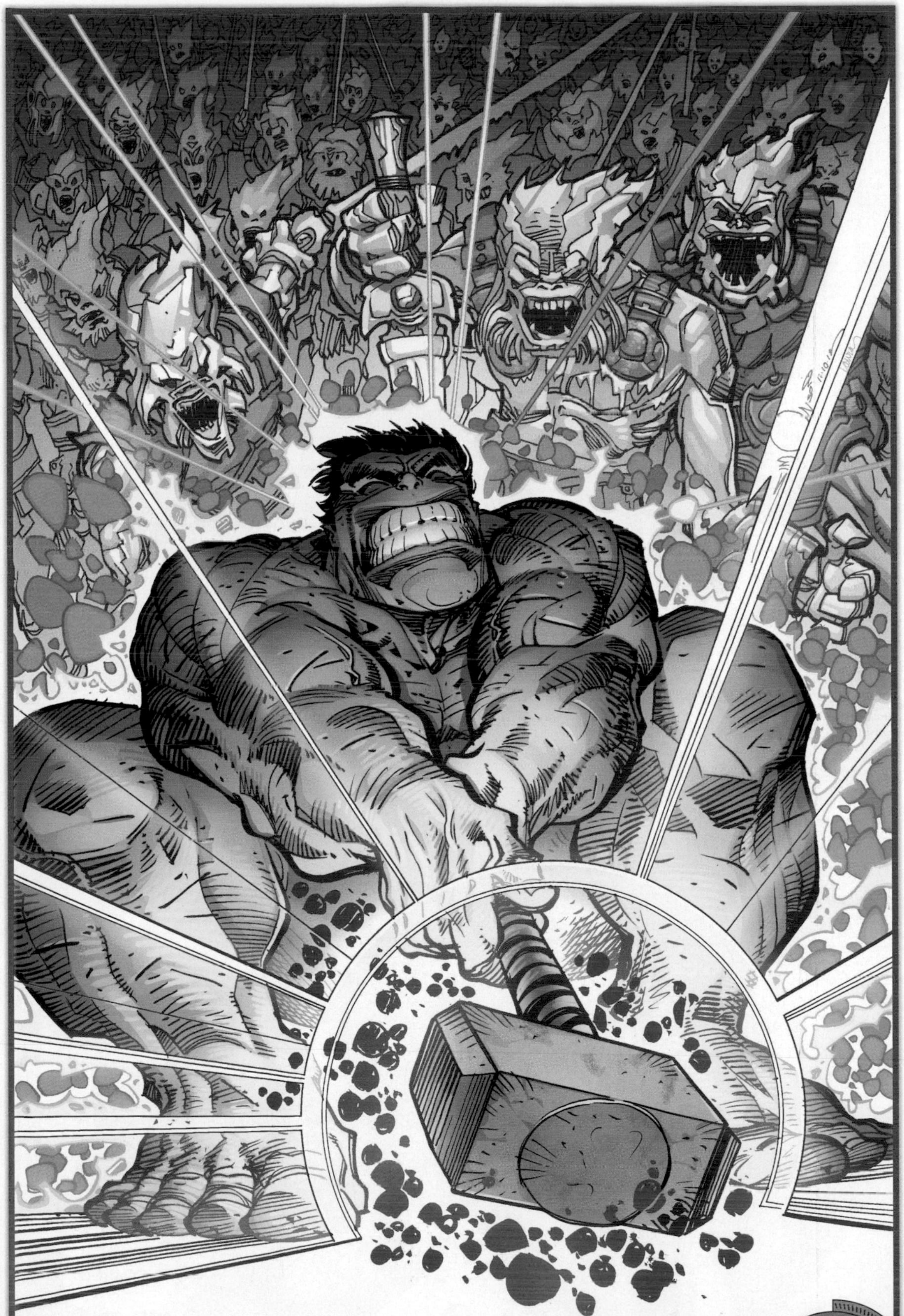

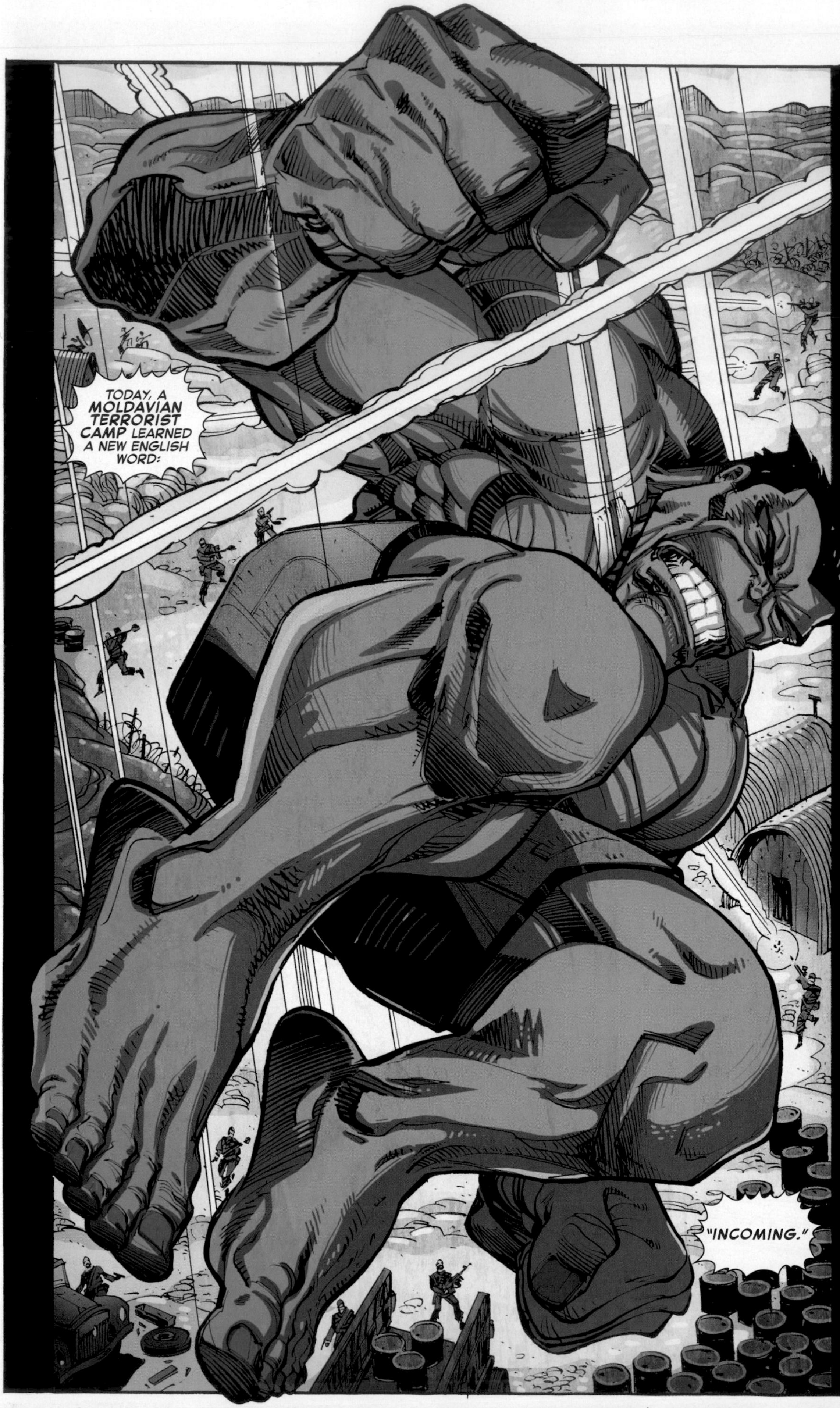
TODAY, A MOLDAVIAN TERRORIST CAMP LEARNED A NEW ENGLISH WORD:
"INCOMING."

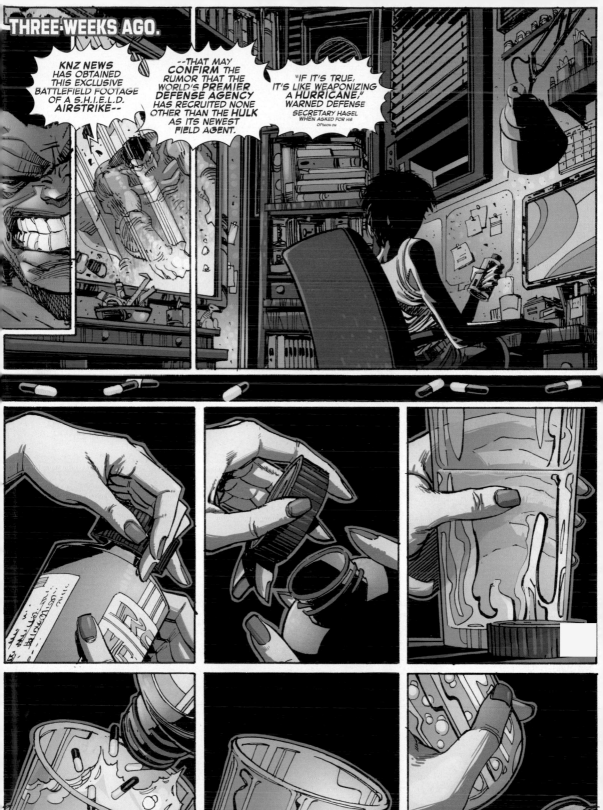

KNZ NEWS HAS OBTAINED THIS EXCLUSIVE BATTLEFIELD FOOTAGE OF A S.H.I.E.L.D. AIRSTRIKE--

--THAT MAY CONFIRM THE RUMOR THAT THE WORLD'S PREMIER DEFENSE AGENCY HAS RECRUITED NONE OTHER THAN THE HULK AS ITS NEWEST FIELD AGENT.

"IF IT'S TRUE, IT'S LIKE WEAPONIZING A HURRICANE," WARNED DEFENSE SECRETARY HAGEL WHEN ASKED FOR HIS OPINION ON

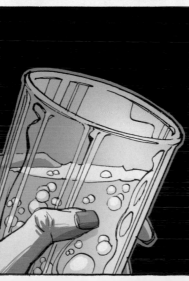

DING

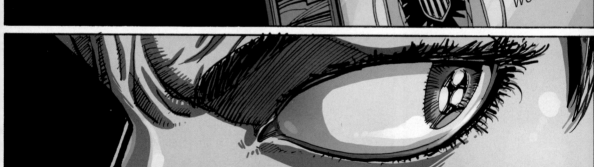

1 NEW EMAIL

FROM:
S.H.I.E.L.D.

ATTN:
DR. PATRICIA WOLMAN

EYES ONLY

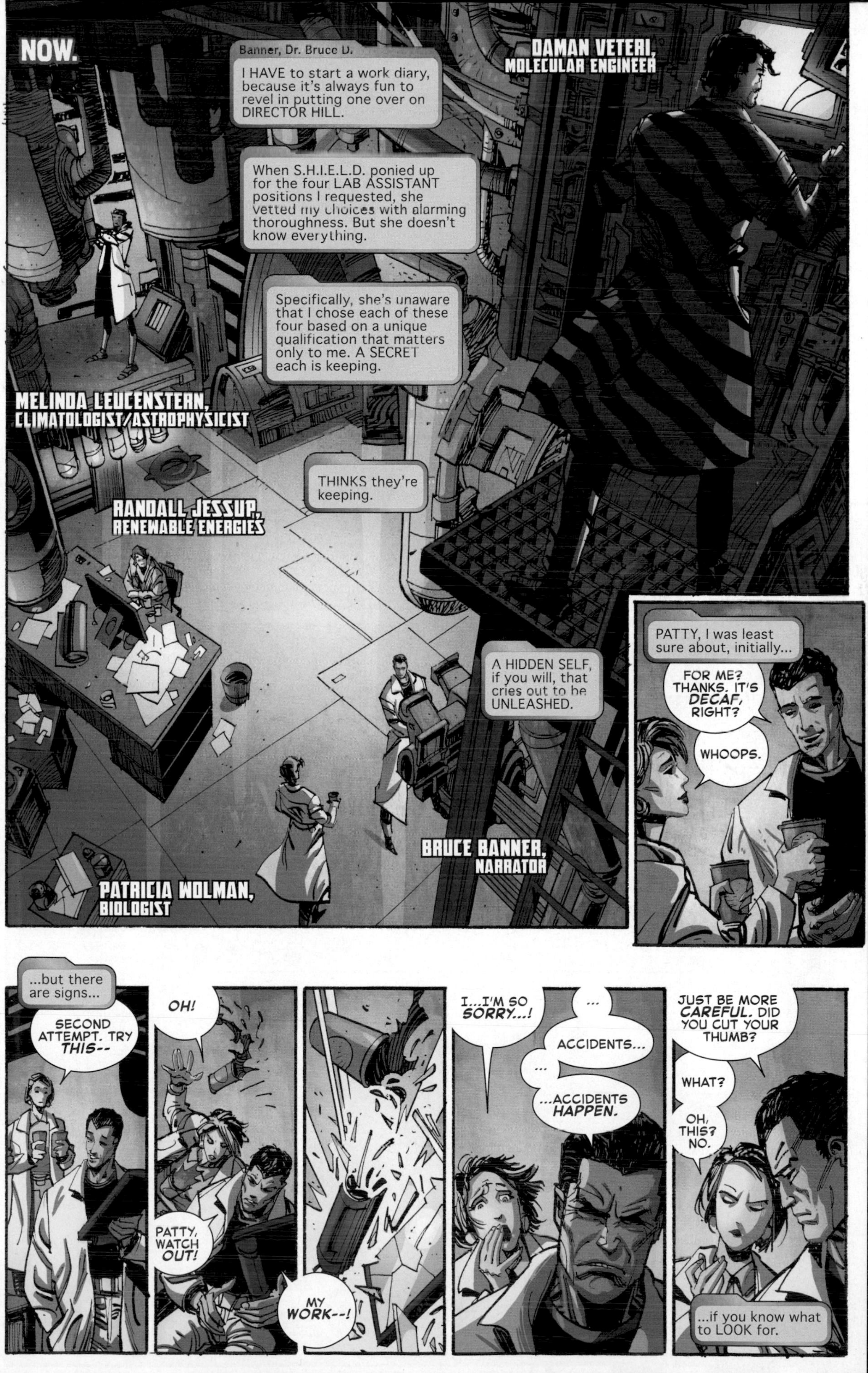

NOW.
Banner, Dr. Bruce D.
I HAVE to start a work diary, because it's always fun to revel in putting one over on DIRECTOR HILL.
DAMAN VETERI, MOLECULAR ENGINEER
When S.H.I.E.L.D. ponied up for the four LAB ASSISTANT positions I requested, she vetted my choices with alarming thoroughness. But she doesn't know everything.
Specifically, she's unaware that I chose each of these four based on a unique qualification that matters only to me. A SECRET each is keeping.
MELINDA LEUCENSTERN, CLIMATOLOGIST/ASTROPHYSICIST
THINKS they're keeping.
RANDALL JESSUP, RENEWABLE ENERGIES
A HIDDEN SELF, if you will, that cries out to be UNLEASHED.
BRUCE BANNER, NARRATOR
PATRICIA WOLMAN, BIOLOGIST
PATTY, I was least sure about, initially...
FOR ME? THANKS. IT'S DECAF, RIGHT?
WHOOPS.
...but there are signs...
SECOND ATTEMPT. TRY THIS--
OH!
PATTY, WATCH OUT!
MY WORK--!
I...I'M SO SORRY...!
...
ACCIDENTS...
...
...ACCIDENTS HAPPEN.
JUST BE MORE CAREFUL. DID YOU CUT YOUR THUMB?
WHAT?
OH, THIS? NO.
...if you know what to LOOK for.

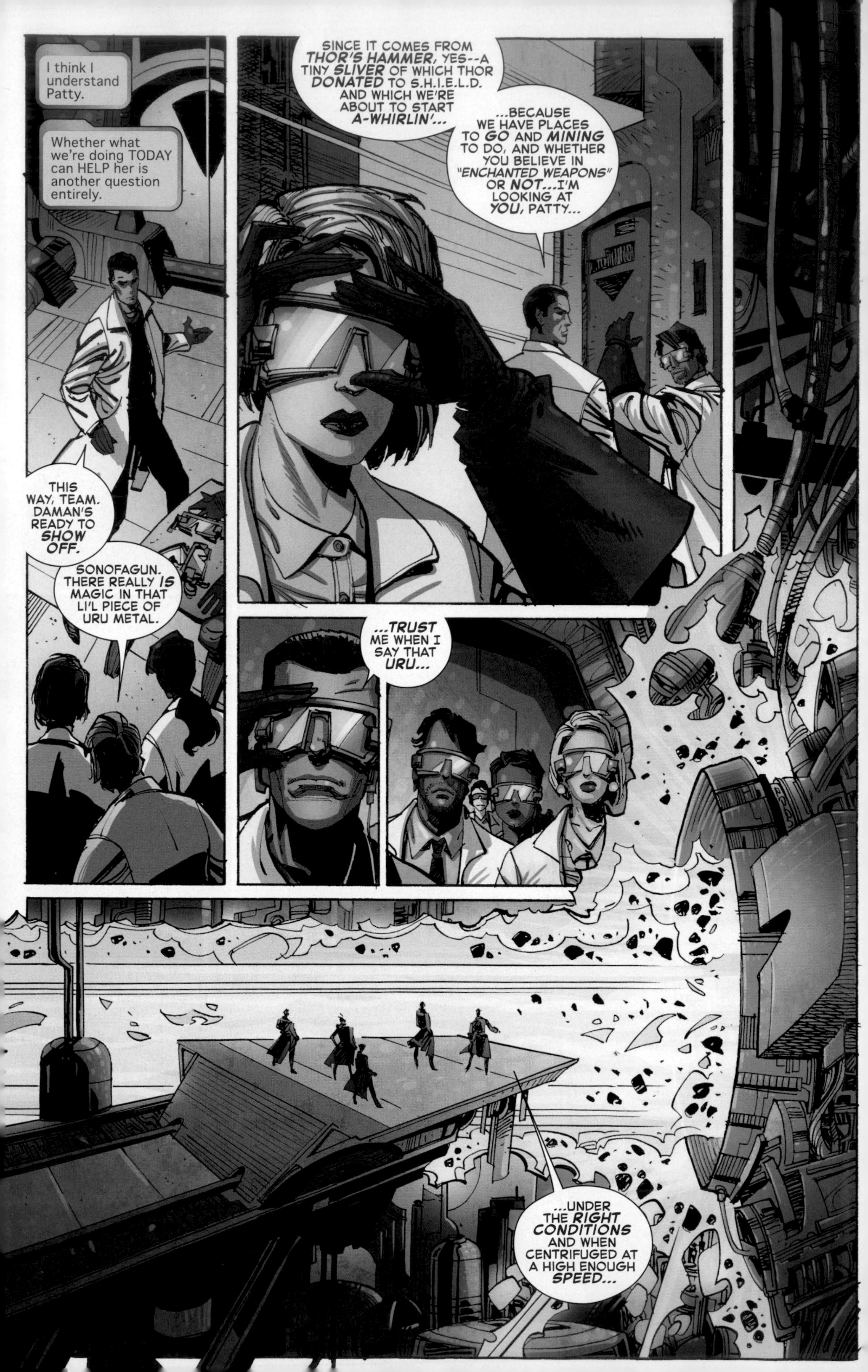
I think I understand Patty.
Whether what we're doing TODAY can HELP her is another question entirely.
SINCE IT COMES FROM THOR'S HAMMER, YES--A TINY SLIVER OF WHICH THOR DONATED TO S.H.I.E.L.D. AND WHICH WE'RE ABOUT TO START A-WHIRLIN'...
...BECAUSE WE HAVE PLACES TO GO AND MINING TO DO, AND WHETHER YOU BELIEVE IN "ENCHANTED WEAPONS" OR NOT...I'M LOOKING AT YOU, PATTY...
THIS WAY, TEAM. DAMAN'S READY TO SHOW OFF.
SONOFAGUN. THERE REALLY IS MAGIC IN THAT LI'L PIECE OF URU METAL.
...TRUST ME WHEN I SAY THAT URU...
...UNDER THE RIGHT CONDITIONS AND WHEN CENTRIFUGED AT A HIGH ENOUGH SPEED...

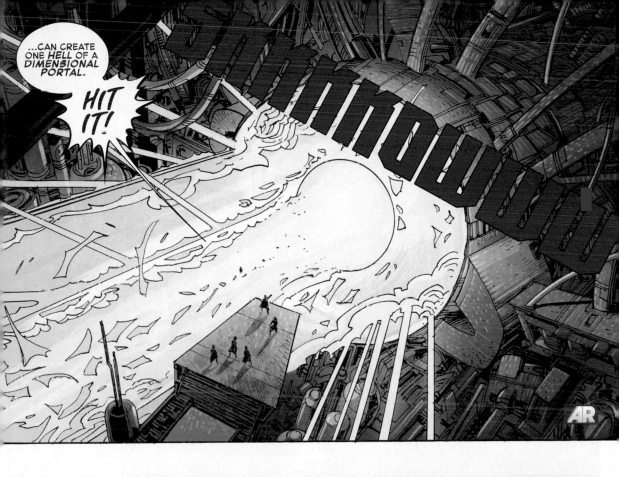

...CAN CREATE ONE *HELL* OF A DIMENSIONAL PORTAL.

HIT IT!

ELSEWHERE.

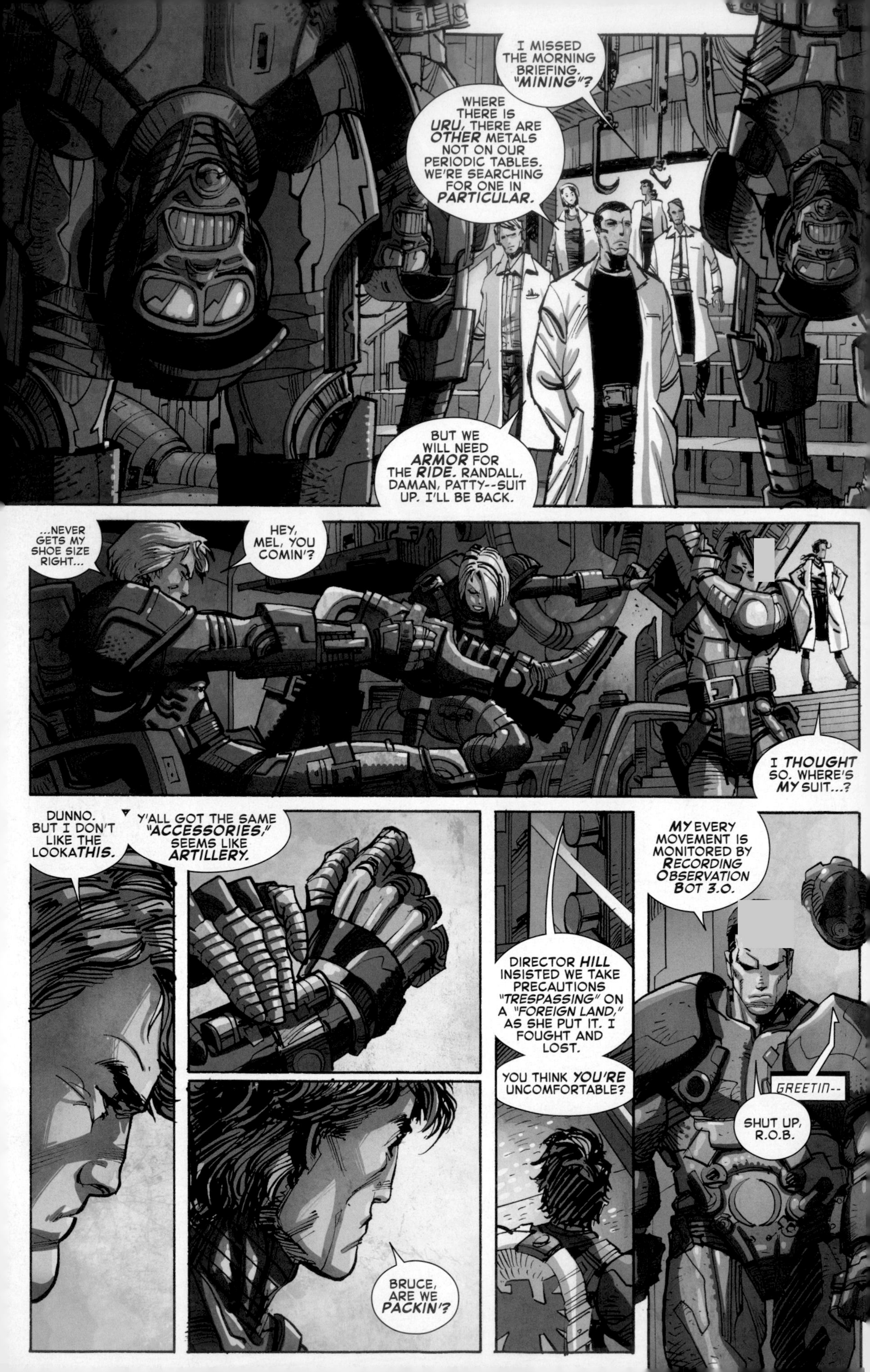
I MISSED THE MORNING BRIEFING. "MINING"?
WHERE THERE IS URU, THERE ARE OTHER METALS NOT ON OUR PERIODIC TABLES. WE'RE SEARCHING FOR ONE IN PARTICULAR.
BUT WE WILL NEED ARMOR FOR THE RIDE. RANDALL, DAMAN, PATTY--SUIT UP. I'LL BE BACK.
...NEVER GETS MY SHOE SIZE RIGHT...
HEY, MEL, YOU COMIN'?
I THOUGHT SO. WHERE'S MY SUIT...?
DUNNO. BUT I DON'T LIKE THE LOOKATHIS.
Y'ALL GOT THE SAME "ACCESSORIES," SEEMS LIKE ARTILLERY.
BRUCE, ARE WE PACKIN'?
DIRECTOR HILL INSISTED WE TAKE PRECAUTIONS "TRESPASSING" ON A "FOREIGN LAND," AS SHE PUT IT. I FOUGHT AND LOST.
YOU THINK YOU'RE UNCOMFORTABLE?
MY EVERY MOVEMENT IS MONITORED BY RECORDING OBSERVATION BOT 3.0.
GREETIN--
SHUT UP, R.O.B.

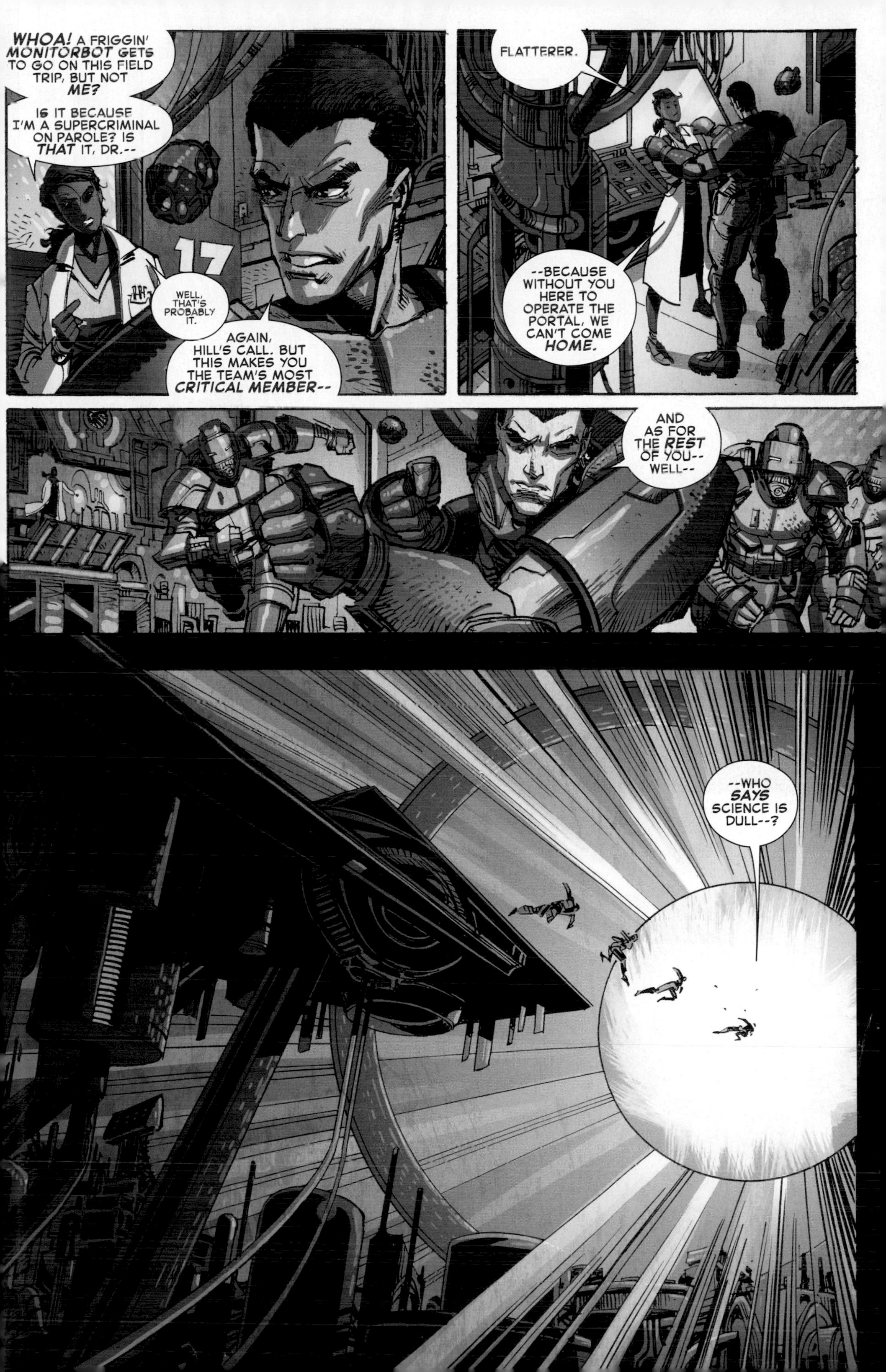
WHOA! A FRIGGIN' MONITORBOT GETS TO GO ON THIS FIELD TRIP, BUT NOT ME?
IS IT BECAUSE I'M A SUPERCRIMINAL ON PAROLE? IS THAT IT, DR.--
WELL, THAT'S PROBABLY IT.
AGAIN, HILL'S CALL. BUT THIS MAKES YOU THE TEAM'S MOST CRITICAL MEMBER--
FLATTERER.
--BECAUSE WITHOUT YOU HERE TO OPERATE THE PORTAL, WE CAN'T COME HOME.
AND AS FOR THE REST OF YOU-- WELL--
--WHO SAYS SCIENCE IS DULL--?

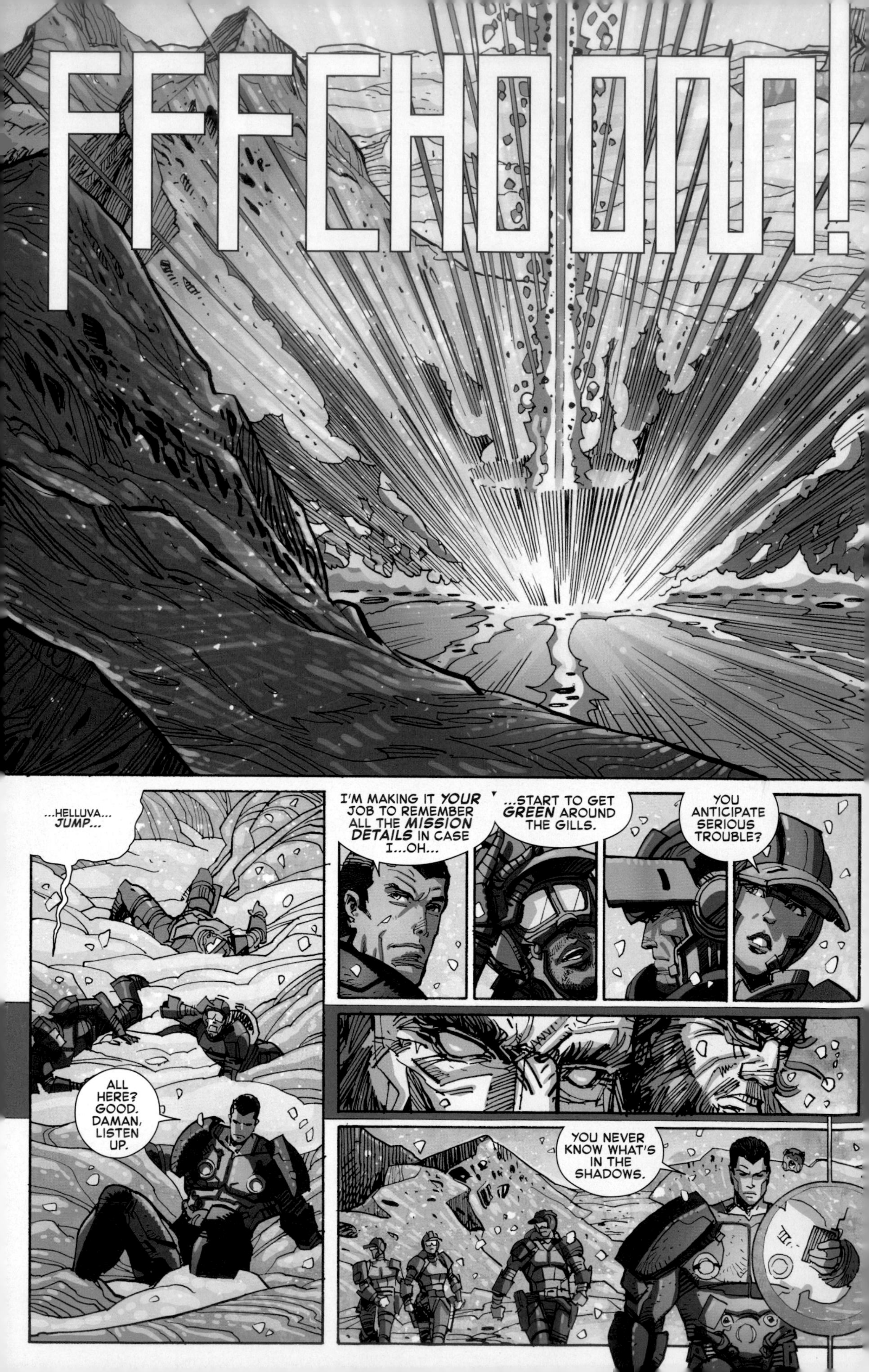
FFFCHOOM!
...HELLUVA... JUMP...
ALL HERE? GOOD. DAMAN, LISTEN UP.
I'M MAKING IT YOUR JOB TO REMEMBER ALL THE MISSION DETAILS IN CASE I...OH...
...START TO GET GREEN AROUND THE GILLS.
YOU ANTICIPATE SERIOUS TROUBLE?
YOU NEVER KNOW WHAT'S IN THE SHADOWS.

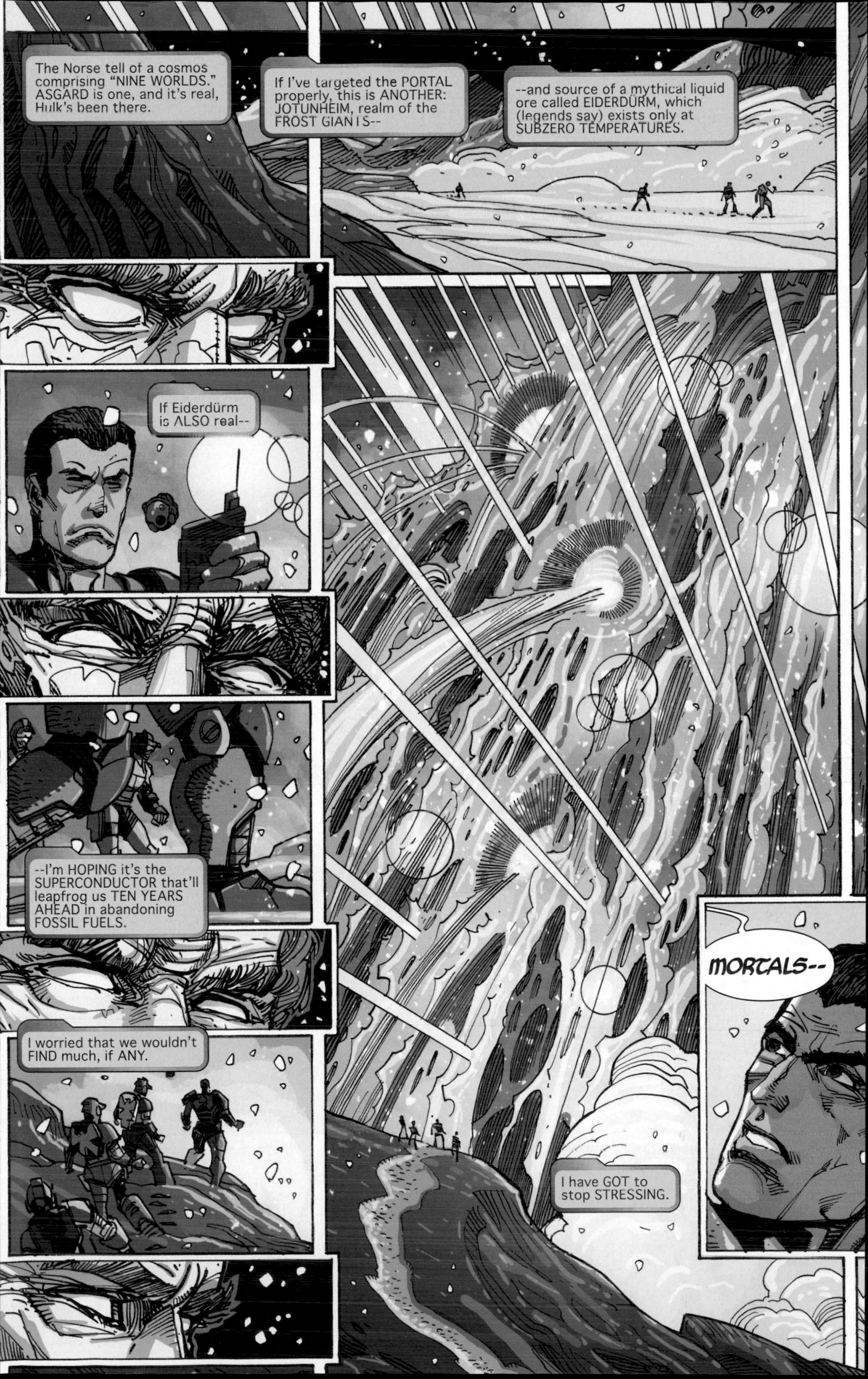

The Norse tell of a cosmos comprising "NINE WORLDS." ASGARD is one, and it's real, Hulk's been there.
If I've targeted the PORTAL properly, this is ANOTHER: JOTUNHEIM, realm of the FROST GIANTS--
--and source of a mythical liquid ore called EIDERDÜRM, which (legends say) exists only at SUBZERO TEMPERATURES.
If Eiderdürm is ALSO real--
--I'm HOPING it's the SUPERCONDUCTOR that'll leapfrog us TEN YEARS AHEAD in abandoning FOSSIL FUELS.
I worried that we wouldn't FIND much, if ANY.
I have GOT to stop STRESSING.
MORTALS--

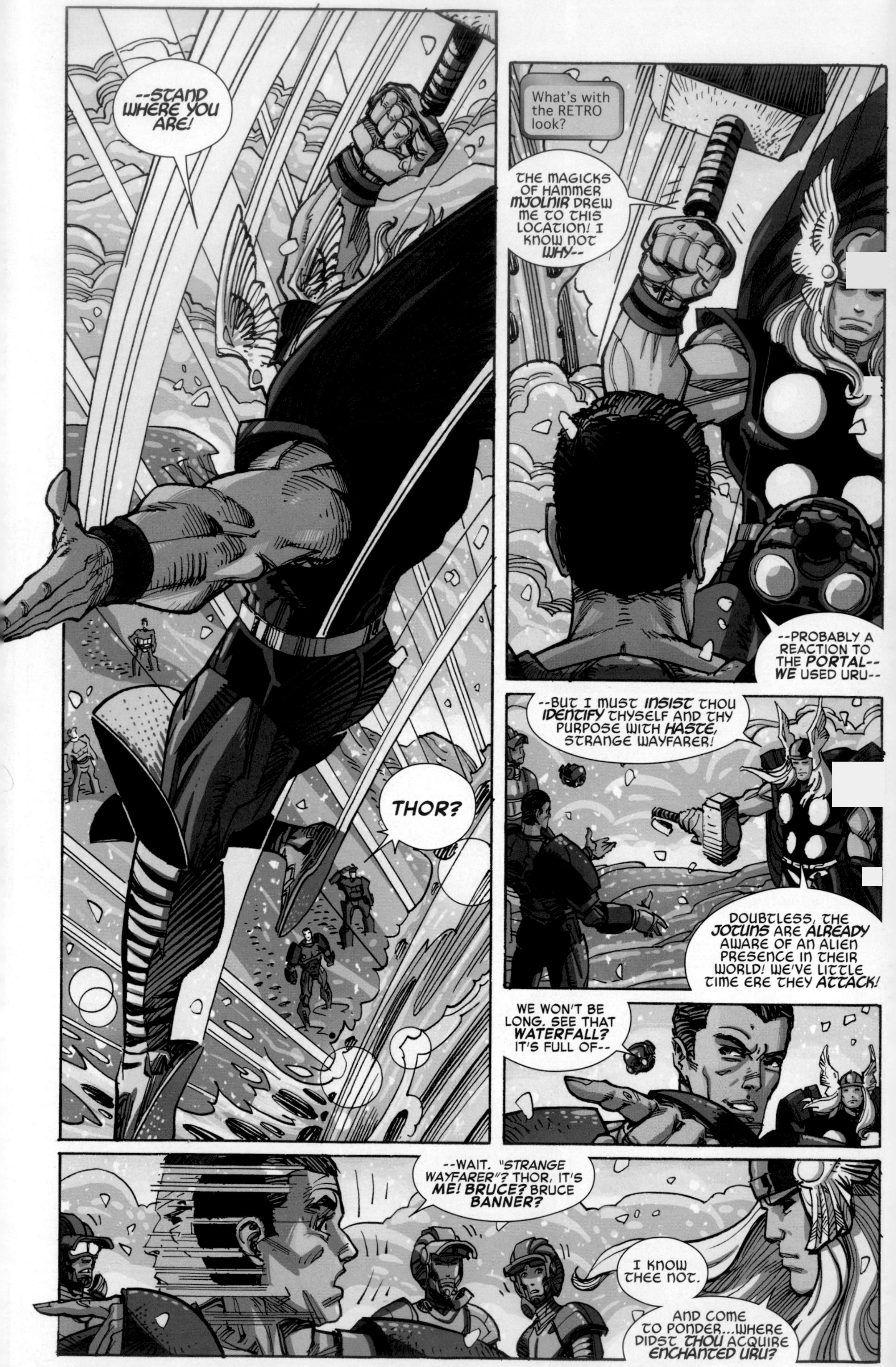
--STAND WHERE YOU ARE!
THOR?
What's with the RETRO look?
THE MAGICKS OF HAMMER MJOLNIR DREW ME TO THIS LOCATION! I KNOW NOT WHY--
--PROBABLY A REACTION TO THE PORTAL--WE USED URU--
--BUT I MUST INSIST THOU IDENTIFY THYSELF AND THY PURPOSE WITH HASTE, STRANGE WAYFARER!
DOUBTLESS, THE JOTUNS ARE ALREADY AWARE OF AN ALIEN PRESENCE IN THEIR WORLD! WE'VE LITTLE TIME ERE THEY ATTACK!
WE WON'T BE LONG. SEE THAT WATERFALL? IT'S FULL OF--
--WAIT. "STRANGE WAYFARER"? THOR, IT'S ME! BRUCE? BRUCE BANNER?
I KNOW THEE NOT.
AND COME TO PONDER...WHERE DIDST THOU ACQUIRE ENCHANTED URU?

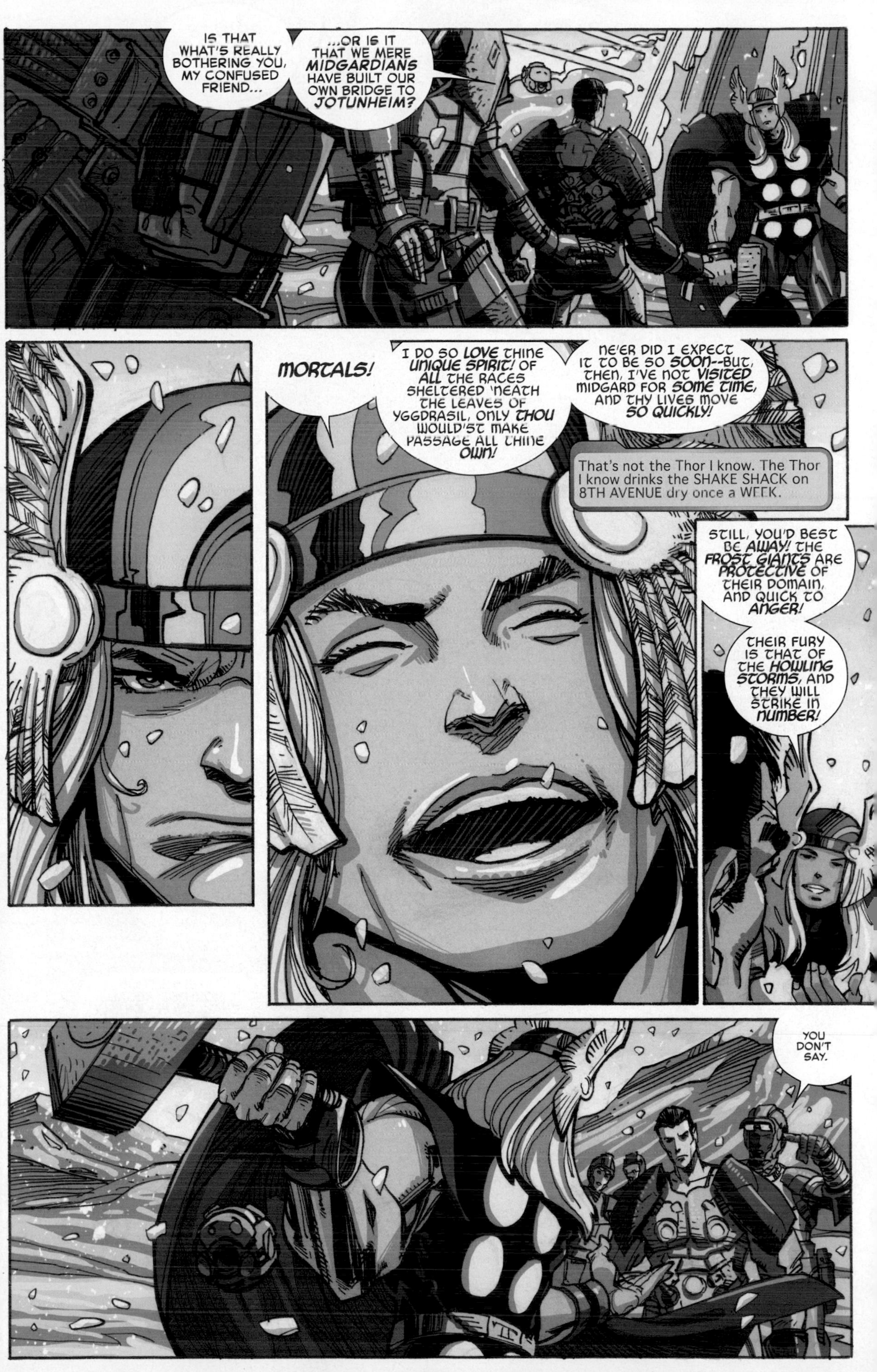
IS THAT WHAT'S REALLY BOTHERING YOU, MY CONFUSED FRIEND...
...OR IS IT THAT WE MERE MIDGARDIANS HAVE BUILT OUR OWN BRIDGE TO JOTUNHEIM?
MORTALS!
I DO SO LOVE THINE UNIQUE SPIRIT! OF ALL THE RACES SHELTERED 'NEATH THE LEAVES OF YGGDRASIL, ONLY THOU WOULD'ST MAKE PASSAGE ALL THINE OWN!
NE'ER DID I EXPECT IT TO BE SO SOON--BUT, THEN, I'VE NOT VISITED MIDGARD FOR SOME TIME, AND THY LIVES MOVE SO QUICKLY!
That's not the Thor I know. The Thor I know drinks the SHAKE SHACK on 8TH AVENUE dry once a WEEK.
STILL, YOU'D BEST BE AWAY! THE FROST GIANTS ARE PROTECTIVE OF THEIR DOMAIN, AND QUICK TO ANGER!
THEIR FURY IS THAT OF THE HOWLING STORMS, AND THEY WILL STRIKE IN NUMBER!
YOU DON'T SAY.

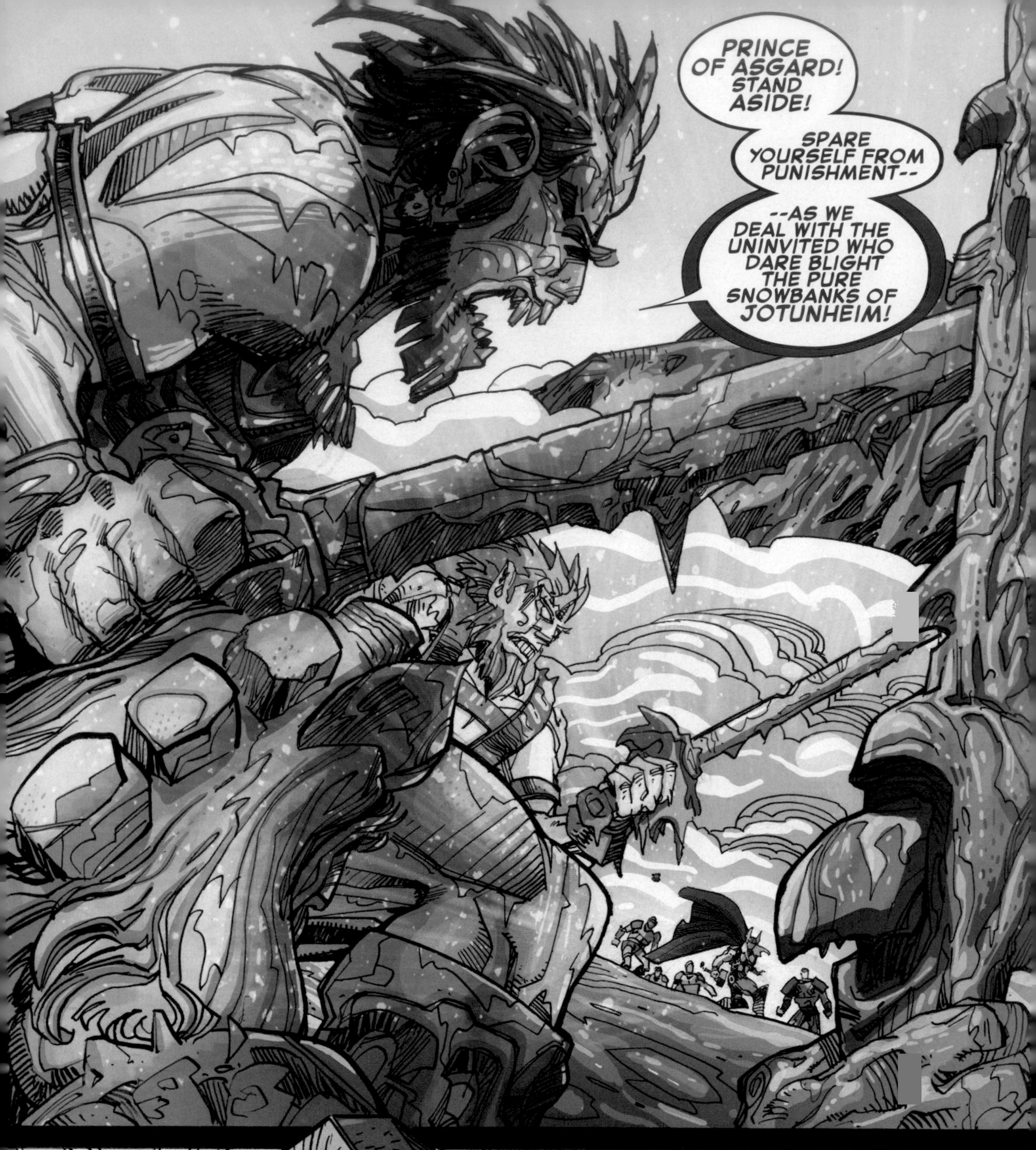
PRINCE OF ASGARD! STAND ASIDE!
SPARE YOURSELF FROM PUNISHMENT--
--AS WE DEAL WITH THE UNINVITED WHO DARE BLIGHT THE PURE SNOWBANKS OF JOTUNHEIM!
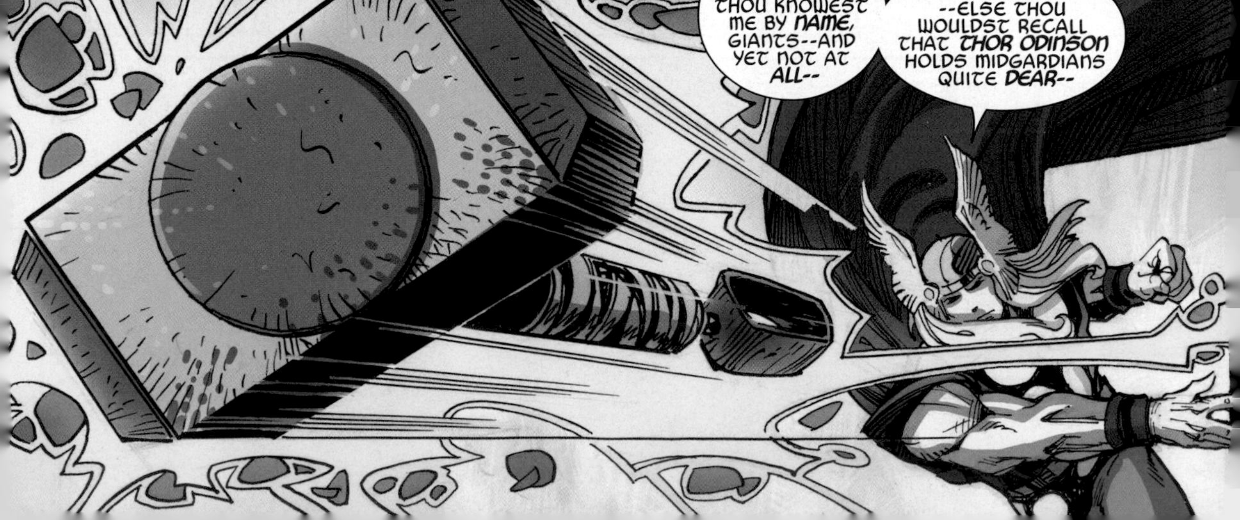
THOU KNOWEST ME BY NAME, GIANTS--AND YET NOT AT ALL--
--ELSE THOU WOULDST RECALL THAT THOR ODINSON HOLDS MIDGARDIANS QUITE DEAR--

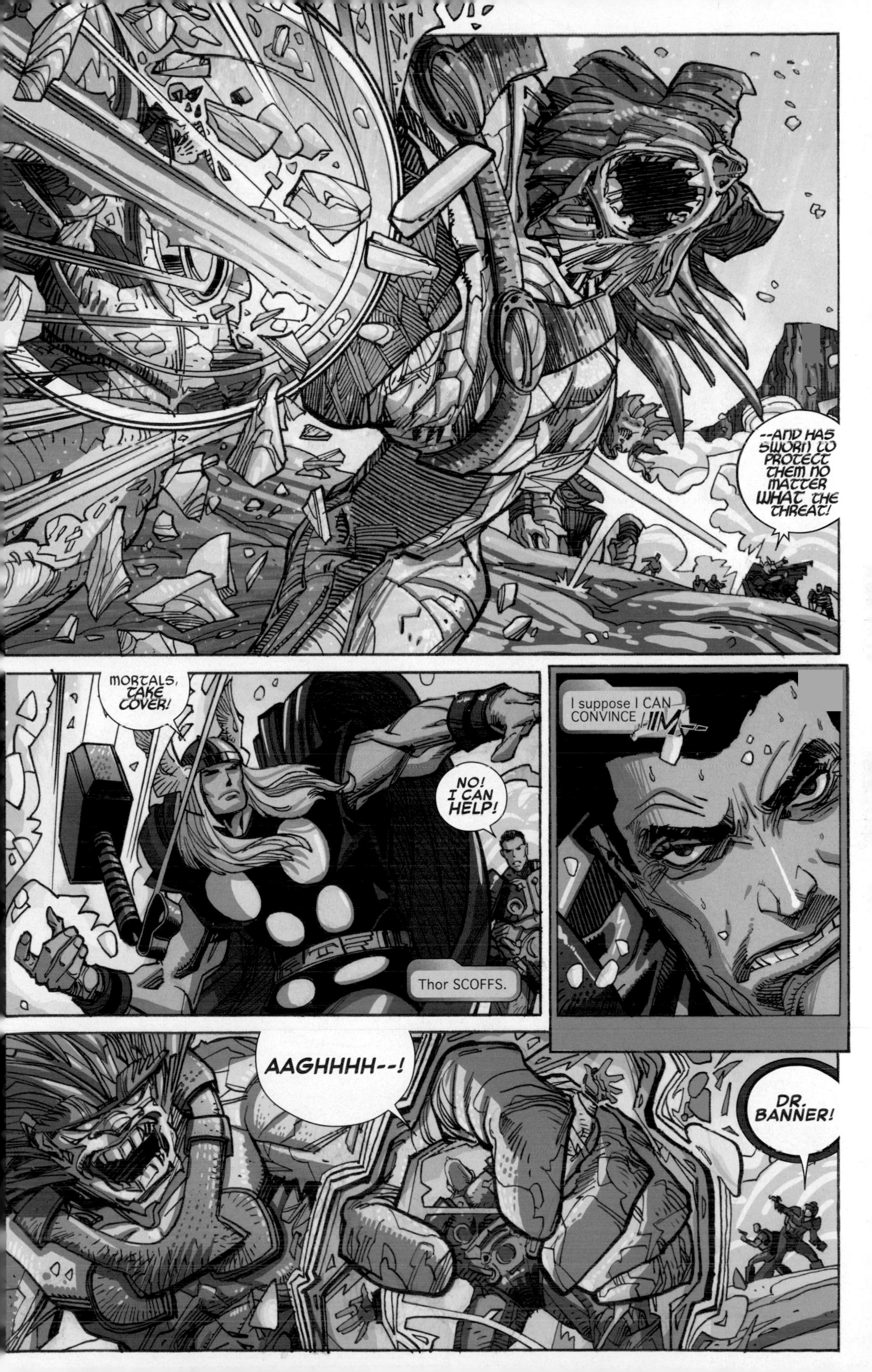
--AND HAS SWORN TO PROTECT THEM NO MATTER WHAT THE THREAT!
MORTALS, TAKE COVER!
NO! I CAN HELP!
Thor SCOFFS.
I suppose I CAN CONVINCE HIM--
AAGHHHH--!
DR. BANNER!

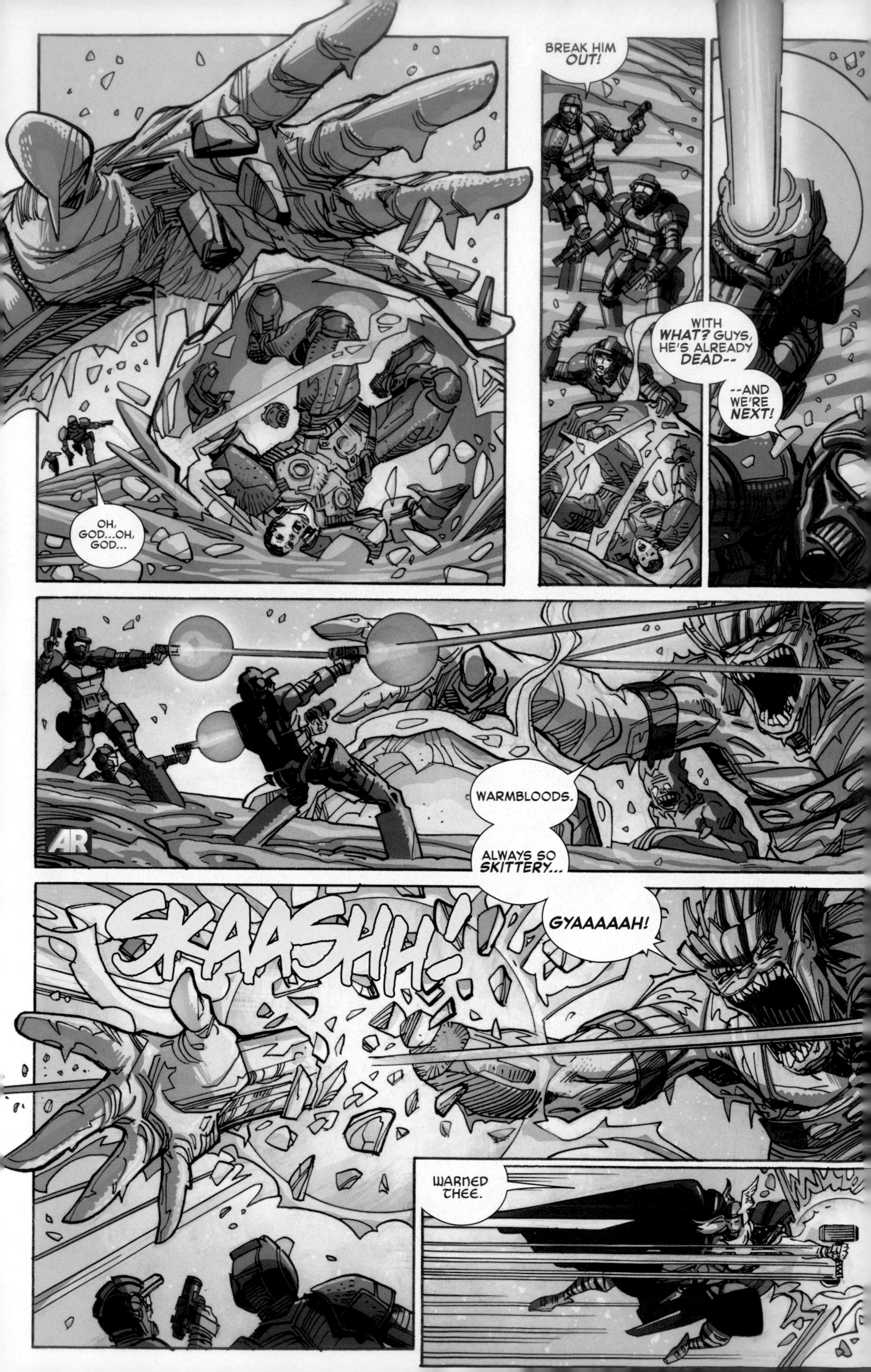
OH, GOD...OH, GOD...
BREAK HIM OUT!
WITH WHAT? GUYS, HE'S ALREADY DEAD--
--AND WE'RE NEXT!
WARMBLOODS.
ALWAYS SO SKITTERY...
SKAASHH!
GYAAAAAH!
WARNED THEE.

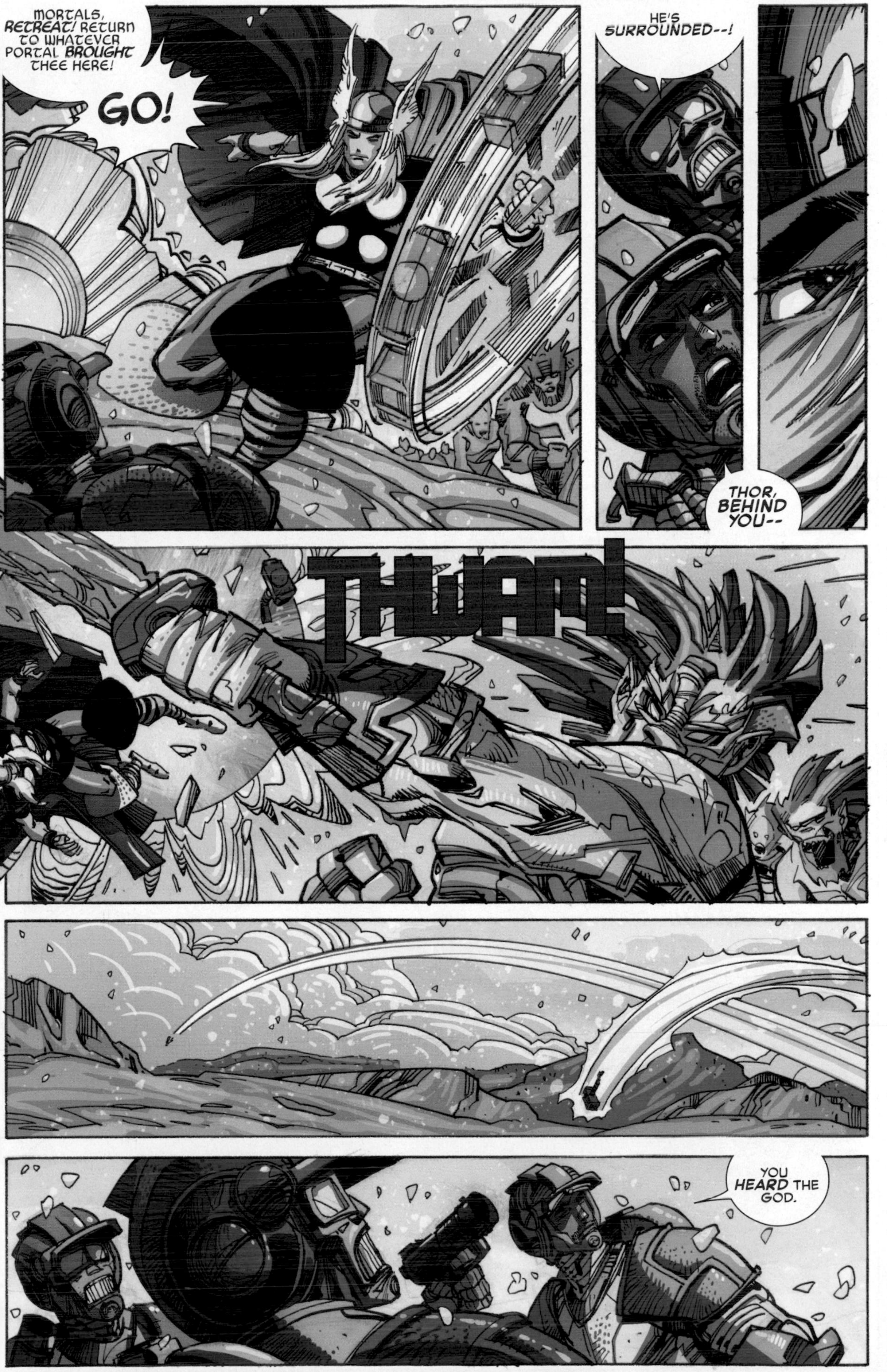
MORTALS, RETREAT! RETURN TO WHATEVER PORTAL BROUGHT THEE HERE!
GO!
HE'S SURROUNDED--!
THOR, BEHIND YOU--
THWAM!
YOU HEARD THE GOD.

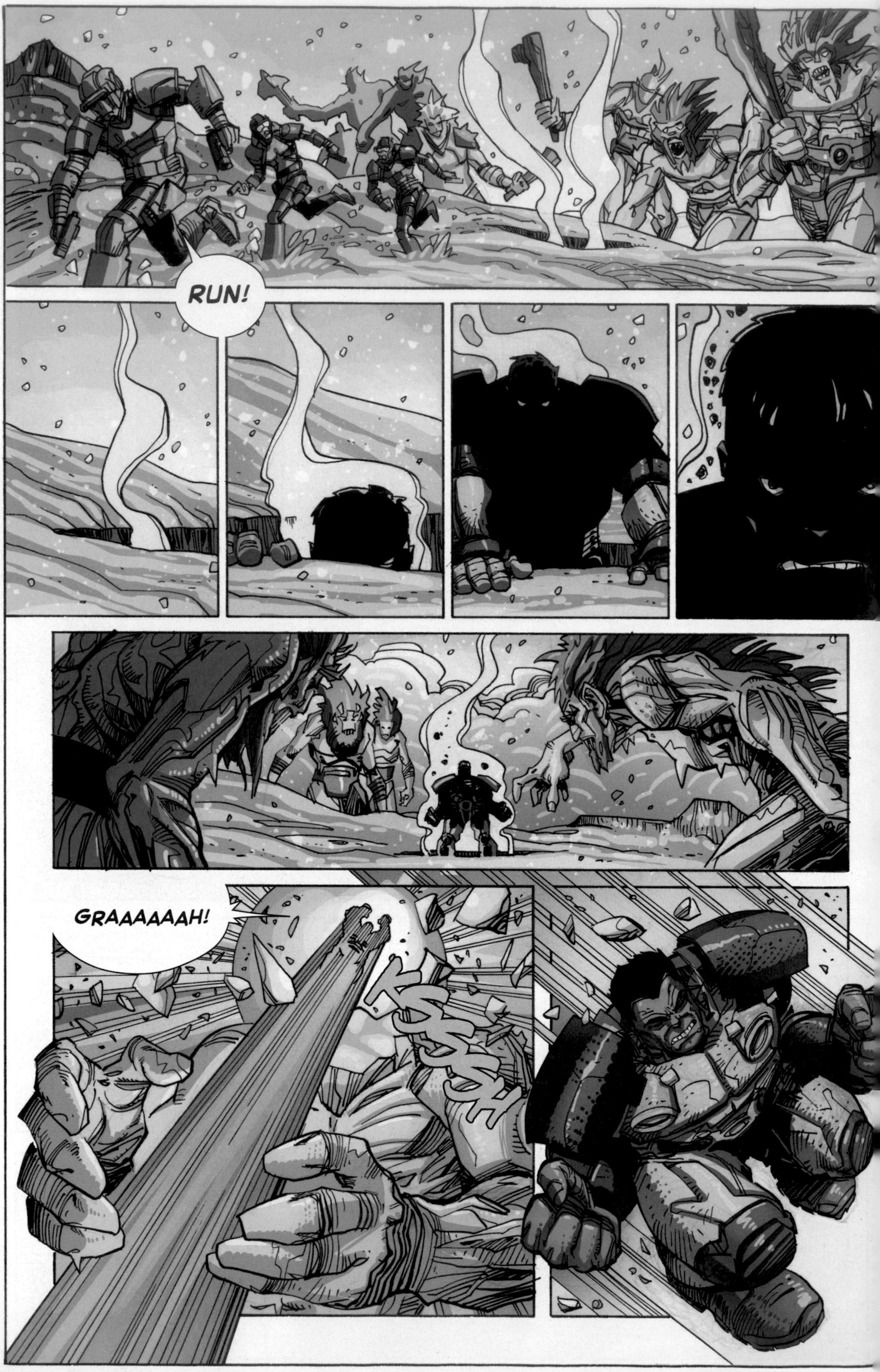
RUN!
GRAAAAAAH!
TSSSH

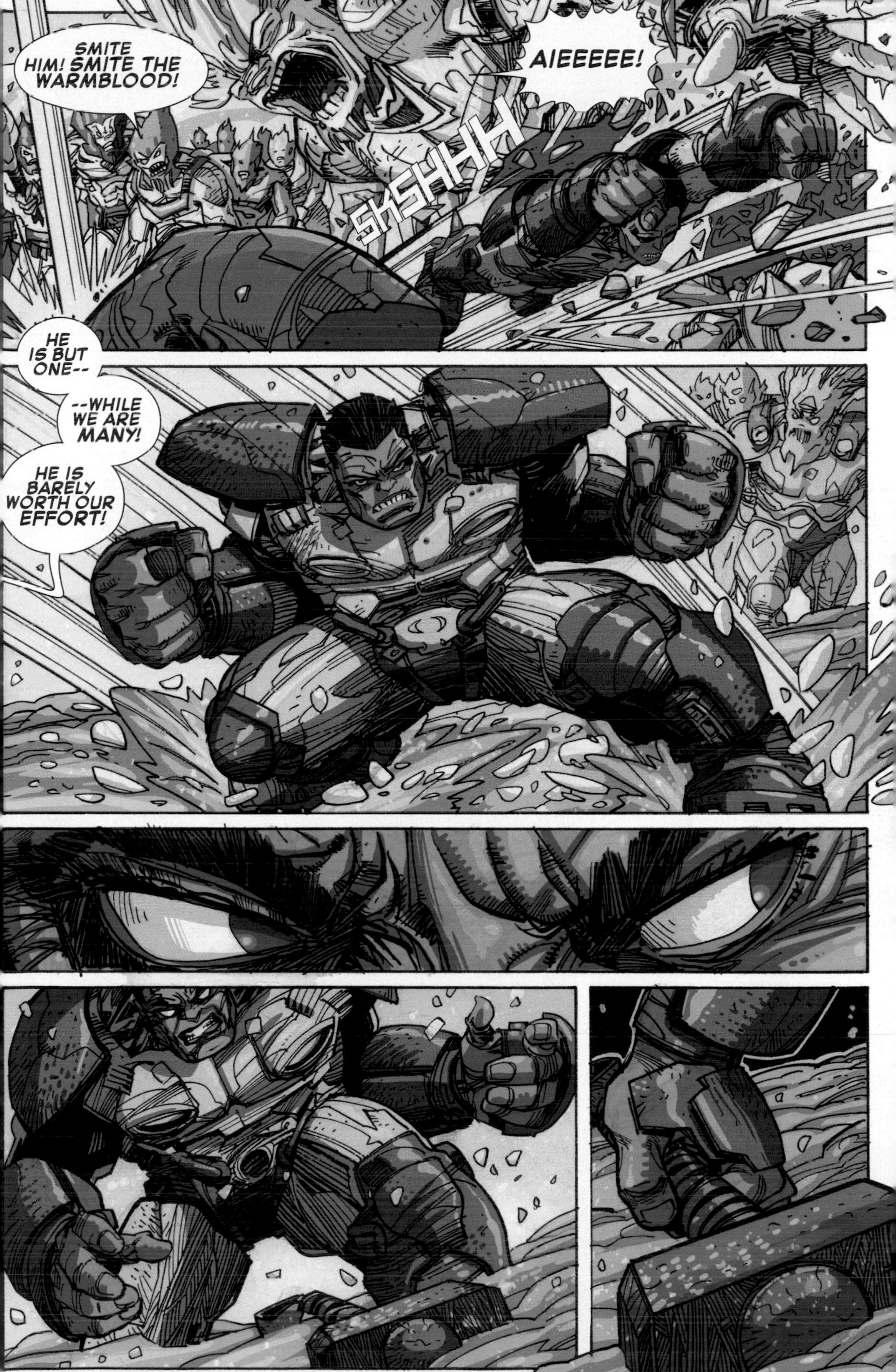
SMITE HIM! SMITE THE WARMBLOOD!
AIEEEEE!
SKSHHH
HE IS BUT ONE--
--WHILE WE ARE MANY!
HE IS BARELY WORTH OUR EFFORT!

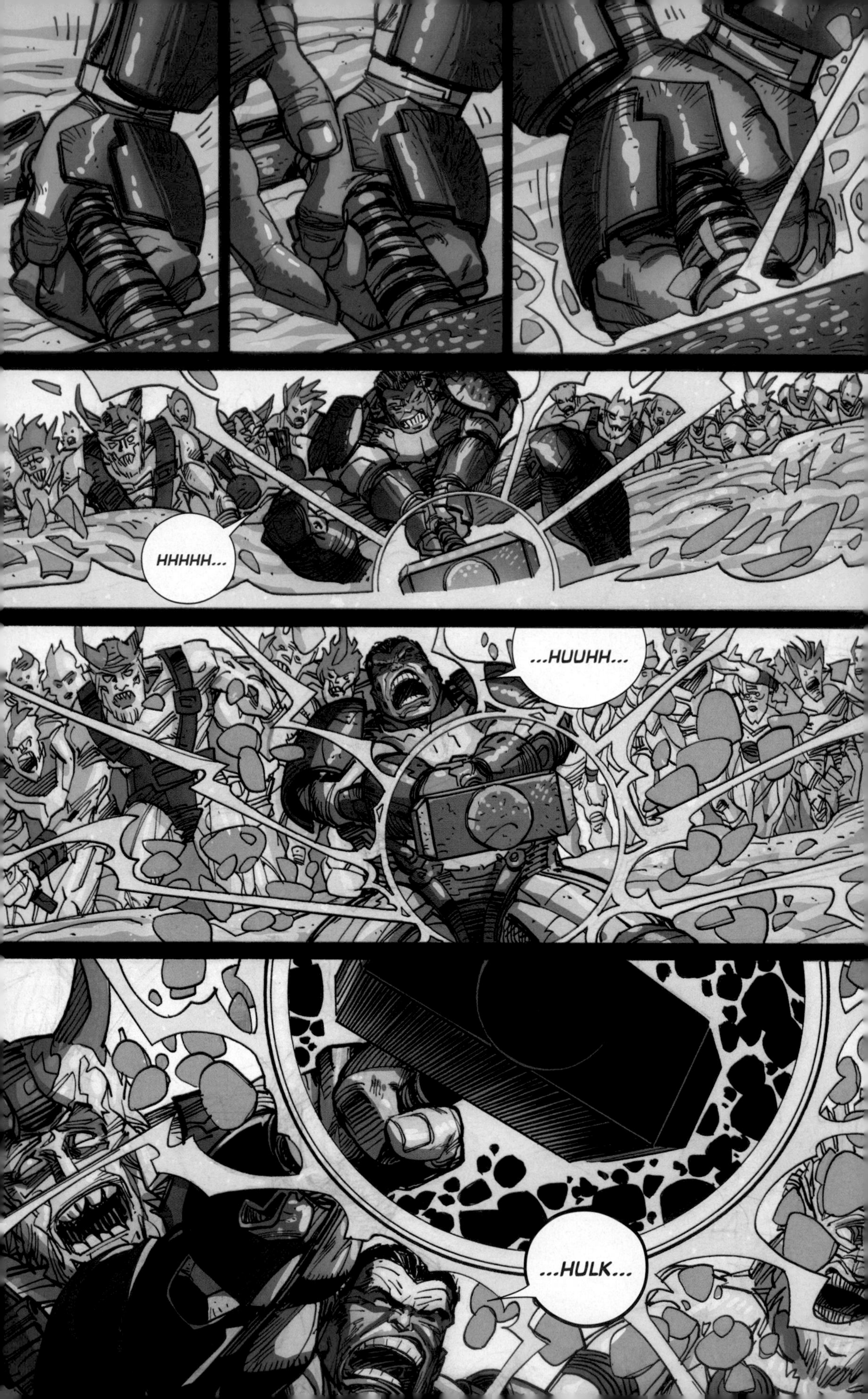
HHHHH...
...HUUHH...
...HULK...

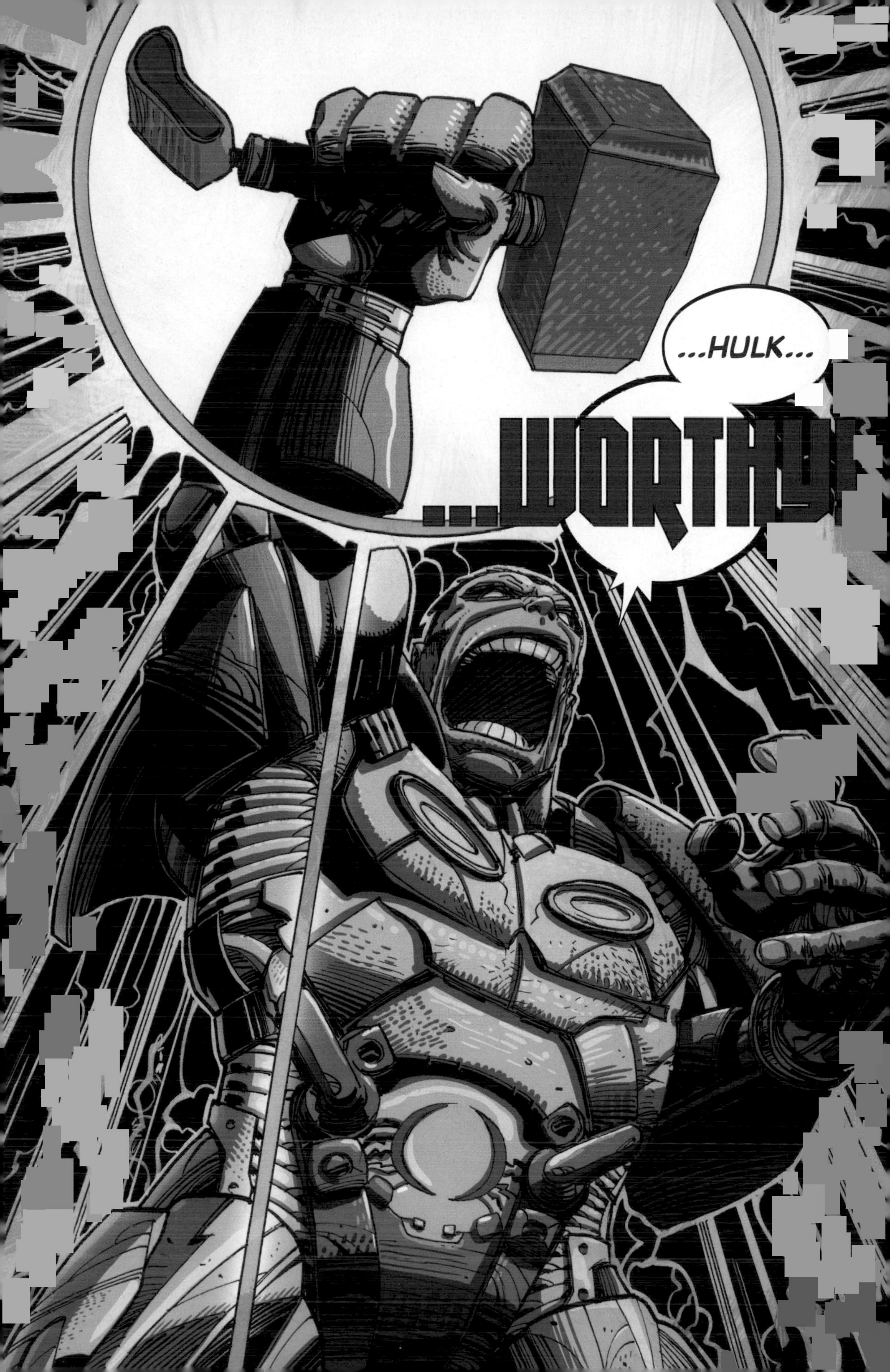

...HULK...
...WORTHY!

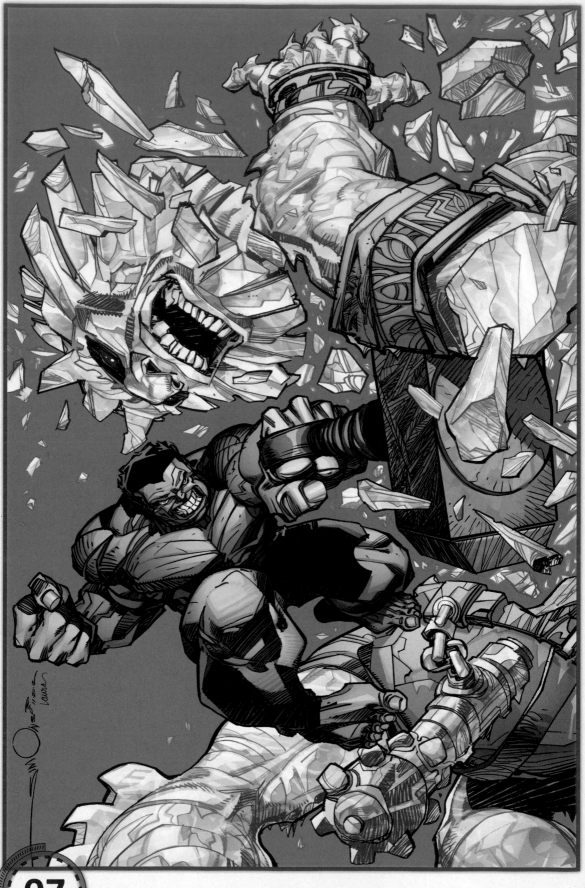

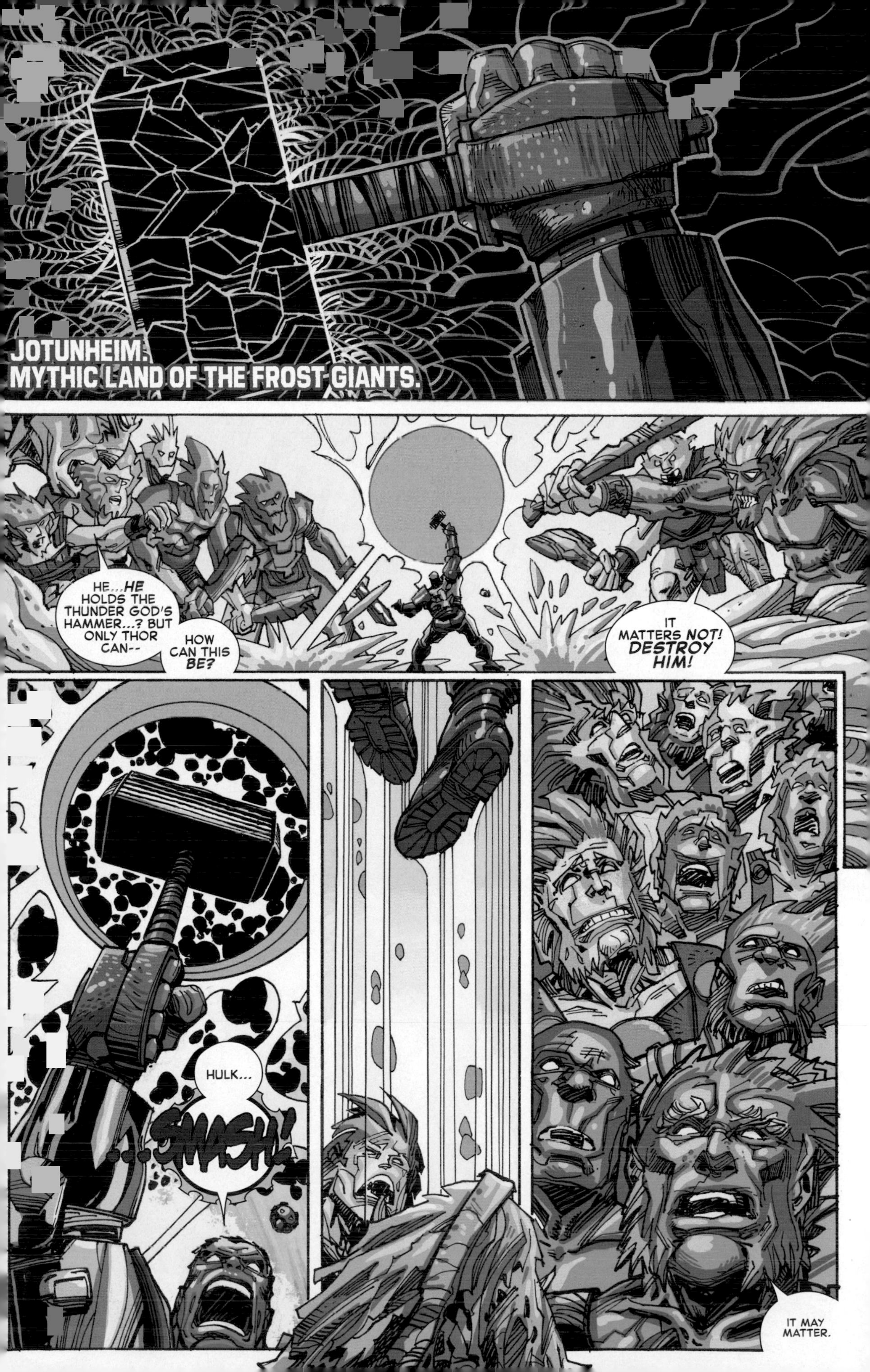
JOTUNHEIM.
MYTHIC LAND OF THE FROST GIANTS.
HE...HE HOLDS THE THUNDER GOD'S HAMMER...? BUT ONLY THOR CAN--
HOW CAN THIS BE?
IT MATTERS NOT! DESTROY HIM!
HULK...
...SMASH!
IT MAY MATTER.

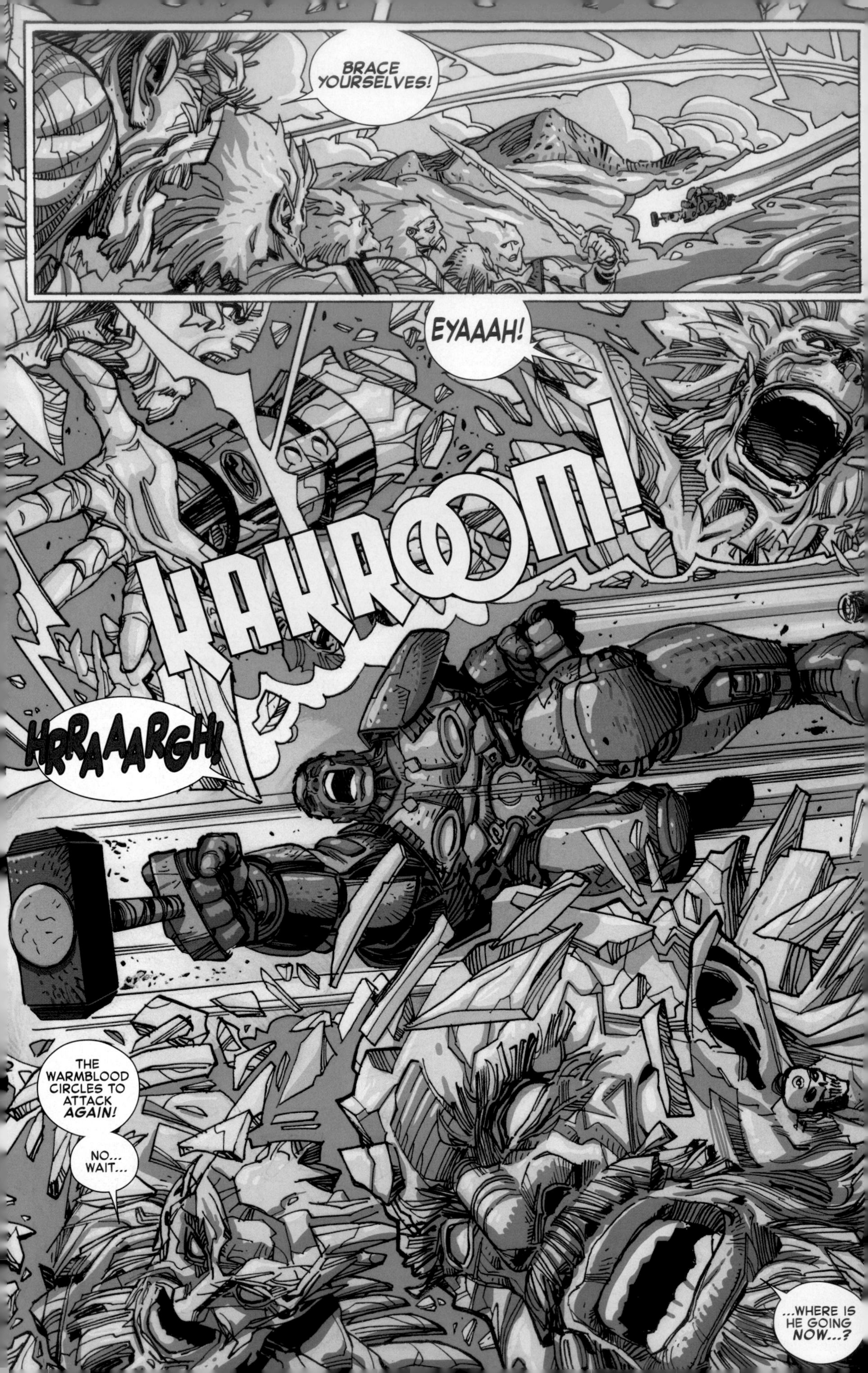
BRACE YOURSELVES!
EYAAAH!
KAKROOM!
HRRAAARGH!
THE WARMBLOOD CIRCLES TO ATTACK AGAIN!
NO... WAIT...
...WHERE IS HE GOING NOW...?

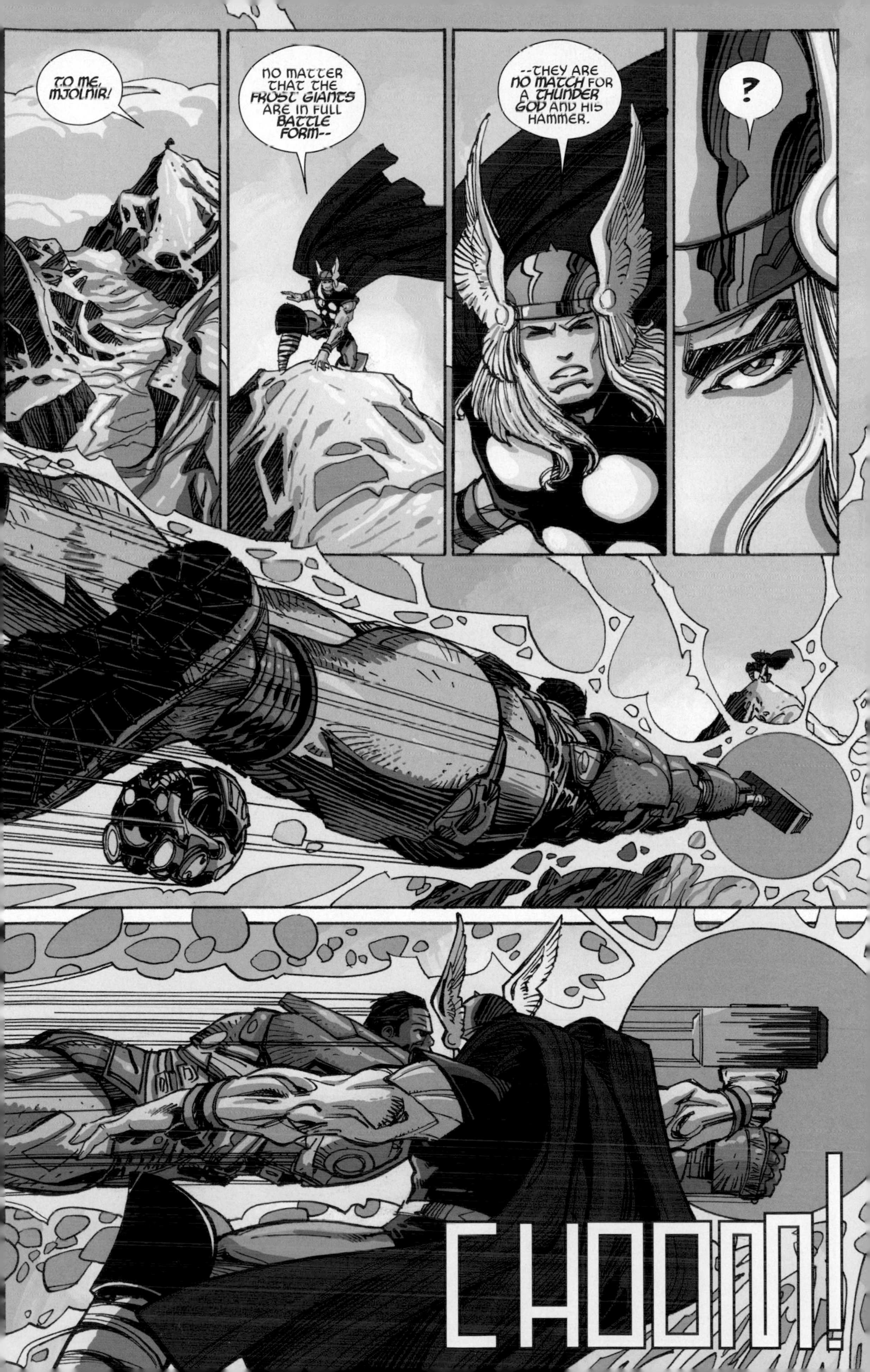
TO ME, MJOLNIR!
NO MATTER THAT THE FROST GIANTS ARE IN FULL BATTLE FORM--
--THEY ARE NO MATCH FOR A THUNDER GOD AND HIS HAMMER.
?
CHOOM!

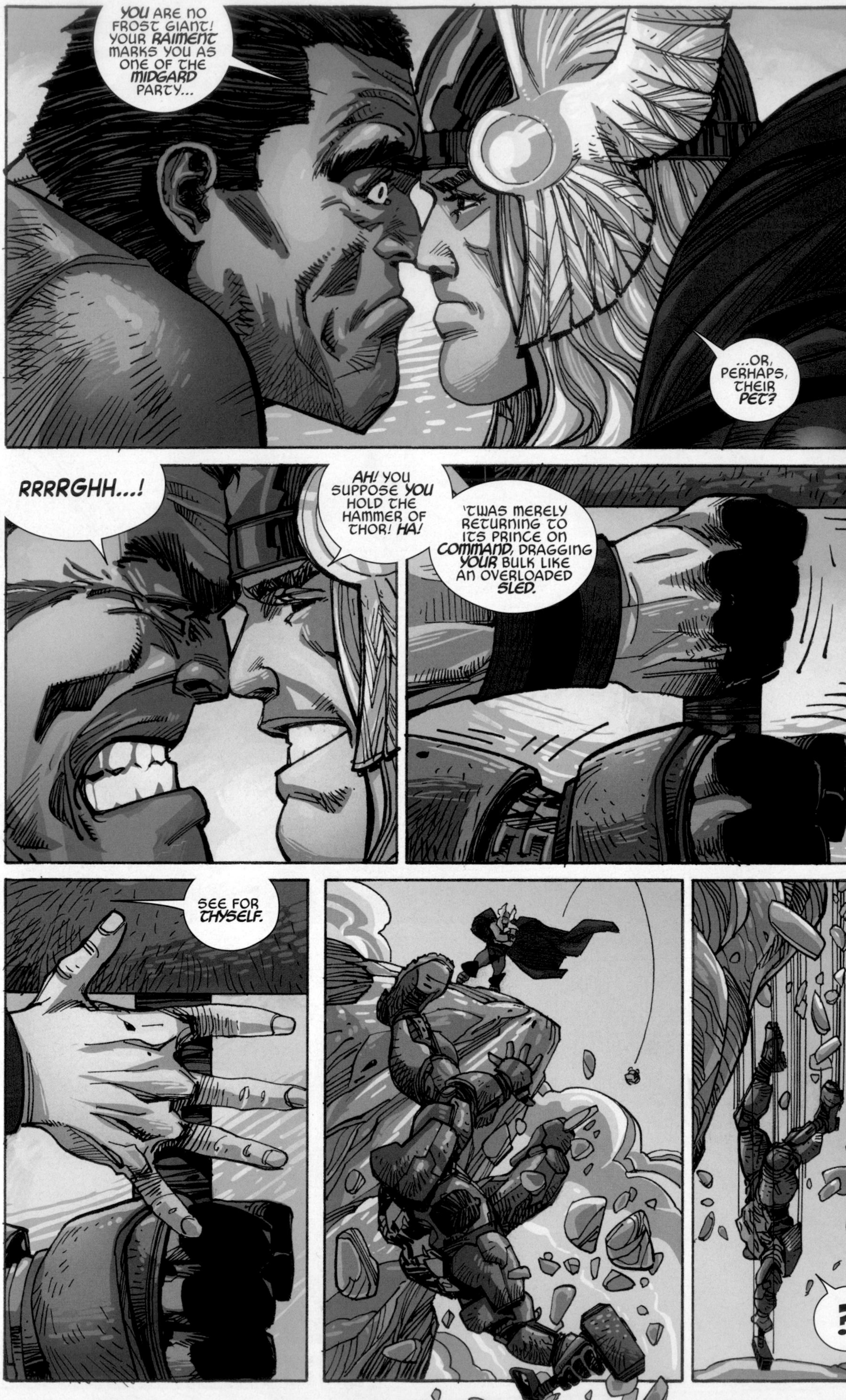

YOU ARE NO FROST GIANT! YOUR RAIMENT MARKS YOU AS ONE OF THE MIDGARD PARTY...
...OR, PERHAPS, THEIR PET?
RRRRGHH...!
AH! YOU SUPPOSE YOU HOLD THE HAMMER OF THOR! HA!
'TWAS MERELY RETURNING TO ITS PRINCE ON COMMAND, DRAGGING YOUR BULK LIKE AN OVERLOADED SLED.
SEE FOR THYSELF.
?

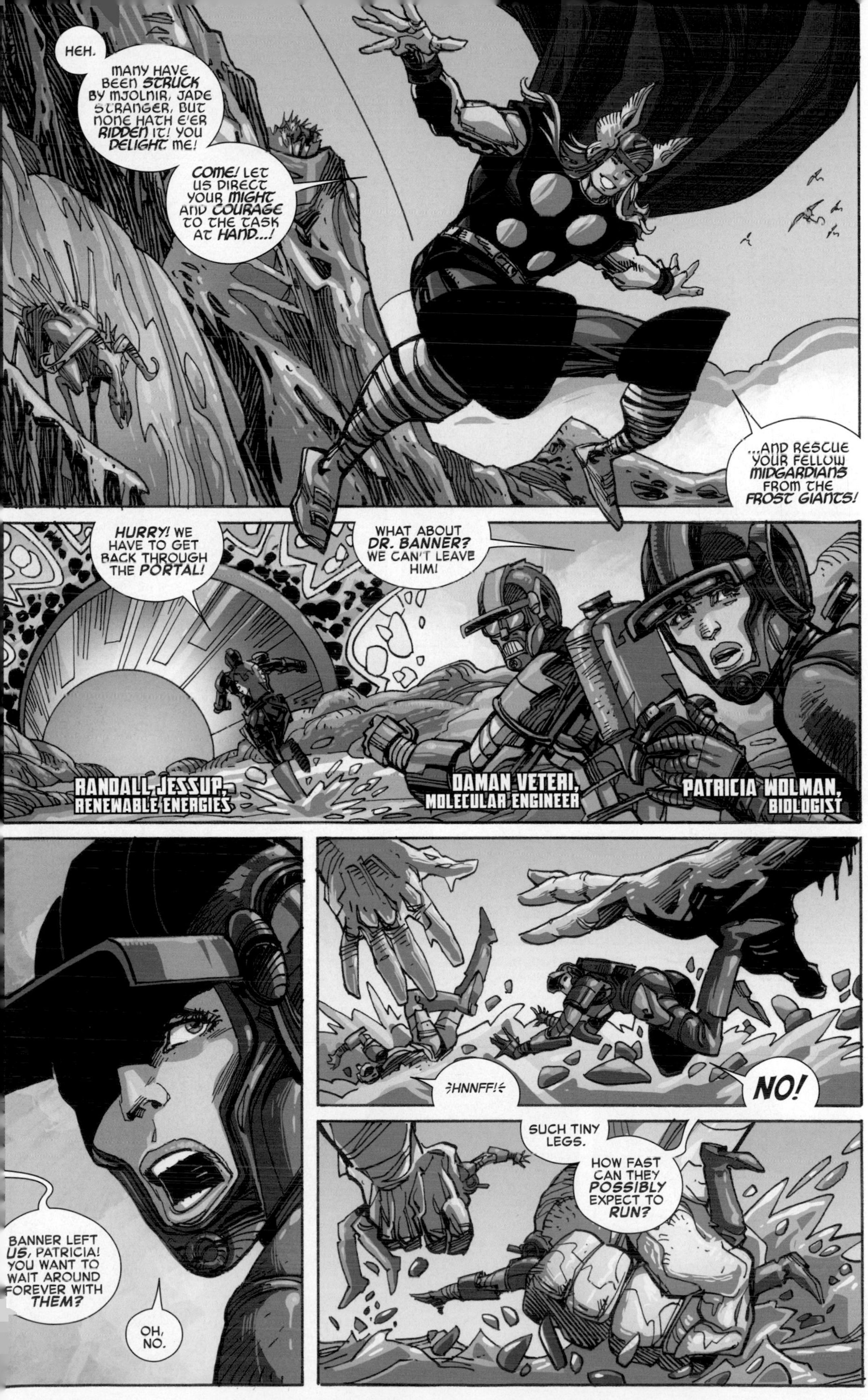
HEH.
MANY HAVE BEEN STRUCK BY MJOLNIR, JADE STRANGER, BUT NONE HATH E'ER RIDDEN IT! YOU DELIGHT ME!
COME! LET US DIRECT YOUR MIGHT AND COURAGE TO THE TASK AT HAND...!
...AND RESCUE YOUR FELLOW MIDGARDIANS FROM THE FROST GIANTS!
HURRY! WE HAVE TO GET BACK THROUGH THE PORTAL!
WHAT ABOUT DR. BANNER? WE CAN'T LEAVE HIM!
RANDALL JESSUP, RENEWABLE ENERGIES
DAMAN VETERI, MOLECULAR ENGINEER
PATRICIA WOLMAN, BIOLOGIST
BANNER LEFT US, PATRICIA! YOU WANT TO WAIT AROUND FOREVER WITH THEM?
OH, NO.
HNNFF!
NO!
SUCH TINY LEGS.
HOW FAST CAN THEY POSSIBLY EXPECT TO RUN?

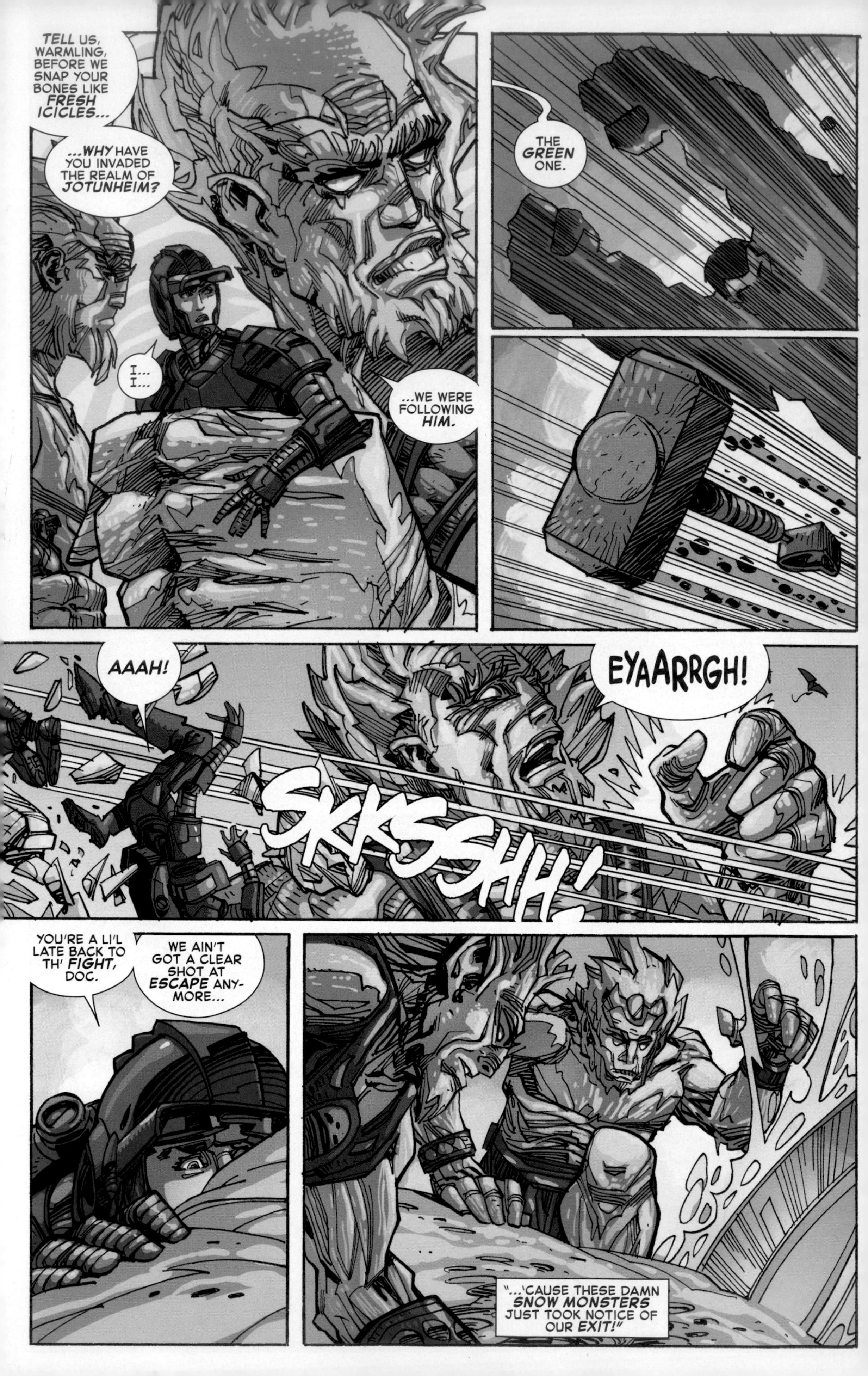
TELL US, WARMLING, BEFORE WE SNAP YOUR BONES LIKE FRESH ICICLES...
...WHY HAVE YOU INVADED THE REALM OF JOTUNHEIM?
I... I...
...WE WERE FOLLOWING HIM.
THE GREEN ONE.
AAAH!
EYAARRGH!
SKKSSHH!
YOU'RE A LI'L LATE BACK TO TH' FIGHT, DOC.
WE AIN'T GOT A CLEAR SHOT AT ESCAPE ANY-MORE...
"...'CAUSE THESE DAMN SNOW MONSTERS JUST TOOK NOTICE OF OUR EXIT!"

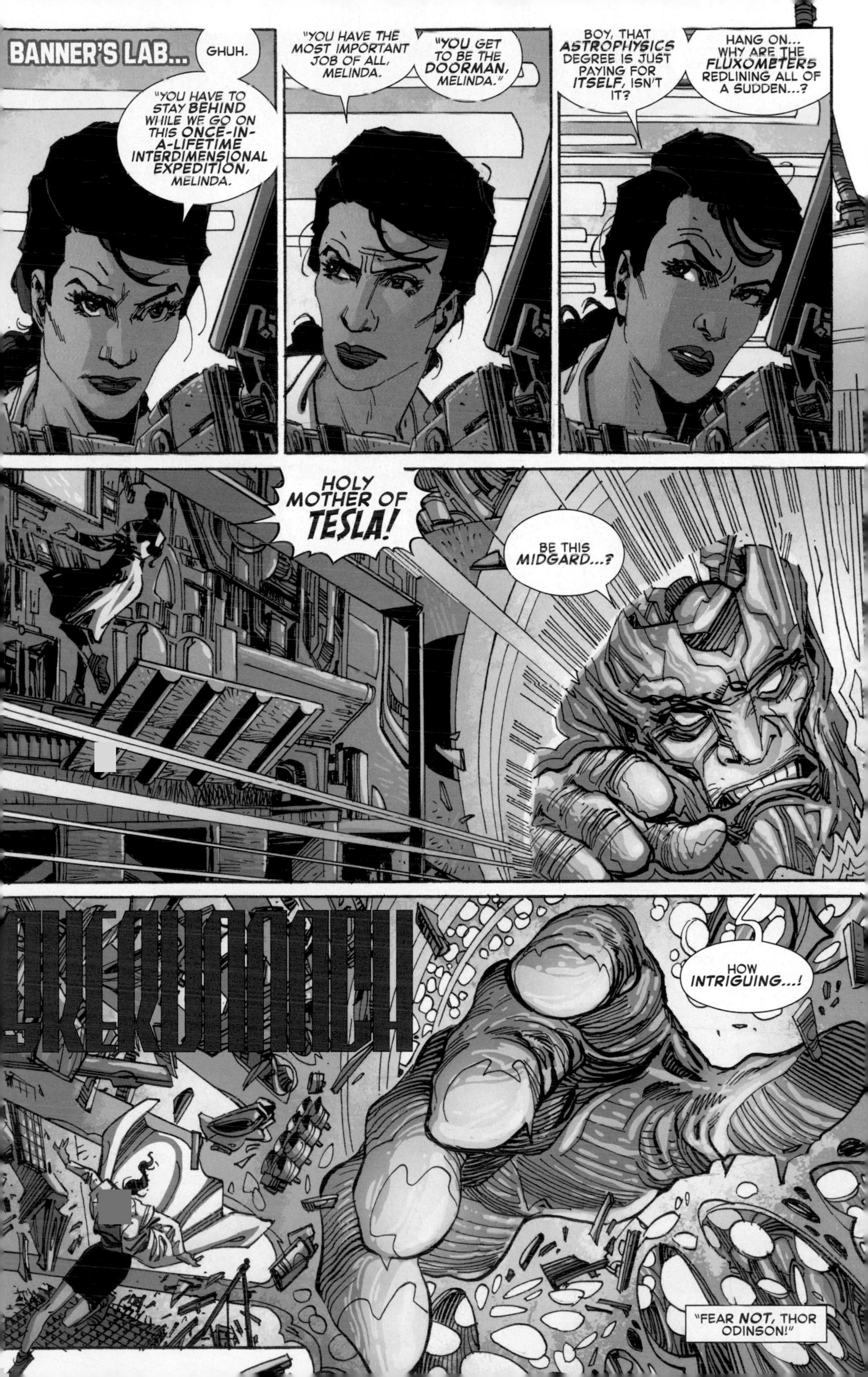
BANNER'S LAB...
GHUH.
"YOU HAVE TO STAY BEHIND WHILE WE GO ON THIS ONCE-IN-A-LIFETIME INTERDIMENSIONAL EXPEDITION, MELINDA.
"YOU HAVE THE MOST IMPORTANT JOB OF ALL, MELINDA.
"YOU GET TO BE THE DOORMAN, MELINDA."
BOY, THAT ASTROPHYSICS DEGREE IS JUST PAYING FOR ITSELF, ISN'T IT?
HANG ON... WHY ARE THE FLUXOMETERS REDLINING ALL OF A SUDDEN...?
HOLY MOTHER OF TESLA!
BE THIS MIDGARD...?
HOW INTRIGUING...!
"FEAR NOT, THOR ODINSON!"

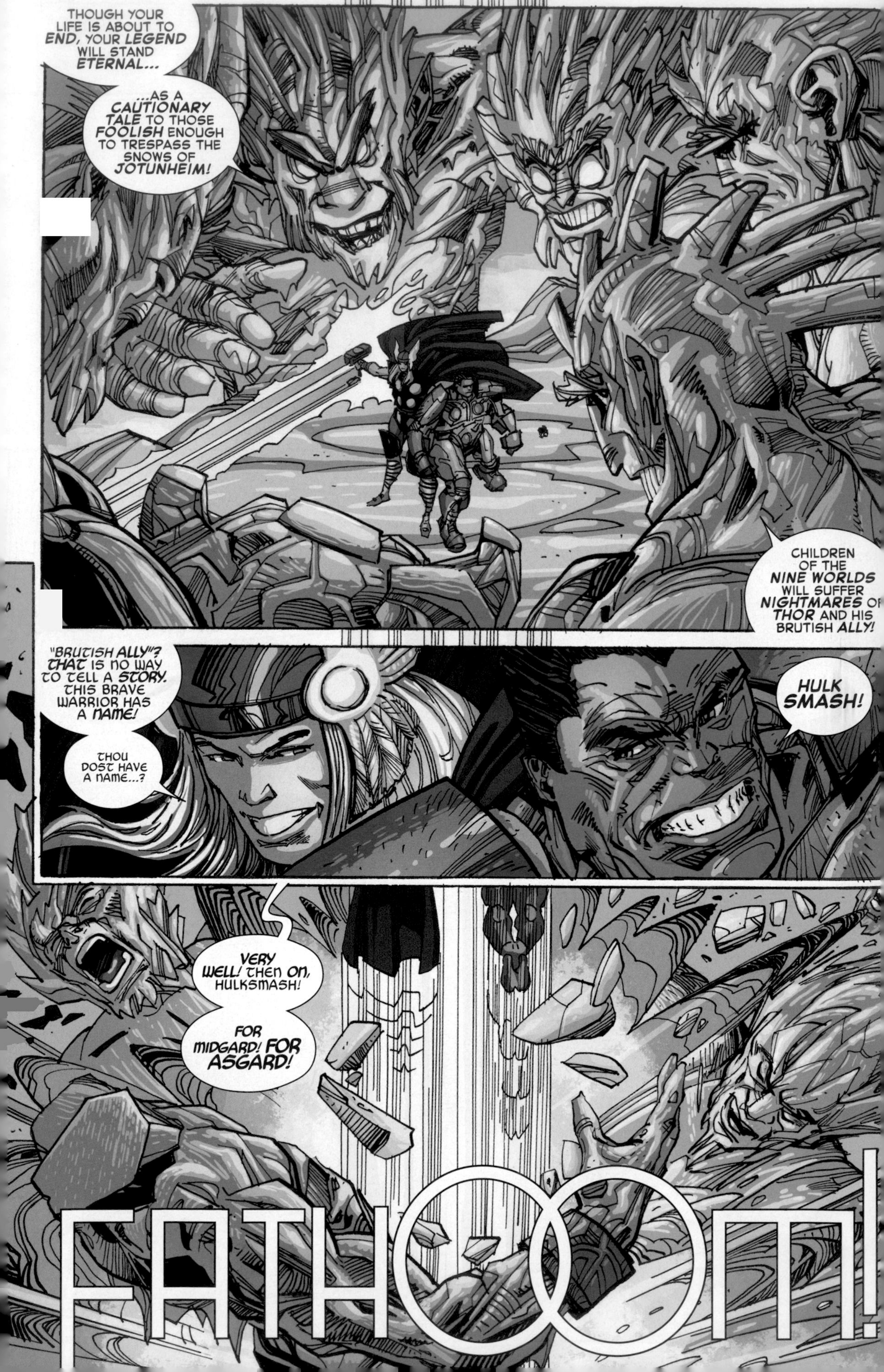
THOUGH YOUR LIFE IS ABOUT TO END, YOUR LEGEND WILL STAND ETERNAL...
...AS A CAUTIONARY TALE TO THOSE FOOLISH ENOUGH TO TRESPASS THE SNOWS OF JOTUNHEIM!
CHILDREN OF THE NINE WORLDS WILL SUFFER NIGHTMARES OF THOR AND HIS BRUTISH ALLY!
"BRUTISH ALLY"? THAT IS NO WAY TO TELL A STORY. THIS BRAVE WARRIOR HAS A NAME!
THOU DOST HAVE A NAME...?
HULK SMASH!
VERY WELL! THEN ON, HULKSMASH!
FOR MIDGARD! FOR ASGARD!
FATHOOM!

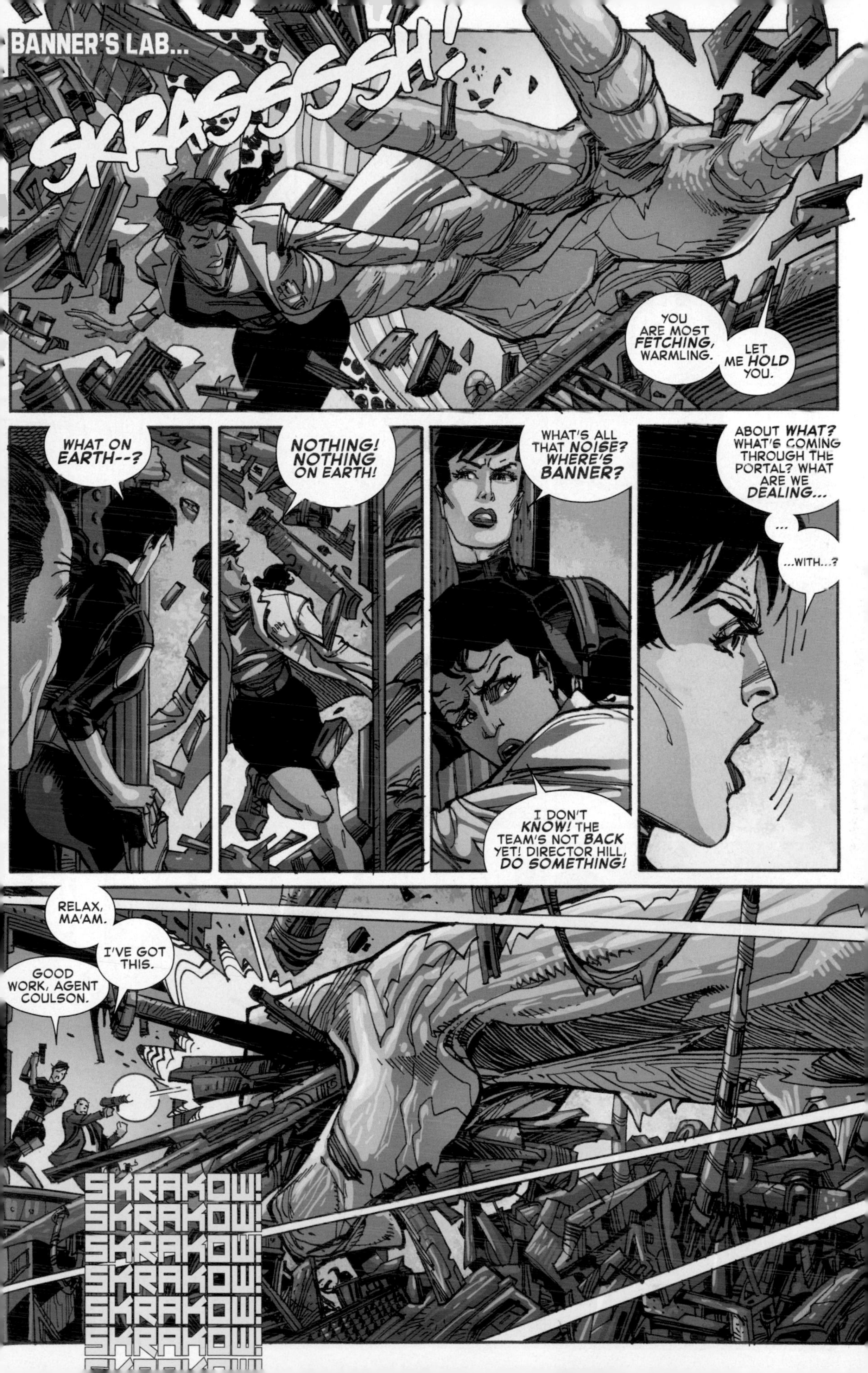
BANNER'S LAB...
SKRASSSSH!
YOU ARE MOST FETCHING, WARMLING.
LET ME HOLD YOU.
WHAT ON EARTH--?
NOTHING! NOTHING ON EARTH!
WHAT'S ALL THAT NOISE? WHERE'S BANNER?
I DON'T KNOW! THE TEAM'S NOT BACK YET! DIRECTOR HILL, DO SOMETHING!
ABOUT WHAT? WHAT'S COMING THROUGH THE PORTAL? WHAT ARE WE DEALING...
...
...WITH...?
RELAX, MA'AM.
I'VE GOT THIS.
GOOD WORK, AGENT COULSON.
SKRAKOW! SKRAKOW! SKRAKOW! SKRAKOW! SKRAKOW! SKRAKOW!

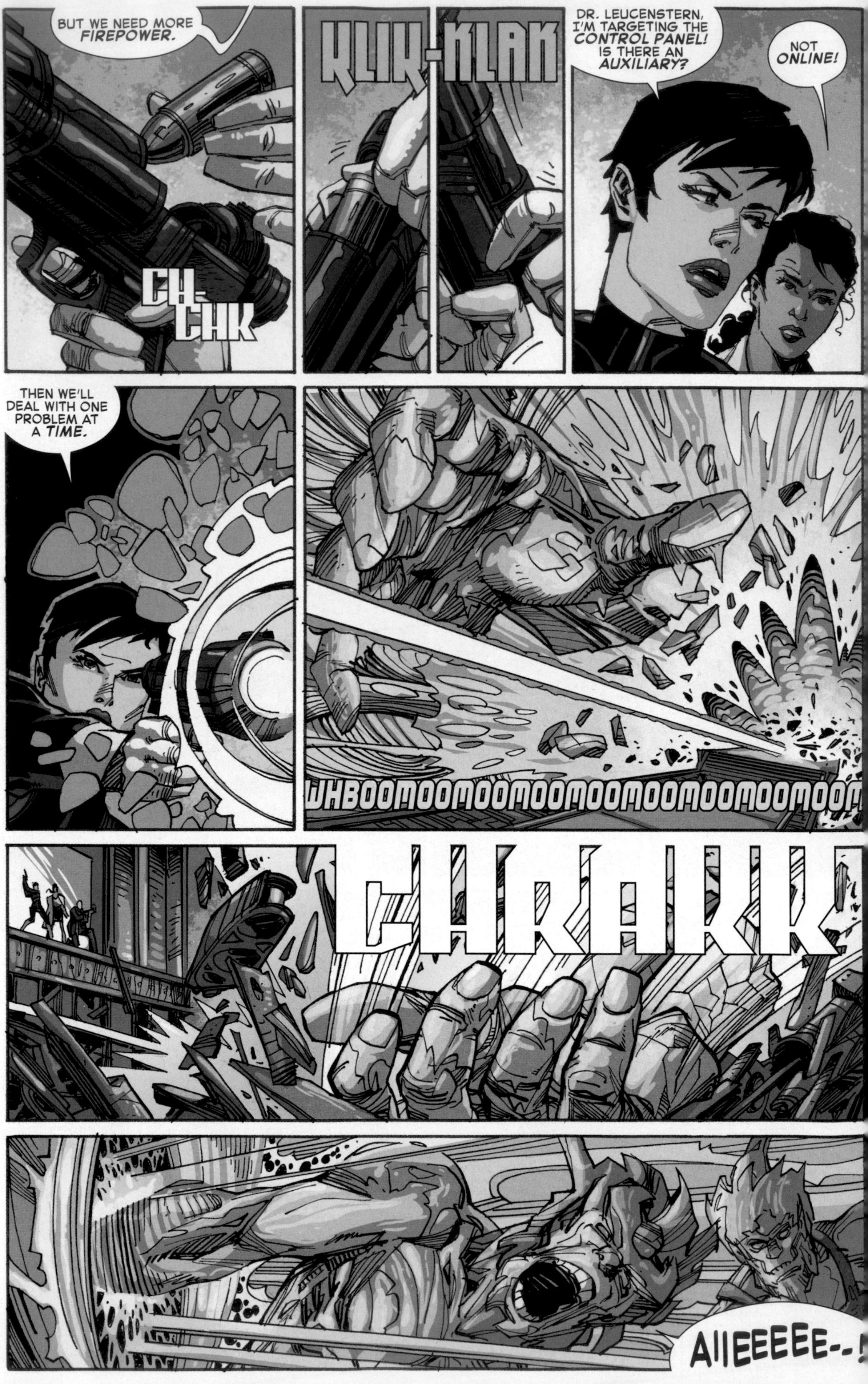
BUT WE NEED MORE FIREPOWER.
CH-CHK
KLIK-KLAK
DR. LEUCENSTERN, I'M TARGETING THE CONTROL PANEL! IS THERE AN AUXILIARY?
NOT ONLINE!
THEN WE'LL DEAL WITH ONE PROBLEM AT A TIME.
WHBOOMOOMOOMOOMOOMOOMOOMOOMOOM
CHRAKK
AIIEEEEE--!

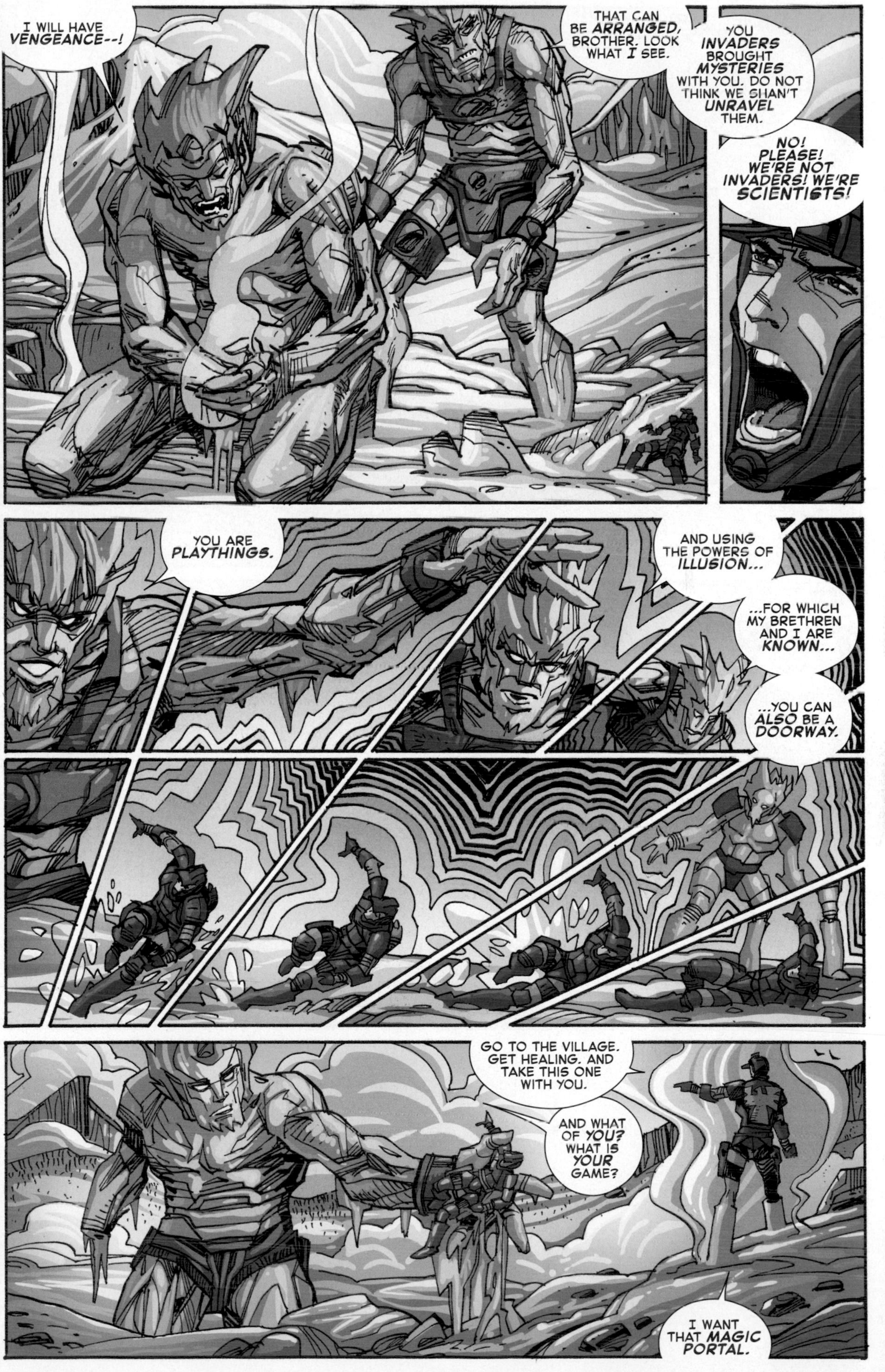
I WILL HAVE VENGEANCE--!
THAT CAN BE ARRANGED, BROTHER. LOOK WHAT I SEE.
YOU INVADERS BROUGHT MYSTERIES WITH YOU. DO NOT THINK WE SHAN'T UNRAVEL THEM.
NO! PLEASE! WE'RE NOT INVADERS! WE'RE SCIENTISTS!
YOU ARE PLAYTHINGS.
AND USING THE POWERS OF ILLUSION...
...FOR WHICH MY BRETHREN AND I ARE KNOWN...
...YOU CAN ALSO BE A DOORWAY.
GO TO THE VILLAGE. GET HEALING. AND TAKE THIS ONE WITH YOU.
AND WHAT OF YOU? WHAT IS YOUR GAME?
I WANT THAT MAGIC PORTAL.

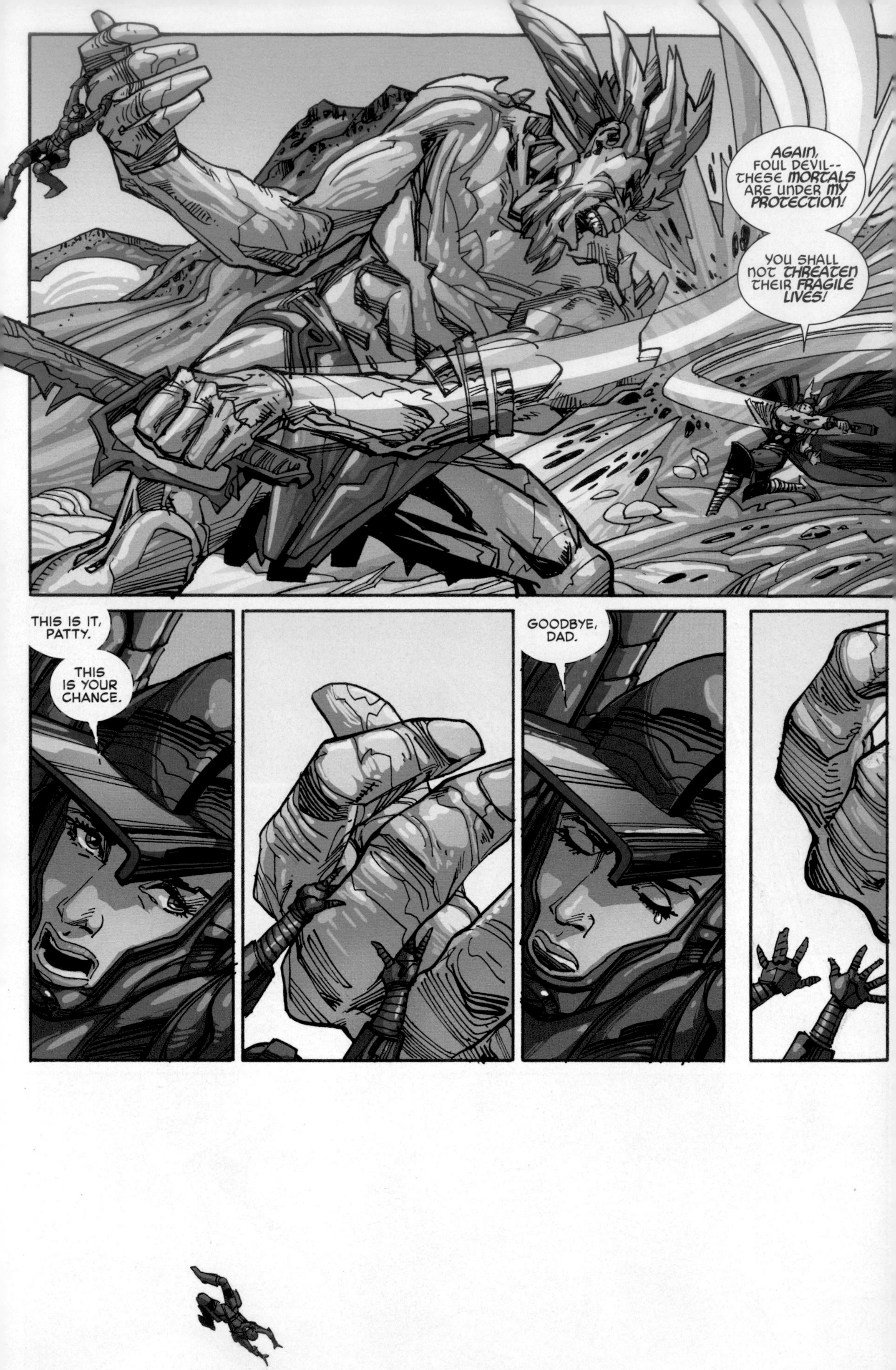
AGAIN, FOUL DEVIL-- THESE MORTALS ARE UNDER MY PROTECTION!
YOU SHALL NOT THREATEN THEIR FRAGILE LIVES!
THIS IS IT, PATTY.
THIS IS YOUR CHANCE.
GOODBYE, DAD.

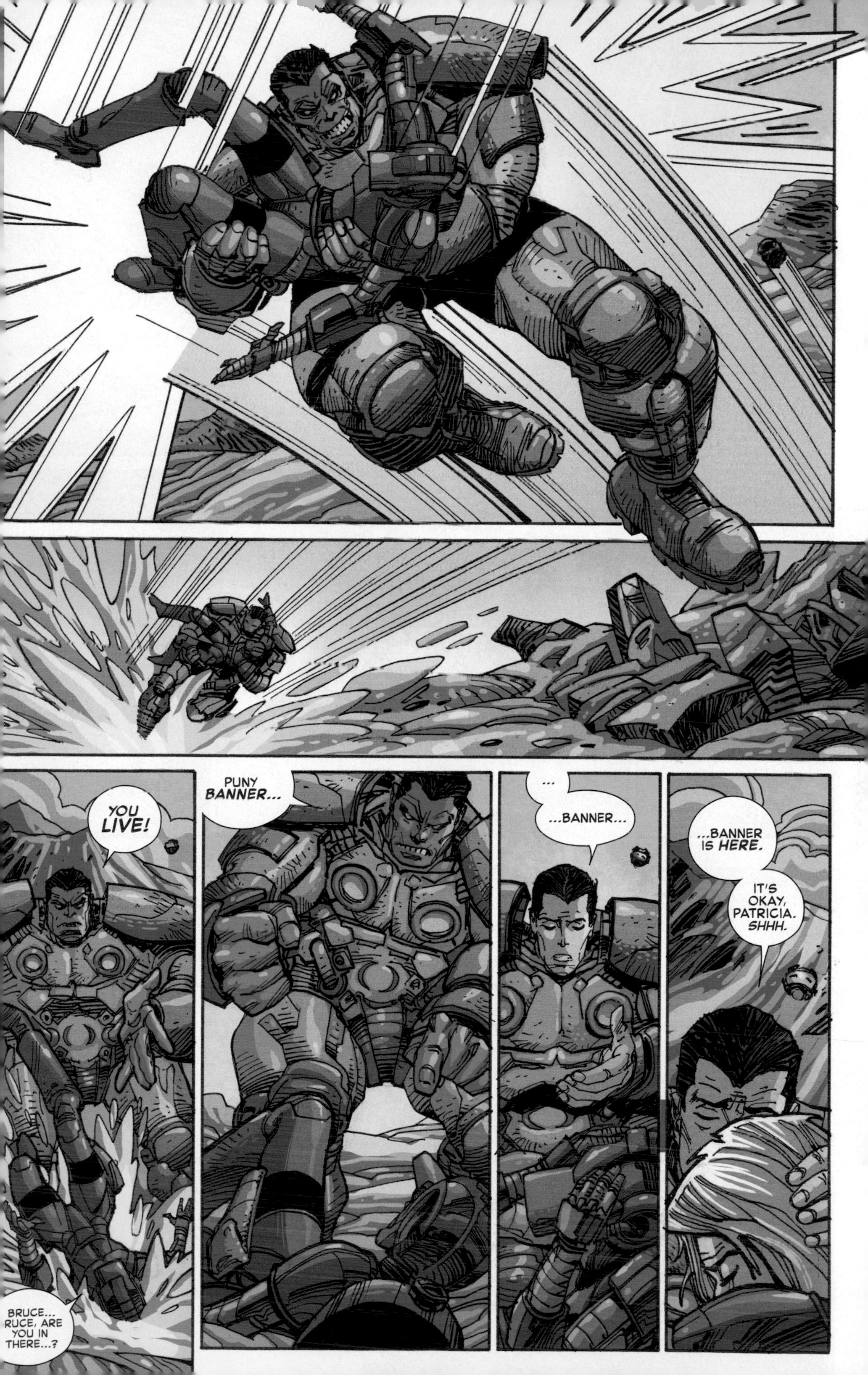
YOU LIVE!
BRUCE... RUCE, ARE YOU IN THERE...?
PUNY BANNER...
...
...BANNER...
...BANNER IS HERE.
IT'S OKAY, PATRICIA. SHHH.

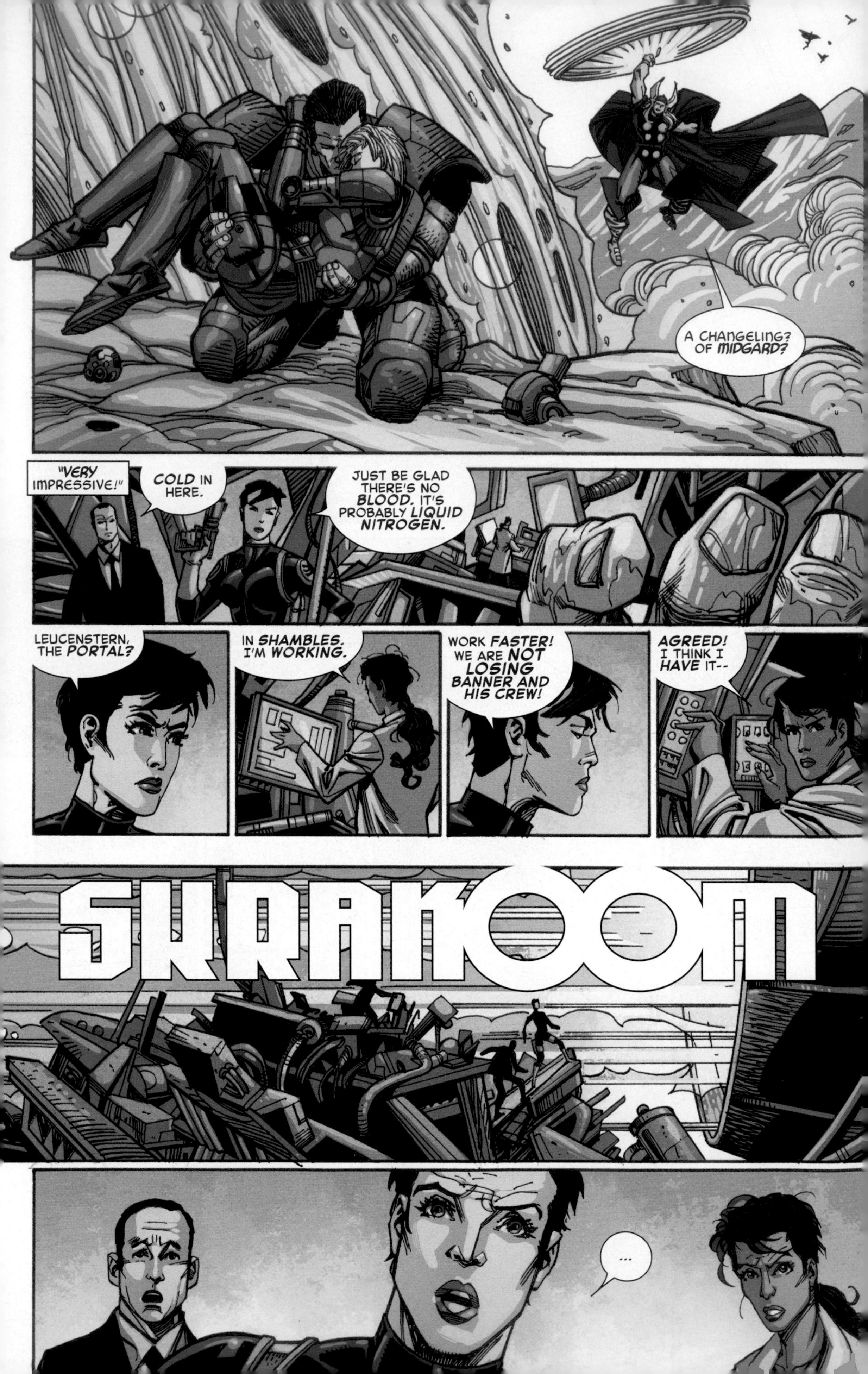
A CHANGELING? OF MIDGARD?
"VERY IMPRESSIVE!"
COLD IN HERE.
JUST BE GLAD THERE'S NO BLOOD. IT'S PROBABLY LIQUID NITROGEN.
LEUCENSTERN, THE PORTAL?
IN SHAMBLES. I'M WORKING.
WORK FASTER! WE ARE NOT LOSING BANNER AND HIS CREW!
AGREED! I THINK I HAVE IT--
SKRAKOOM
...

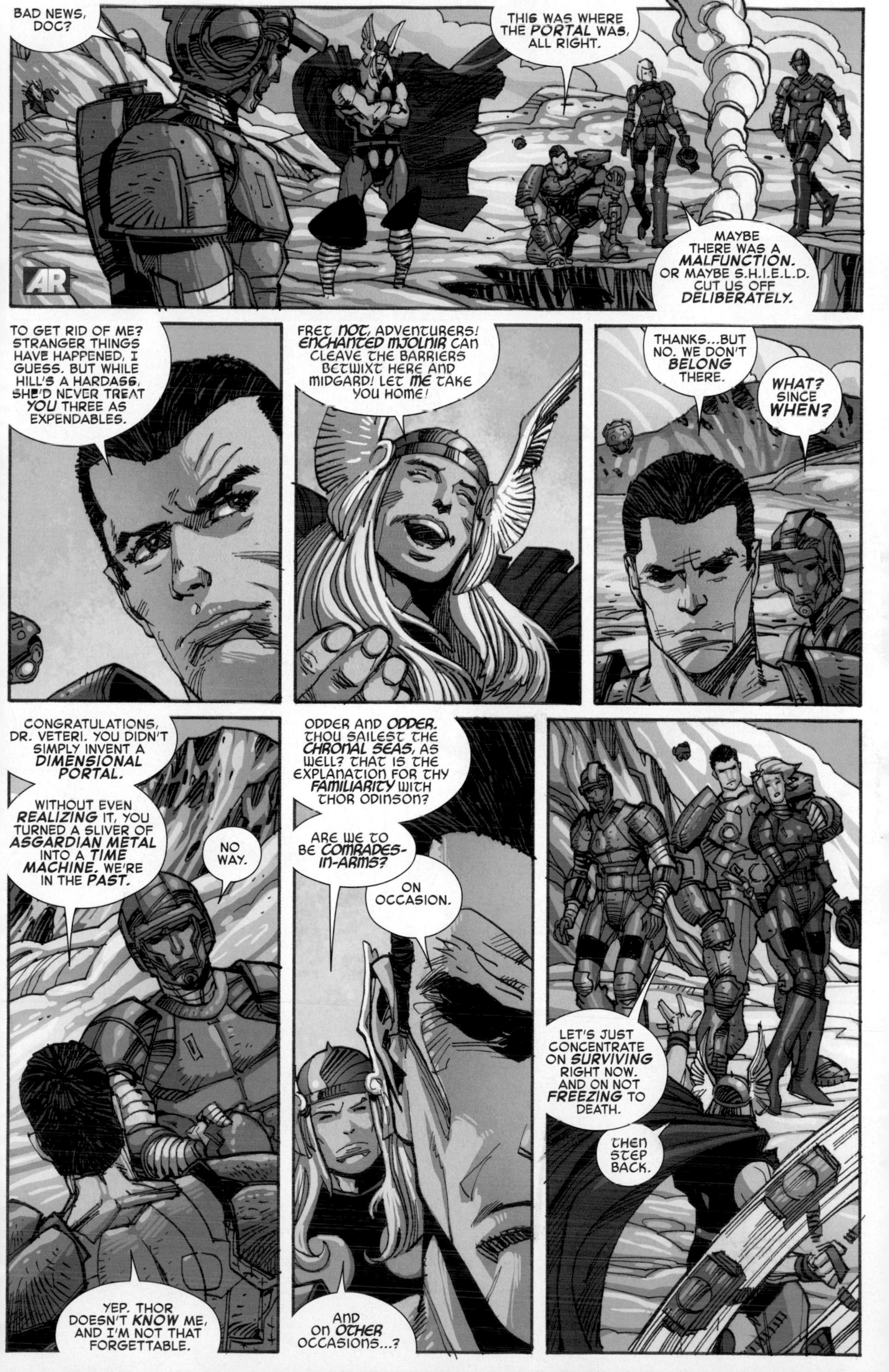
BAD NEWS, DOC?
THIS WAS WHERE THE PORTAL WAS, ALL RIGHT.
MAYBE THERE WAS A MALFUNCTION. OR MAYBE S.H.I.E.L.D. CUT US OFF DELIBERATELY.
AR
TO GET RID OF ME? STRANGER THINGS HAVE HAPPENED, I GUESS. BUT WHILE HILL'S A HARDASS, SHE'D NEVER TREAT YOU THREE AS EXPENDABLES.
FRET NOT, ADVENTURERS! ENCHANTED MJOLNIR CAN CLEAVE THE BARRIERS BETWIXT HERE AND MIDGARD! LET ME TAKE YOU HOME!
THANKS...BUT NO. WE DON'T BELONG THERE.
WHAT? SINCE WHEN?
CONGRATULATIONS, DR. VETERI. YOU DIDN'T SIMPLY INVENT A DIMENSIONAL PORTAL.
WITHOUT EVEN REALIZING IT, YOU TURNED A SLIVER OF ASGARDIAN METAL INTO A TIME MACHINE. WE'RE IN THE PAST.
NO WAY.
YEP. THOR DOESN'T KNOW ME, AND I'M NOT THAT FORGETTABLE.
ODDER AND ODDER. THOU SAILEST THE CHRONAL SEAS, AS WELL? THAT IS THE EXPLANATION FOR THY FAMILIARITY WITH THOR ODINSON?
ARE WE TO BE COMRADES-IN-ARMS?
ON OCCASION.
AND ON OTHER OCCASIONS...?
LET'S JUST CONCENTRATE ON SURVIVING RIGHT NOW. AND ON NOT FREEZING TO DEATH.
THEN STEP BACK.

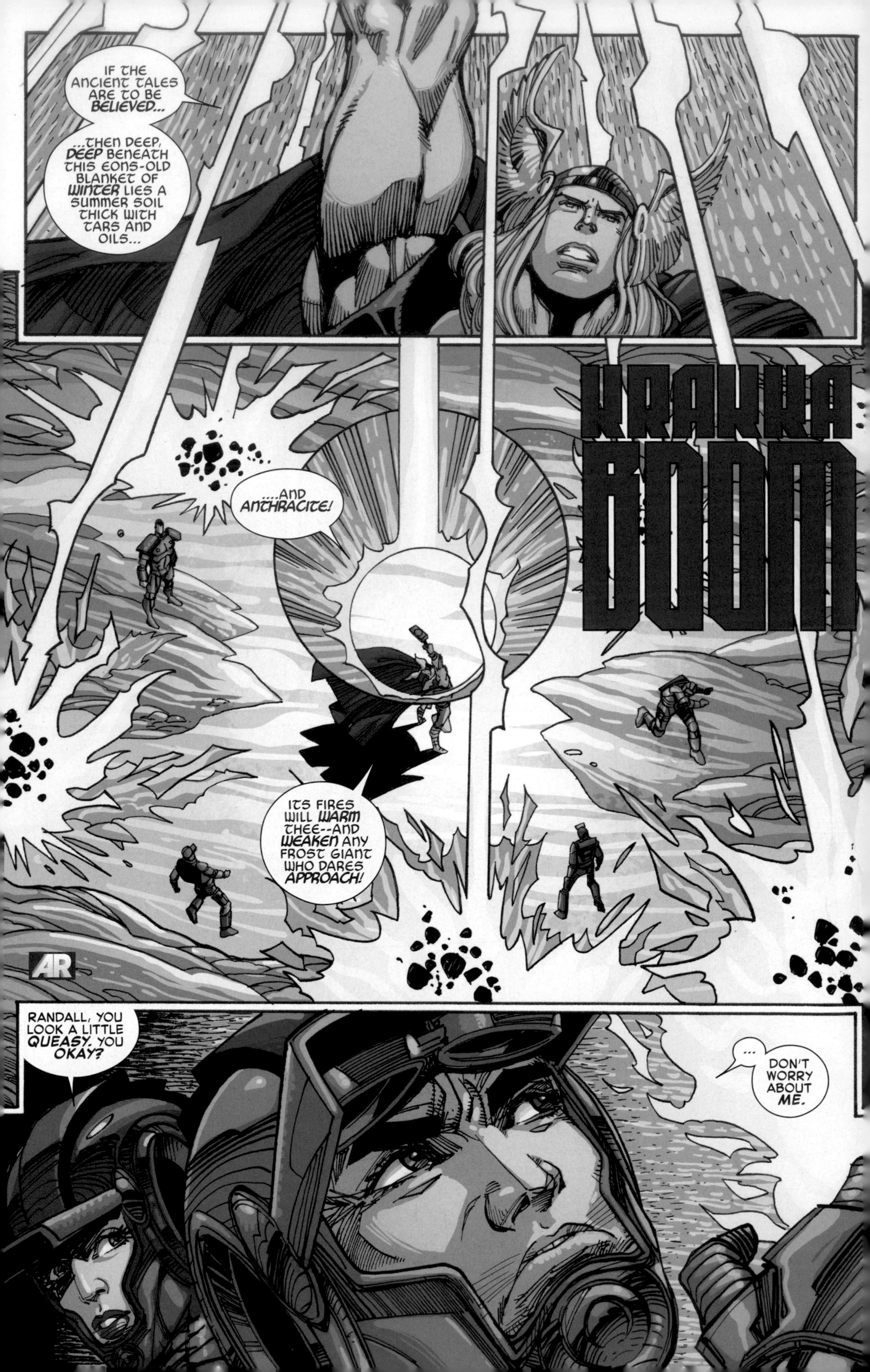
IF THE ANCIENT TALES ARE TO BE BELIEVED...
...THEN DEEP, DEEP BENEATH THIS EONS-OLD BLANKET OF WINTER LIES A SUMMER SOIL THICK WITH TARS AND OILS...
KRAKKA BOOM
....AND ANTHRACITE!
ITS FIRES WILL WARM THEE--AND WEAKEN ANY FROST GIANT WHO DARES APPROACH!
RANDALL, YOU LOOK A LITTLE QUEASY. YOU OKAY?
... DON'T WORRY ABOUT ME.

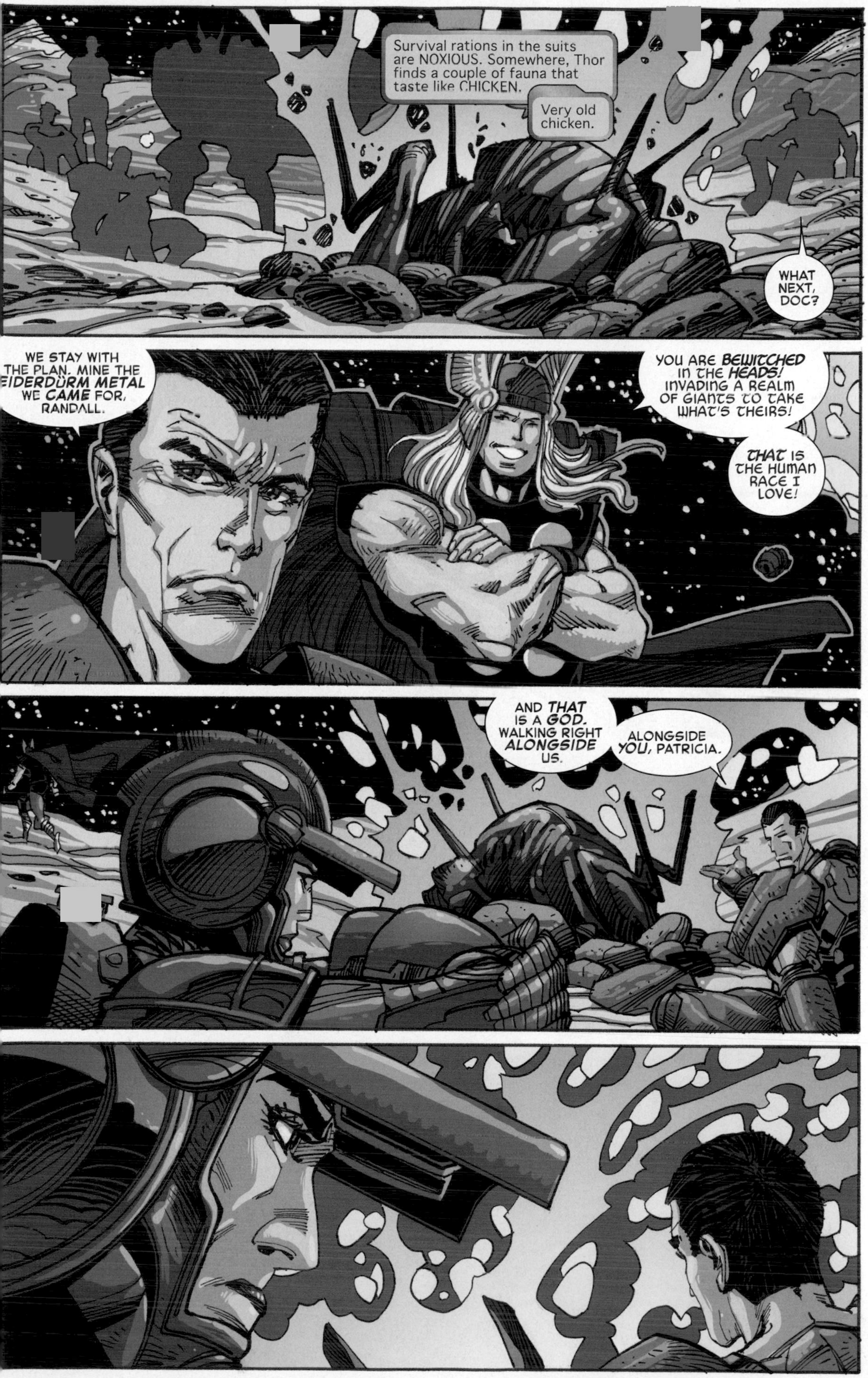
Survival rations in the suits are NOXIOUS. Somewhere, Thor finds a couple of fauna that taste like CHICKEN.
Very old chicken.
WHAT NEXT, DOC?
WE STAY WITH THE PLAN. MINE THE EIDERDÜRM METAL WE CAME FOR, RANDALL.
YOU ARE BEWITCHED IN THE HEADS! INVADING A REALM OF GIANTS TO TAKE WHAT'S THEIRS!
THAT IS THE HUMAN RACE I LOVE!
AND THAT IS A GOD. WALKING RIGHT ALONGSIDE US.
ALONGSIDE YOU, PATRICIA.

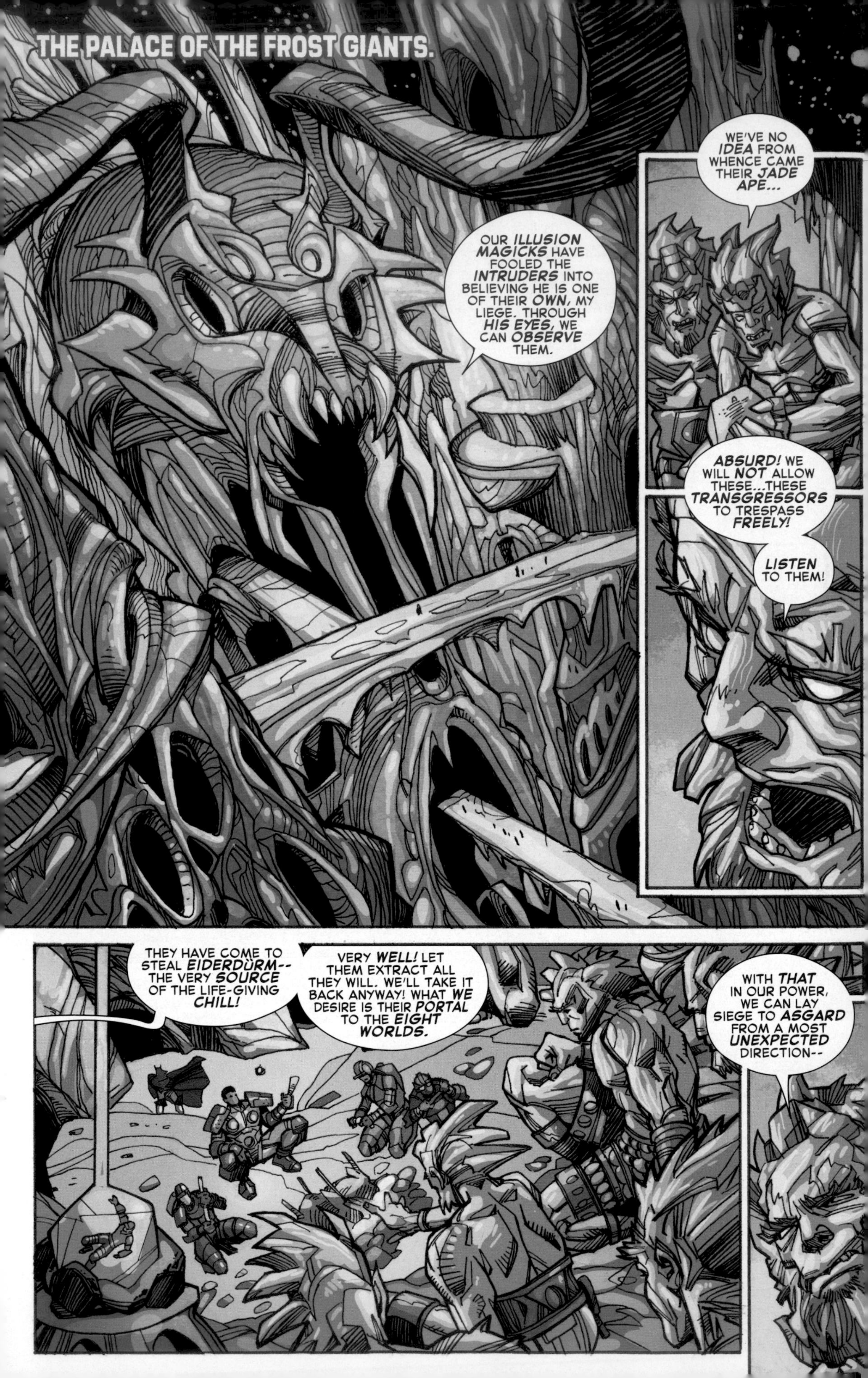
THE PALACE OF THE FROST GIANTS.
OUR ILLUSION MAGICKS HAVE FOOLED THE INTRUDERS INTO BELIEVING HE IS ONE OF THEIR OWN, MY LIEGE. THROUGH HIS EYES, WE CAN OBSERVE THEM.
WE'VE NO IDEA FROM WHENCE CAME THEIR JADE APE...
ABSURD! WE WILL NOT ALLOW THESE...THESE TRANSGRESSORS TO TRESPASS FREELY!
LISTEN TO THEM!
THEY HAVE COME TO STEAL EIDERDÜRM-- THE VERY SOURCE OF THE LIFE-GIVING CHILL!
VERY WELL! LET THEM EXTRACT ALL THEY WILL. WE'LL TAKE IT BACK ANYWAY! WHAT WE DESIRE IS THEIR PORTAL TO THE EIGHT WORLDS.
WITH THAT IN OUR POWER, WE CAN LAY SIEGE TO ASGARD FROM A MOST UNEXPECTED DIRECTION--

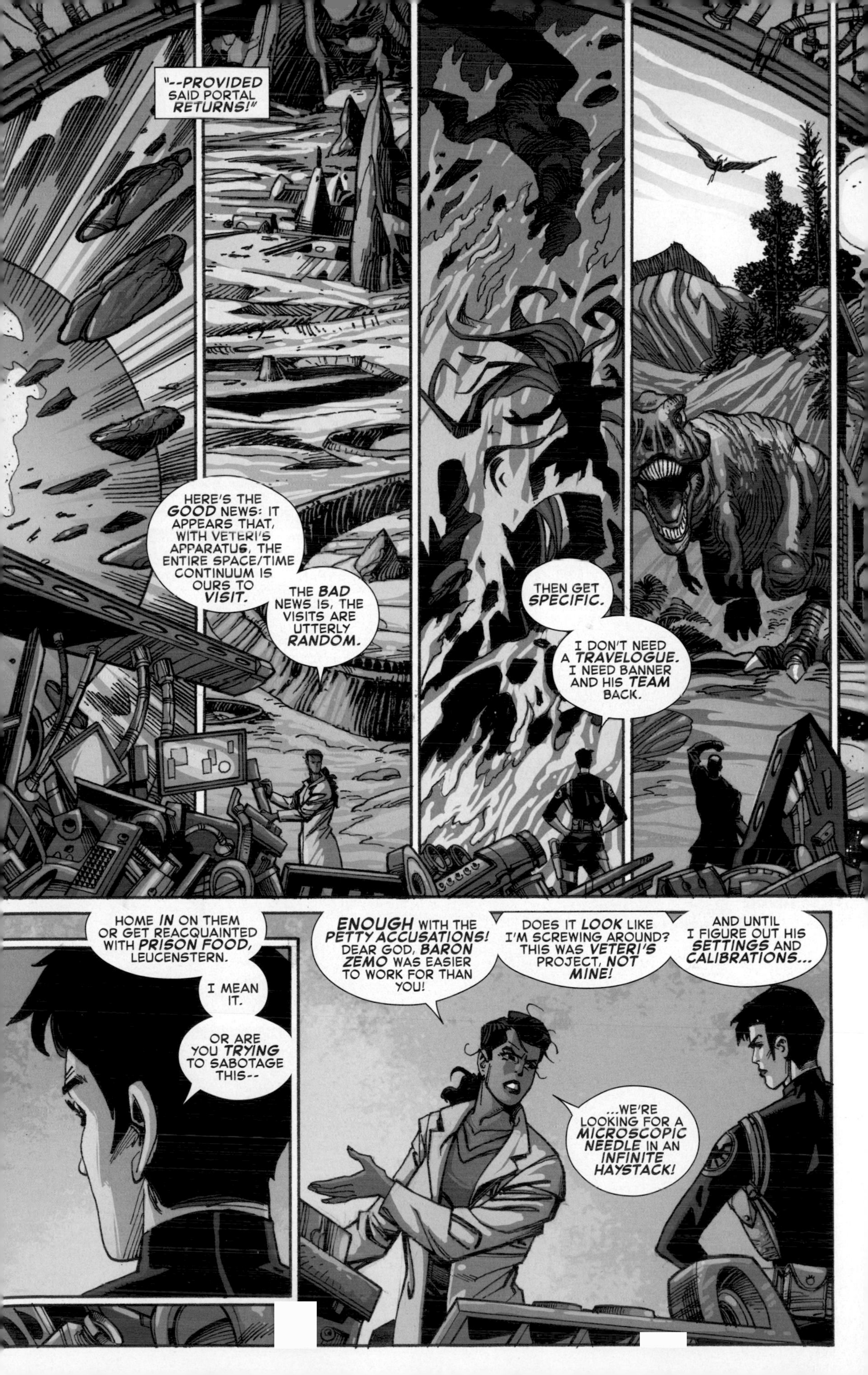
"--PROVIDED SAID PORTAL RETURNS!"
HERE'S THE GOOD NEWS: IT APPEARS THAT, WITH VETERI'S APPARATUS, THE ENTIRE SPACE/TIME CONTINUUM IS OURS TO VISIT.
THE BAD NEWS IS, THE VISITS ARE UTTERLY RANDOM.
THEN GET SPECIFIC.
I DON'T NEED A TRAVELOGUE. I NEED BANNER AND HIS TEAM BACK.
HOME IN ON THEM OR GET REACQUAINTED WITH PRISON FOOD, LEUCENSTERN.
I MEAN IT.
OR ARE YOU TRYING TO SABOTAGE THIS--
ENOUGH WITH THE PETTY ACCUSATIONS! DEAR GOD, BARON ZEMO WAS EASIER TO WORK FOR THAN YOU!
DOES IT LOOK LIKE I'M SCREWING AROUND? THIS WAS VETERI'S PROJECT, NOT MINE!
AND UNTIL I FIGURE OUT HIS SETTINGS AND CALIBRATIONS...
...WE'RE LOOKING FOR A MICROSCOPIC NEEDLE IN AN INFINITE HAYSTACK!

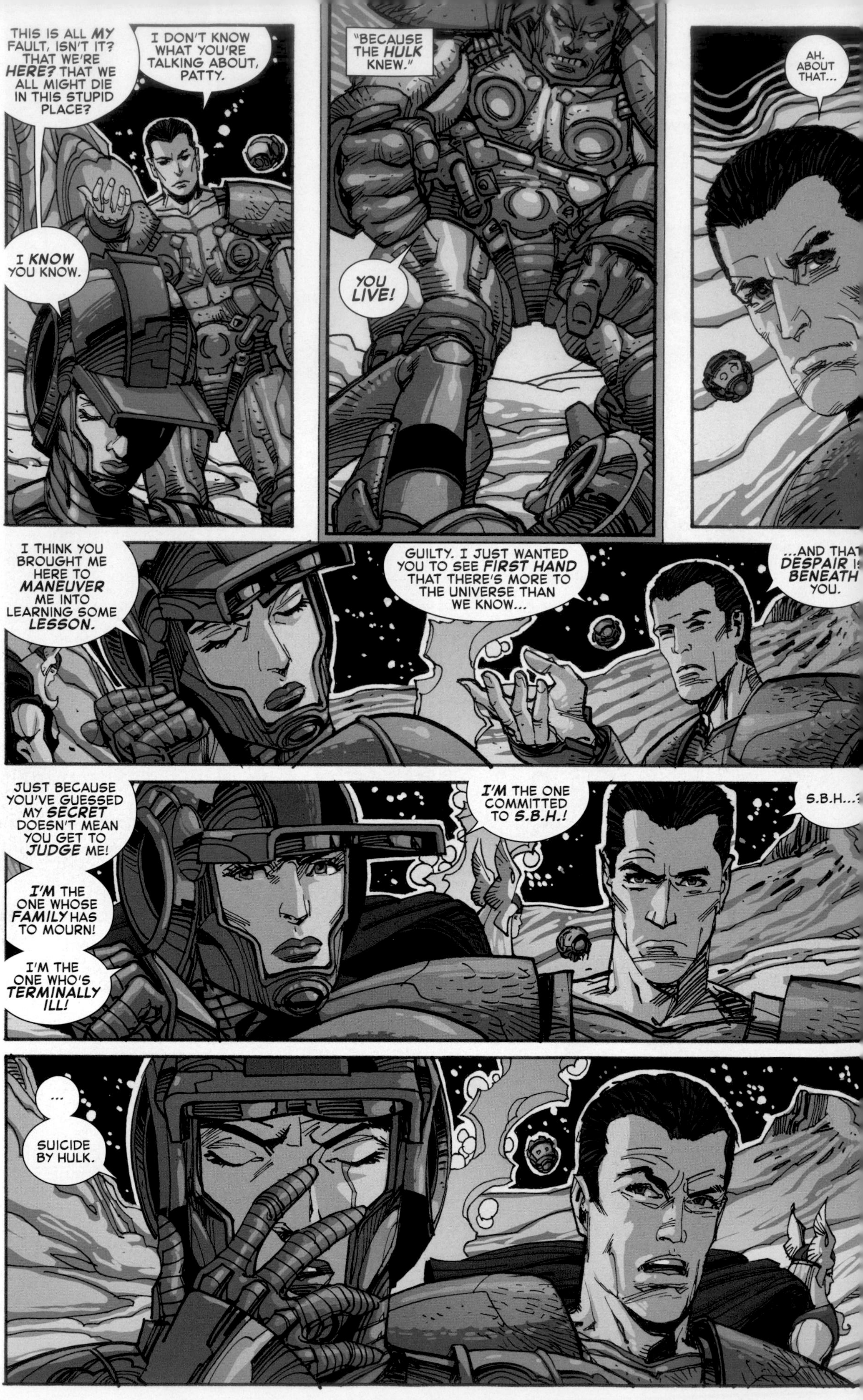
THIS IS ALL MY FAULT, ISN'T IT? THAT WE'RE HERE? THAT WE ALL MIGHT DIE IN THIS STUPID PLACE?
I DON'T KNOW WHAT YOU'RE TALKING ABOUT, PATTY.
I KNOW YOU KNOW.
"BECAUSE THE HULK KNEW."
YOU LIVE!
AH. ABOUT THAT...
I THINK YOU BROUGHT ME HERE TO MANEUVER ME INTO LEARNING SOME LESSON.
GUILTY. I JUST WANTED YOU TO SEE FIRST HAND THAT THERE'S MORE TO THE UNIVERSE THAN WE KNOW...
...AND THAT DESPAIR IS BENEATH YOU.
JUST BECAUSE YOU'VE GUESSED MY SECRET DOESN'T MEAN YOU GET TO JUDGE ME!
I'M THE ONE WHOSE FAMILY HAS TO MOURN!
I'M THE ONE WHO'S TERMINALLY ILL!
I'M THE ONE COMMITTED TO S.B.H.!
S.B.H...?
...
SUICIDE BY HULK.

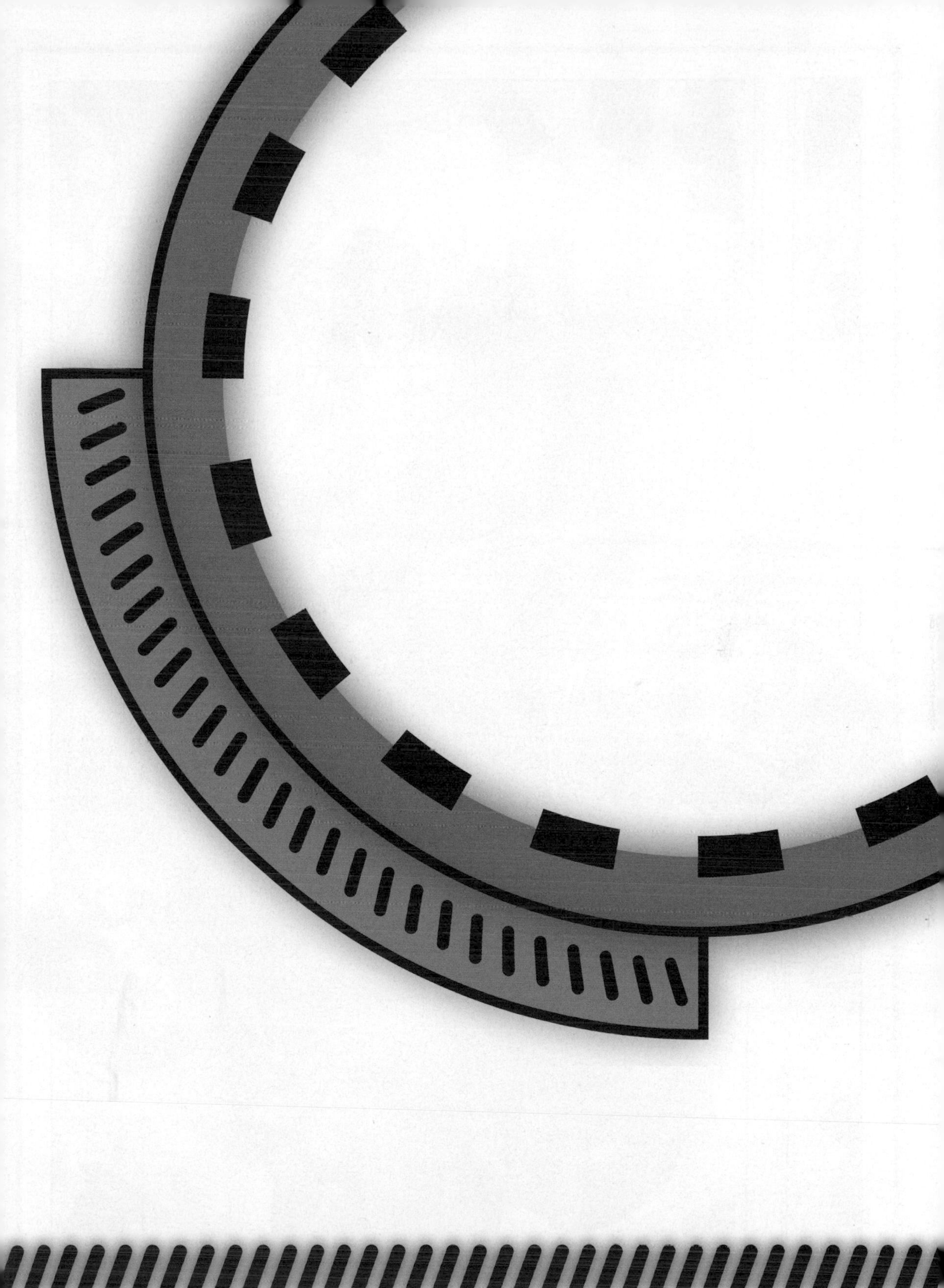

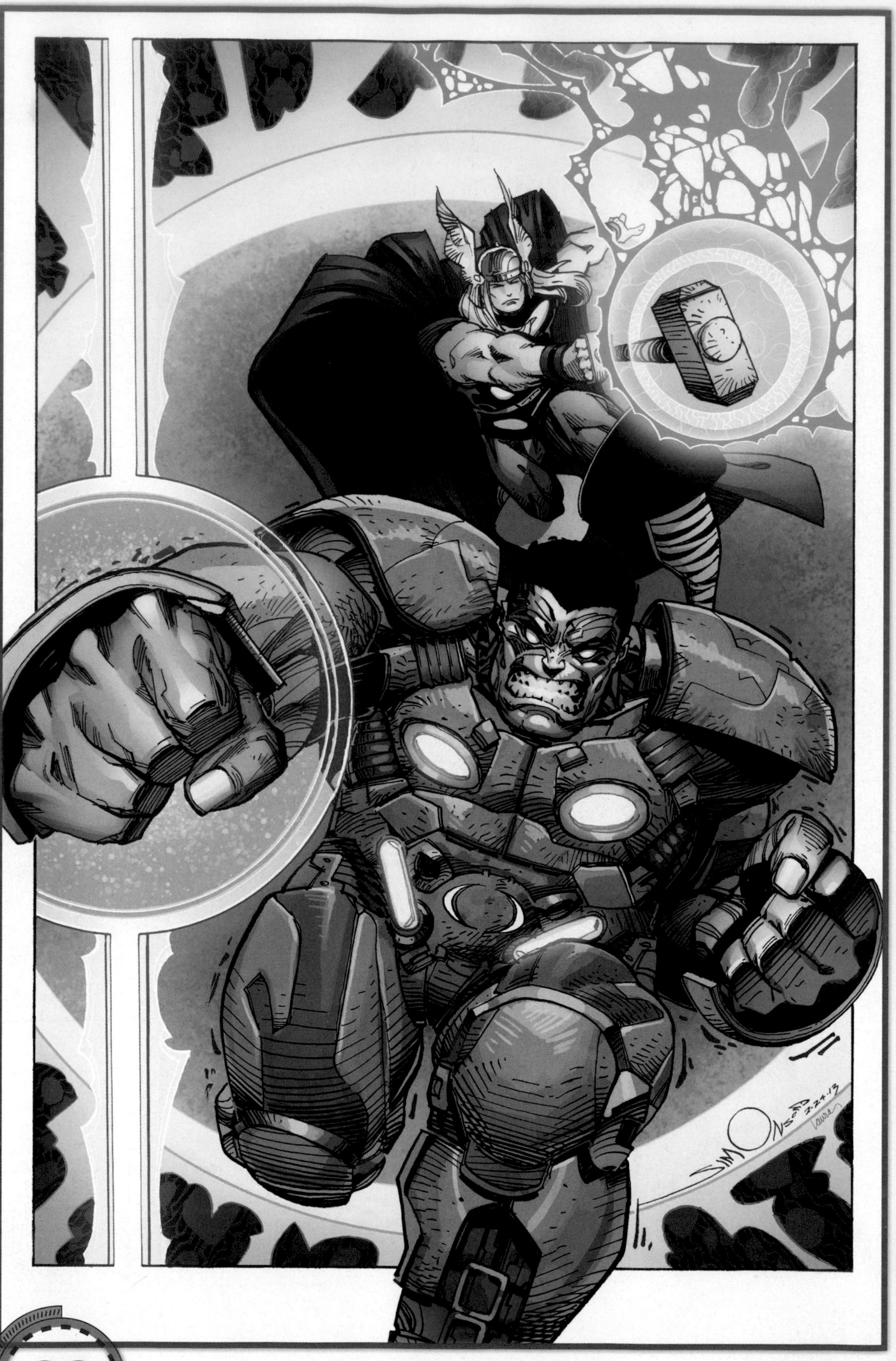

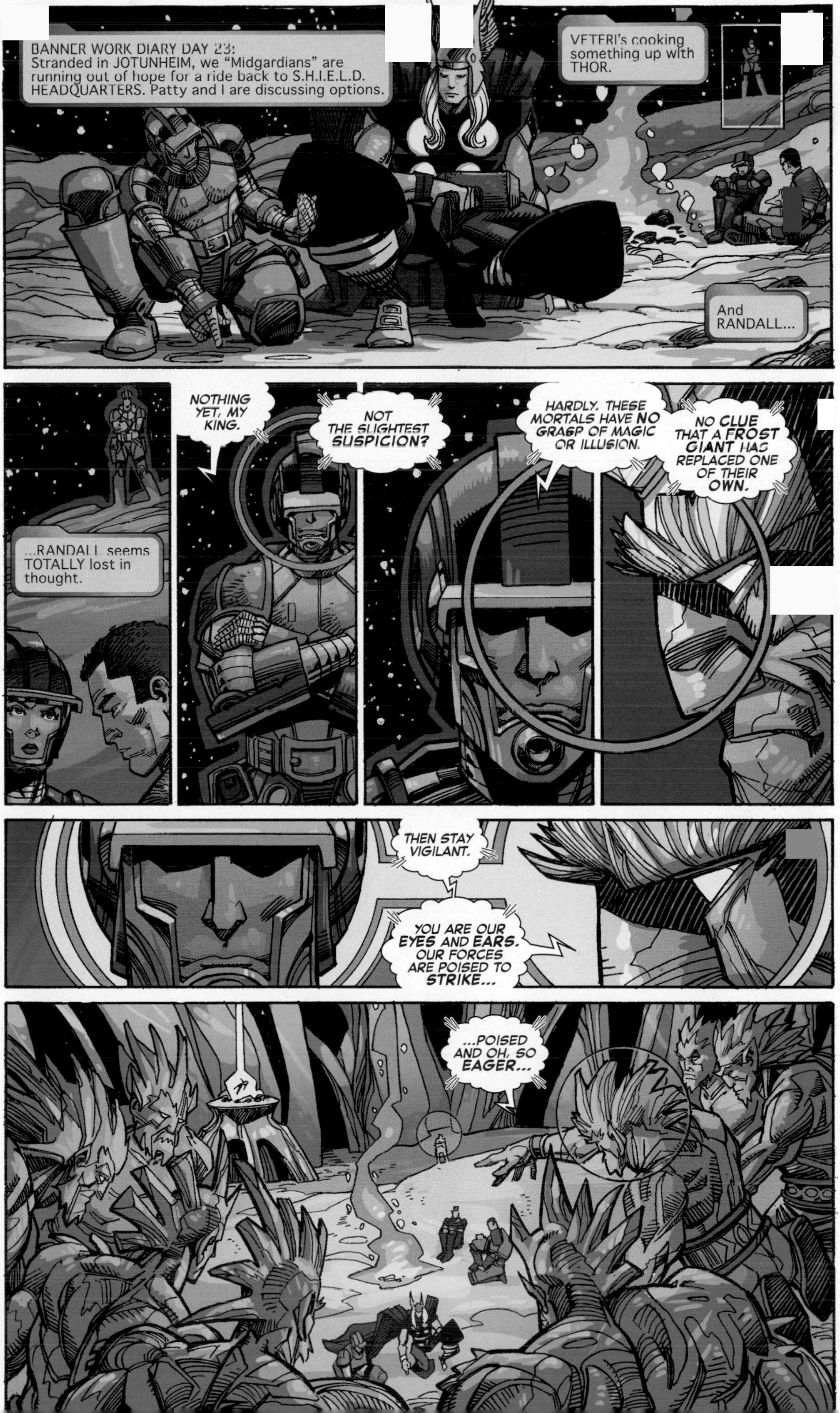

BANNER WORK DIARY DAY 23:
Stranded in JOTUNHEIM, we "Midgardians" are running out of hope for a ride back to S.H.I.E.L.D. HEADQUARTERS. Patty and I are discussing options.
VETERI's cooking something up with THOR.
And RANDALL...
...RANDALL seems TOTALLY lost in thought.
NOTHING YET, MY KING.
NOT THE SLIGHTEST SUSPICION?
HARDLY. THESE MORTALS HAVE NO GRASP OF MAGIC OR ILLUSION.
NO CLUE THAT A FROST GIANT HAS REPLACED ONE OF THEIR OWN.
THEN STAY VIGILANT.
YOU ARE OUR EYES AND EARS. OUR FORCES ARE POISED TO STRIKE...
...POISED AND OH, SO EAGER...

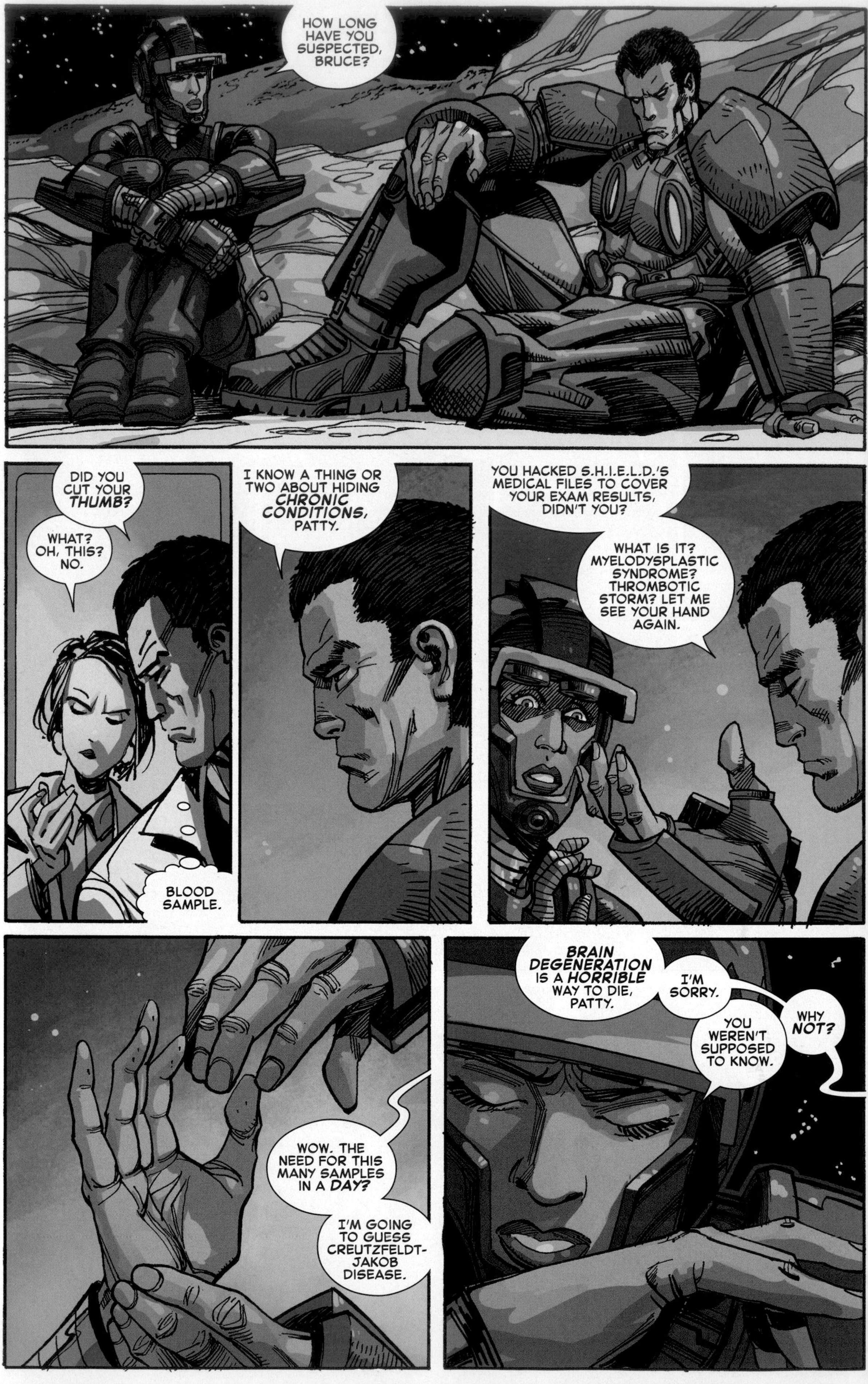

HOW LONG HAVE YOU SUSPECTED, BRUCE?
DID YOU CUT YOUR *THUMB?*
WHAT? OH, THIS? NO.
BLOOD SAMPLE.
I KNOW A THING OR TWO ABOUT HIDING *CHRONIC CONDITIONS,* PATTY.
YOU HACKED S.H.I.E.L.D.'S MEDICAL FILES TO COVER YOUR EXAM RESULTS, DIDN'T YOU?
WHAT IS IT? MYELODYSPLASTIC SYNDROME? THROMBOTIC STORM? LET ME SEE YOUR HAND AGAIN.
WOW. THE NEED FOR THIS MANY SAMPLES IN A *DAY?*
I'M GOING TO GUESS CREUTZFELDT-JAKOB DISEASE.
BRAIN DEGENERATION IS A *HORRIBLE* WAY TO DIE, PATTY.
I'M SORRY.
YOU WEREN'T SUPPOSED TO KNOW.
WHY *NOT?*

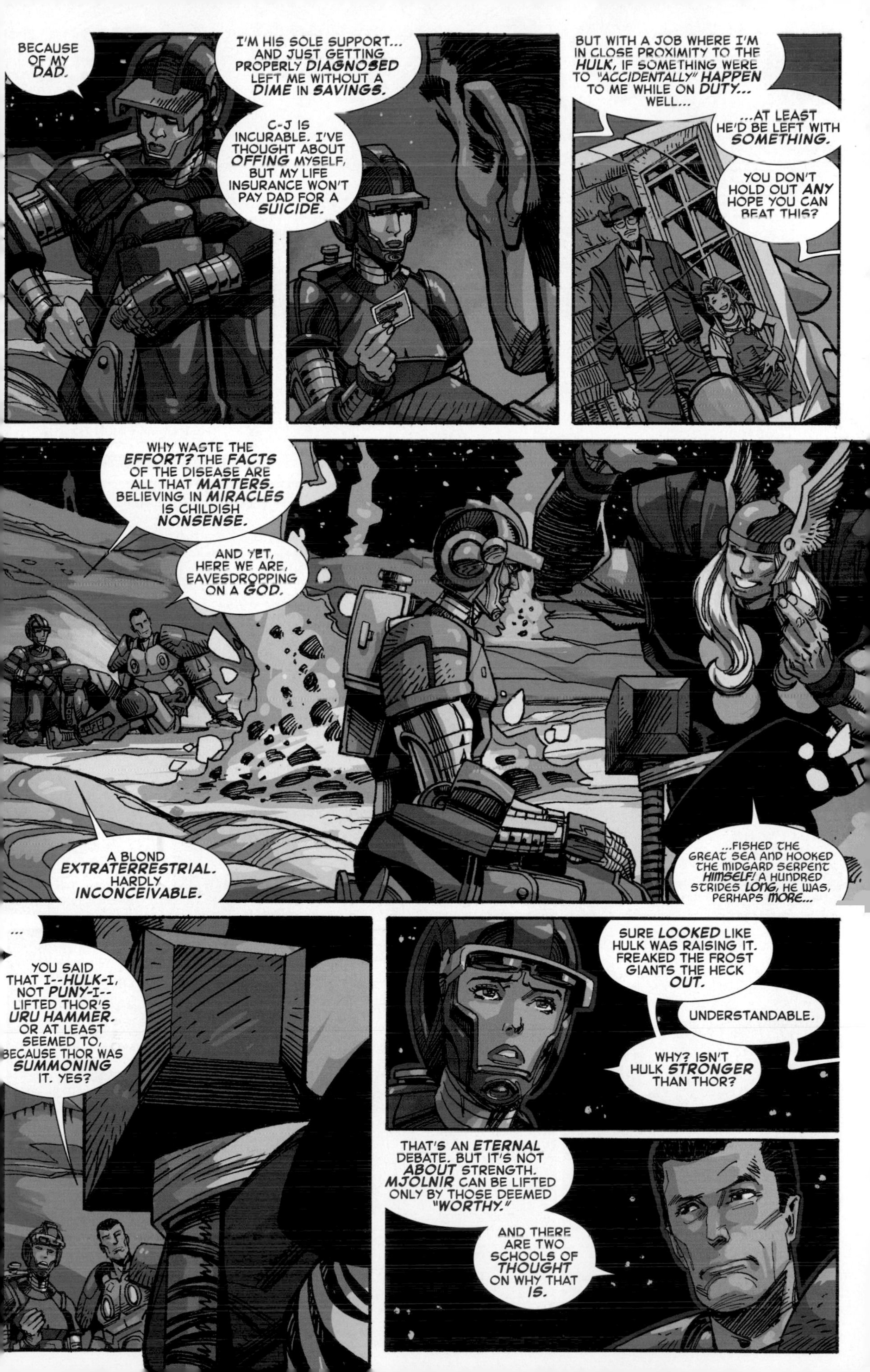

BECAUSE OF MY DAD.
I'M HIS SOLE SUPPORT... AND JUST GETTING PROPERLY DIAGNOSED LEFT ME WITHOUT A DIME IN SAVINGS.
C-J IS INCURABLE. I'VE THOUGHT ABOUT OFFING MYSELF, BUT MY LIFE INSURANCE WON'T PAY DAD FOR A SUICIDE.
BUT WITH A JOB WHERE I'M IN CLOSE PROXIMITY TO THE HULK, IF SOMETHING WERE TO "ACCIDENTALLY" HAPPEN TO ME WHILE ON DUTY... WELL...
...AT LEAST HE'D BE LEFT WITH SOMETHING.
YOU DON'T HOLD OUT ANY HOPE YOU CAN BEAT THIS?
WHY WASTE THE EFFORT? THE FACTS OF THE DISEASE ARE ALL THAT MATTERS. BELIEVING IN MIRACLES IS CHILDISH NONSENSE.
AND YET, HERE WE ARE, EAVESDROPPING ON A GOD.
A BLOND EXTRATERRESTRIAL. HARDLY INCONCEIVABLE.
...FISHED THE GREAT SEA AND HOOKED THE MIDGARD SERPENT HIMSELF! A HUNDRED STRIDES LONG, HE WAS, PERHAPS MORE...
...
YOU SAID THAT I--HULK-I, NOT PUNY-I-- LIFTED THOR'S URU HAMMER. OR AT LEAST SEEMED TO, BECAUSE THOR WAS SUMMONING IT. YES?
SURE LOOKED LIKE HULK WAS RAISING IT. FREAKED THE FROST GIANTS THE HECK OUT.
UNDERSTANDABLE.
WHY? ISN'T HULK STRONGER THAN THOR?
THAT'S AN ETERNAL DEBATE. BUT IT'S NOT ABOUT STRENGTH. MJOLNIR CAN BE LIFTED ONLY BY THOSE DEEMED "WORTHY."
AND THERE ARE TWO SCHOOLS OF THOUGHT ON WHY THAT IS.

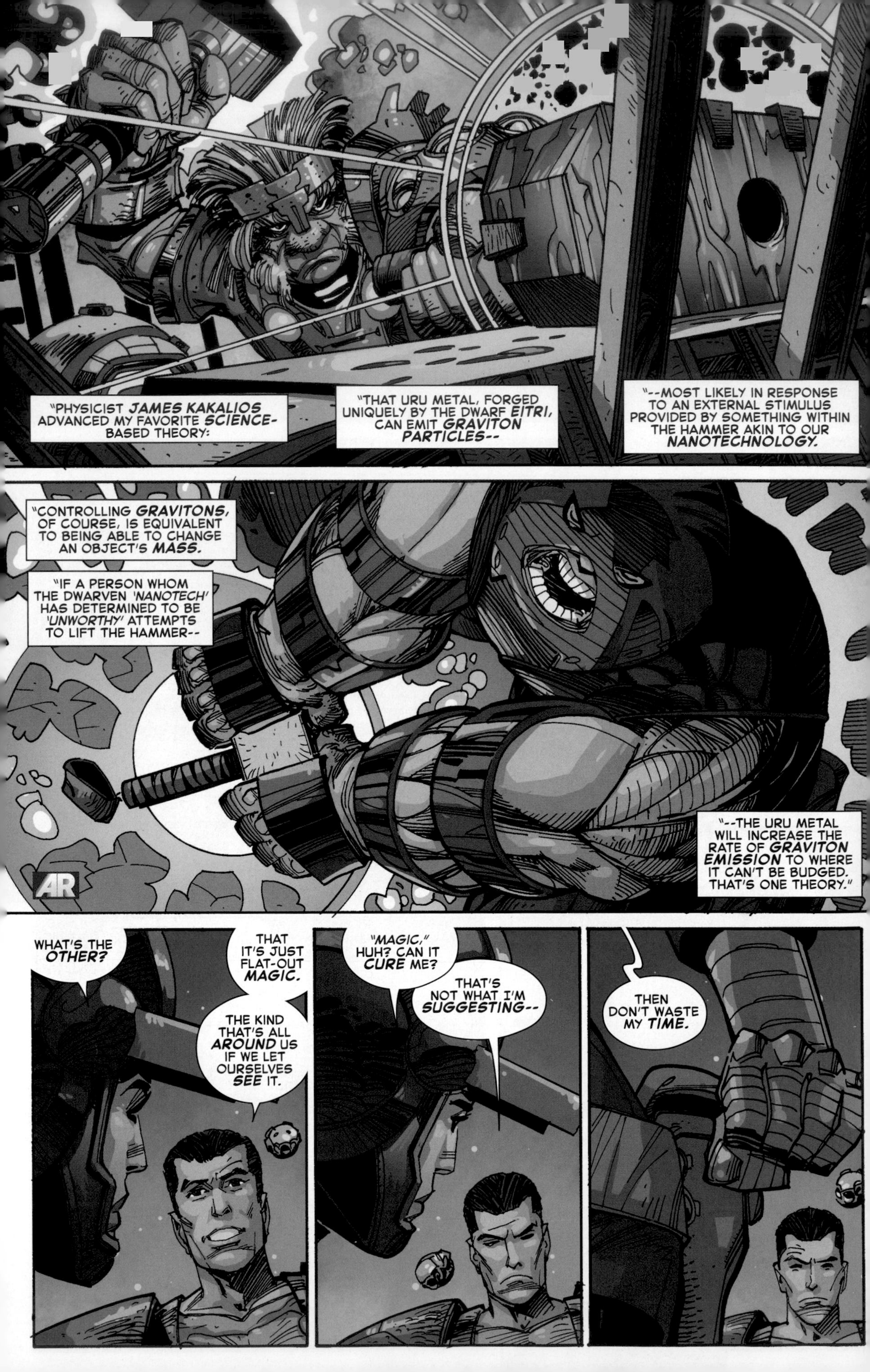
"PHYSICIST JAMES KAKALIOS ADVANCED MY FAVORITE SCIENCE-BASED THEORY:
"THAT URU METAL, FORGED UNIQUELY BY THE DWARF EITRI, CAN EMIT GRAVITON PARTICLES--
"--MOST LIKELY IN RESPONSE TO AN EXTERNAL STIMULUS PROVIDED BY SOMETHING WITHIN THE HAMMER AKIN TO OUR NANOTECHNOLOGY.
"CONTROLLING GRAVITONS, OF COURSE, IS EQUIVALENT TO BEING ABLE TO CHANGE AN OBJECT'S MASS.
"IF A PERSON WHOM THE DWARVEN 'NANOTECH' HAS DETERMINED TO BE 'UNWORTHY' ATTEMPTS TO LIFT THE HAMMER--
"--THE URU METAL WILL INCREASE THE RATE OF GRAVITON EMISSION TO WHERE IT CAN'T BE BUDGED. THAT'S ONE THEORY."
AR
WHAT'S THE OTHER?
THAT IT'S JUST FLAT-OUT MAGIC.
THE KIND THAT'S ALL AROUND US IF WE LET OURSELVES SEE IT.
"MAGIC," HUH? CAN IT CURE ME?
THAT'S NOT WHAT I'M SUGGESTING--
THEN DON'T WASTE MY TIME.

THE LIQUID ORE EIDERDÜRM IS A SUPERCONDUCTOR, RIGHT?

SO HERE'S WHAT I PROPOSE.

SEEING YOU COMMAND LIGHTNING GAVE ME THE IDEA.

BY USING A PROCESS CALLED ELECTROSTATIC SEPARATION, WE COULD CONCEIVABLY EXTRACT PURE EIDERDÜRM SAMPLES FROM THAT WATERFALL--

--IF YOUR WHIRLING HAMMER CAN CREATE A STRONG ENOUGH ELECTROMAGNETIC FIELD.

THOU DOST REALIZE THAT SHOULD THE EIDERDÜRM TOUCH THEE, THOU SHALT REMAIN HERE IN JOTUNHEIM FOREVER, A FROZEN STATUE?

I...DID NOT KNOW THAT.

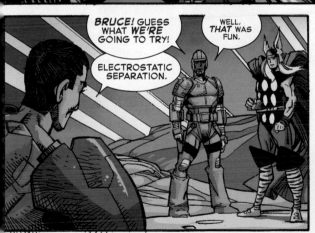

BUT I ALWAYS SAY: LIVE FAST, DIE YOUNG, AND LEAVE A GOOD-LOOKING CORPSE.

HA! WHAT A MAGNIFICENT SENTIMENT! AN ALCHEMIST AND A POET, THOU ART! WELL-SAID! I SHALL QUOTE THEE!

I...DIDN'T REALLY COIN THE...

WHATEVER. OKAY, I'M A GENIUS.

BRUCE! GUESS WHAT WE'RE GOING TO TRY!

ELECTROSTATIC SEPARATION.

WELL, THAT WAS FUN.

PERHAPS AN ENDEAVOR OF THIS MAGNITUDE CALLS FOR THE MIGHT OF THE JADE GIANT! CAREST THOU TO TRANSFORM?

LET'S CALL THAT PLAN "B."

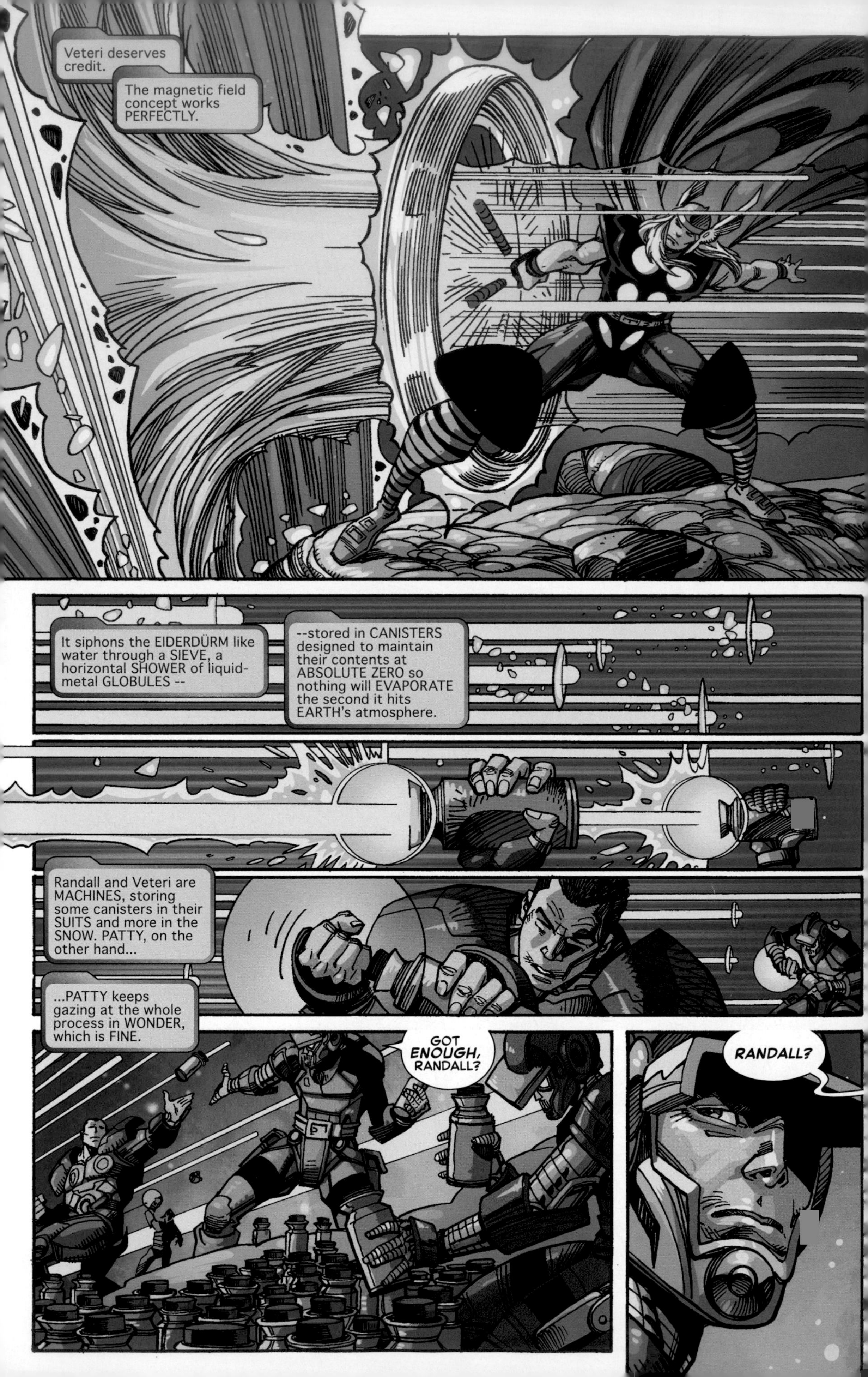

Veteri deserves credit.
The magnetic field concept works PERFECTLY.
It siphons the EIDERDÜRM like water through a SIEVE, a horizontal SHOWER of liquid-metal GLOBULES --
--stored in CANISTERS designed to maintain their contents at ABSOLUTE ZERO so nothing will EVAPORATE the second it hits EARTH's atmosphere.
Randall and Veteri are MACHINES, storing some canisters in their SUITS and more in the SNOW. PATTY, on the other hand...
...PATTY keeps gazing at the whole process in WONDER, which is FINE.
GOT ENOUGH, RANDALL?
RANDALL?

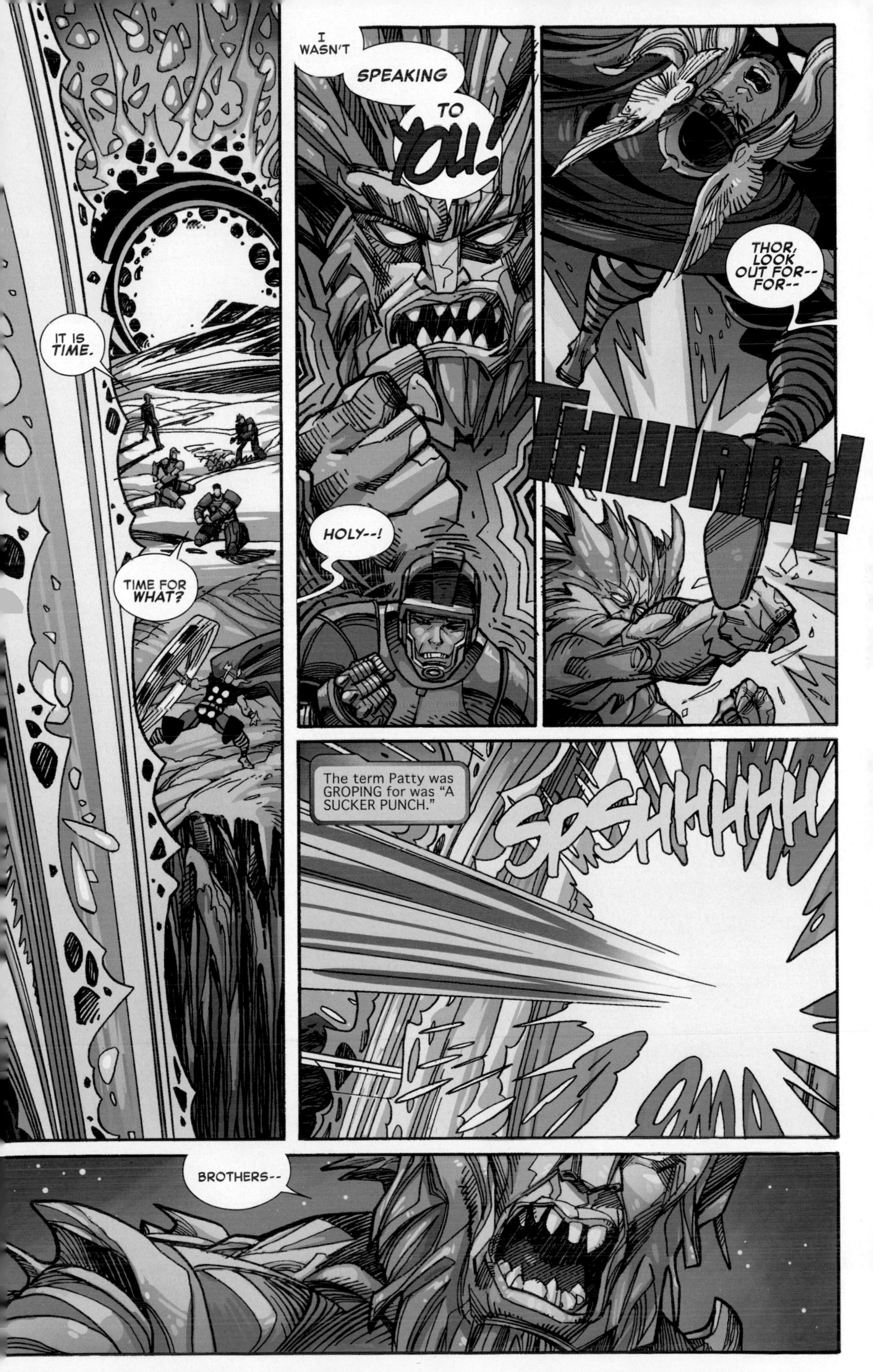
IT IS TIME.
TIME FOR WHAT?
I WASN'T
SPEAKING
TO
YOU!
HOLY--!
THOR, LOOK OUT FOR-- FOR--
THWAMM!
The term Patty was GROPING for was "A SUCKER PUNCH."
SPSHHHHH
BROTHERS--

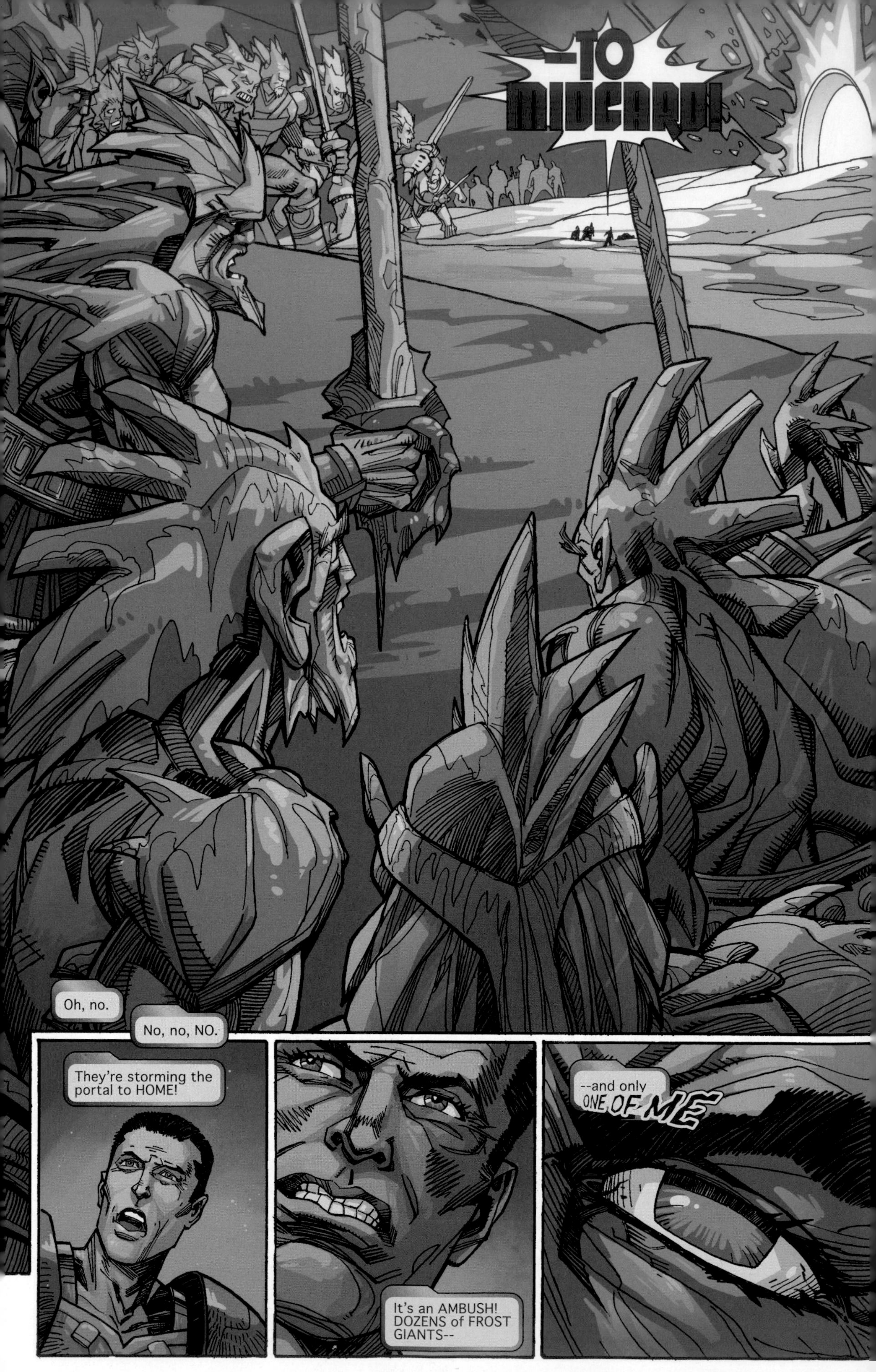
--TO MIDGARD!
Oh, no.
No, no, NO.
They're storming the portal to HOME!
It's an AMBUSH! DOZENS of FROST GIANTS--
--and only ONE OF ME

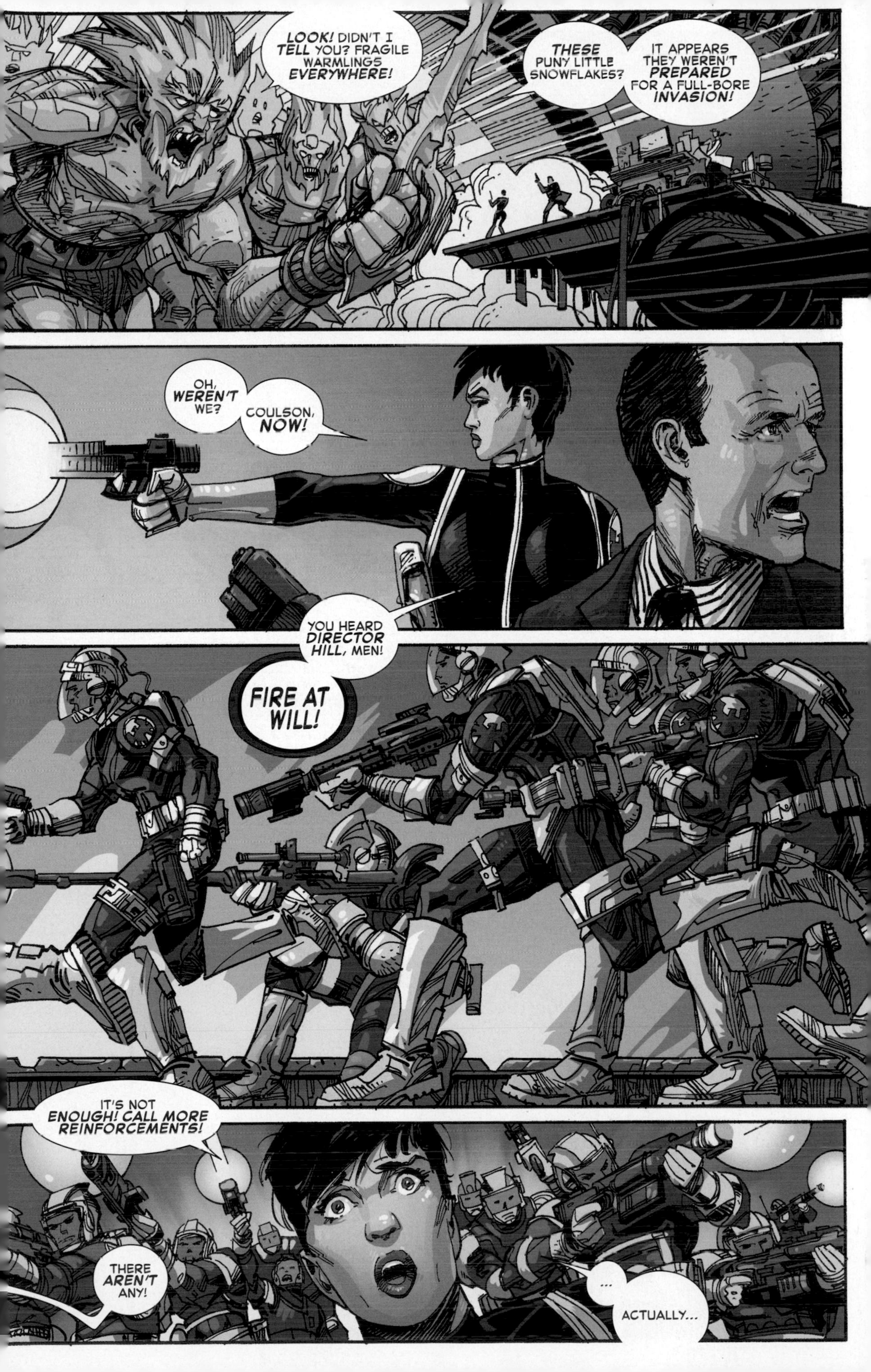
LOOK! DIDN'T I TELL YOU? FRAGILE WARMLINGS EVERYWHERE!
THESE PUNY LITTLE SNOWFLAKES?
IT APPEARS THEY WEREN'T PREPARED FOR A FULL-BORE INVASION!
OH, WEREN'T WE?
COULSON, NOW!
YOU HEARD DIRECTOR HILL, MEN!
FIRE AT WILL!
IT'S NOT ENOUGH! CALL MORE REINFORCEMENTS!
THERE AREN'T ANY!
...
ACTUALLY...

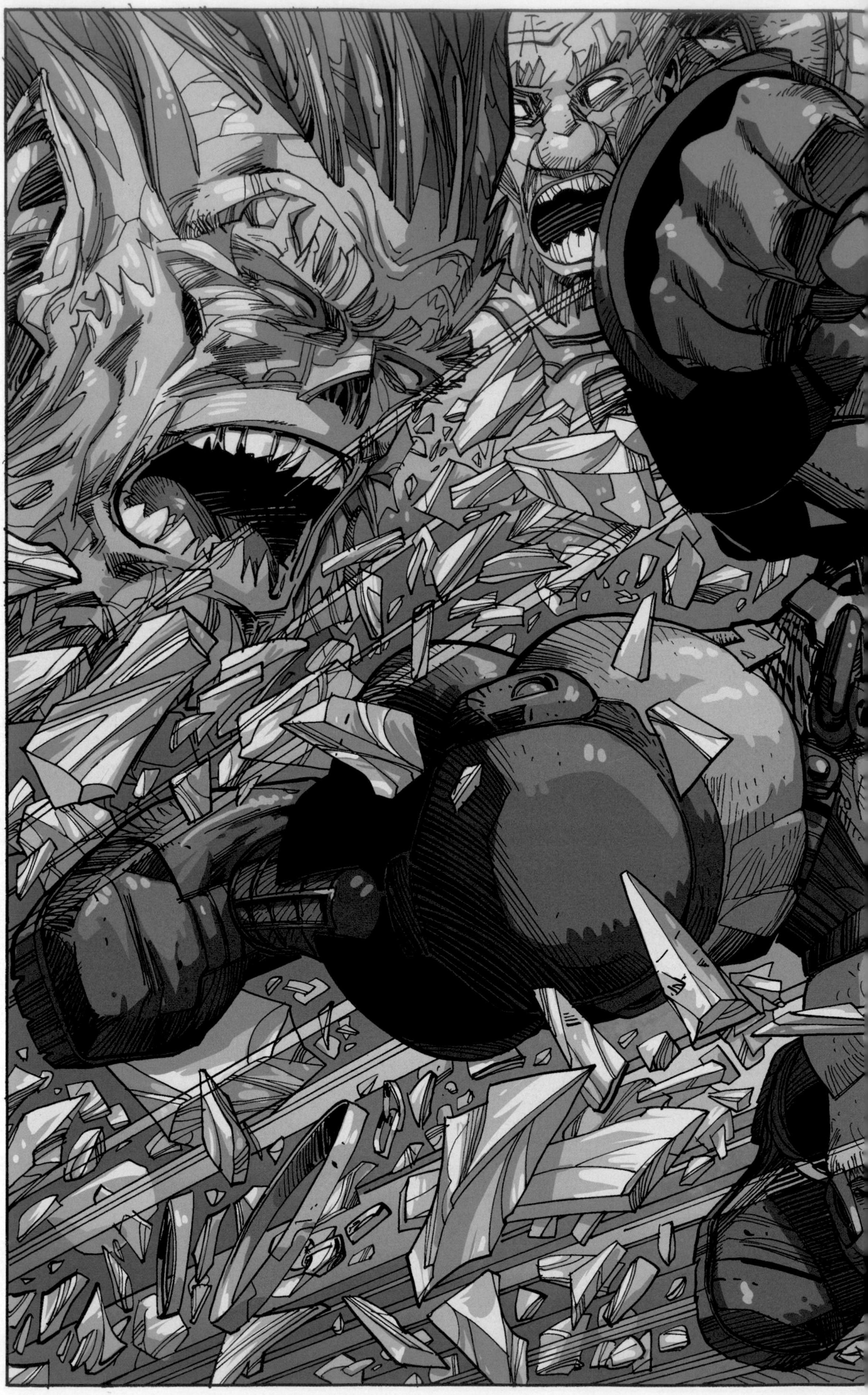

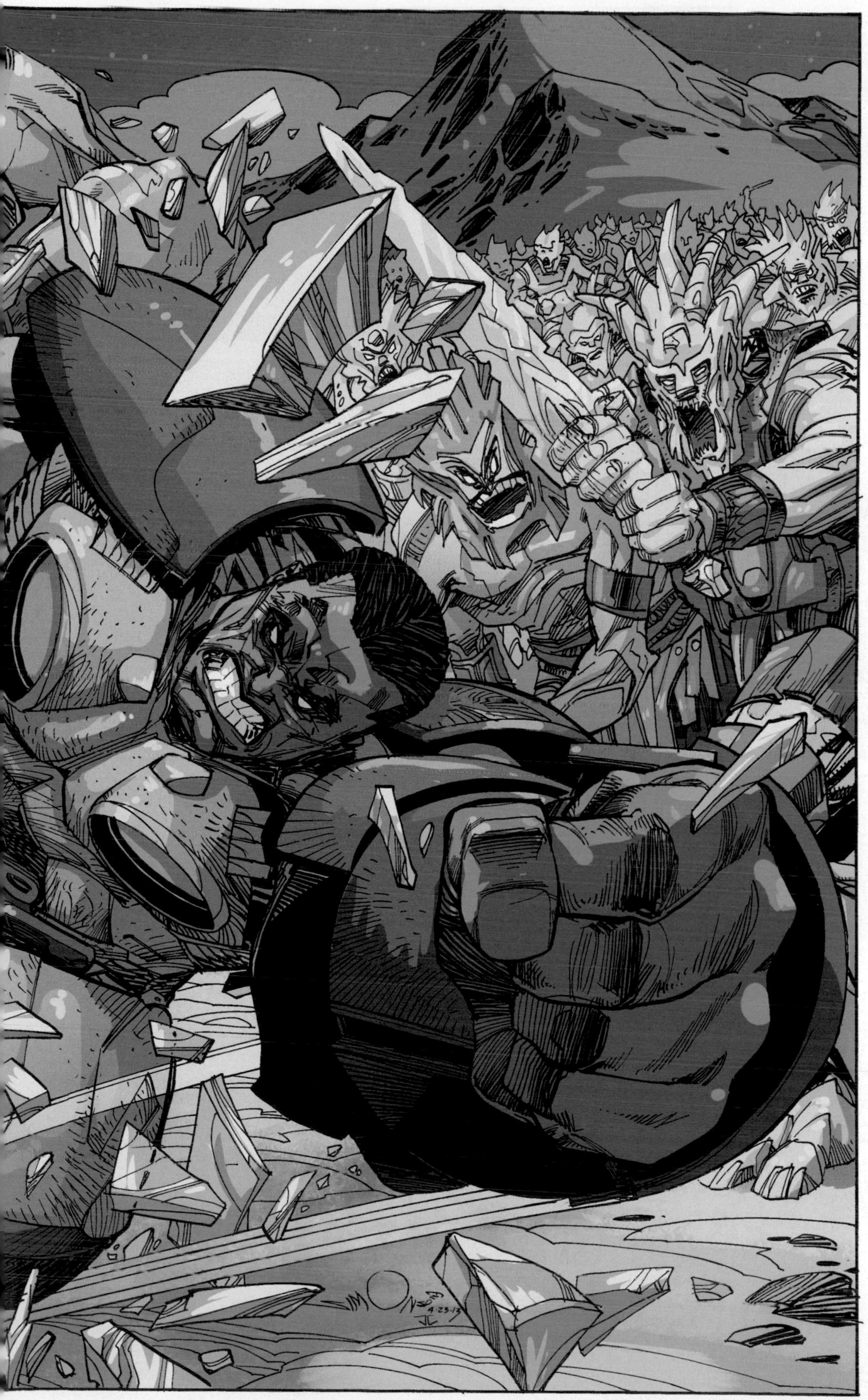

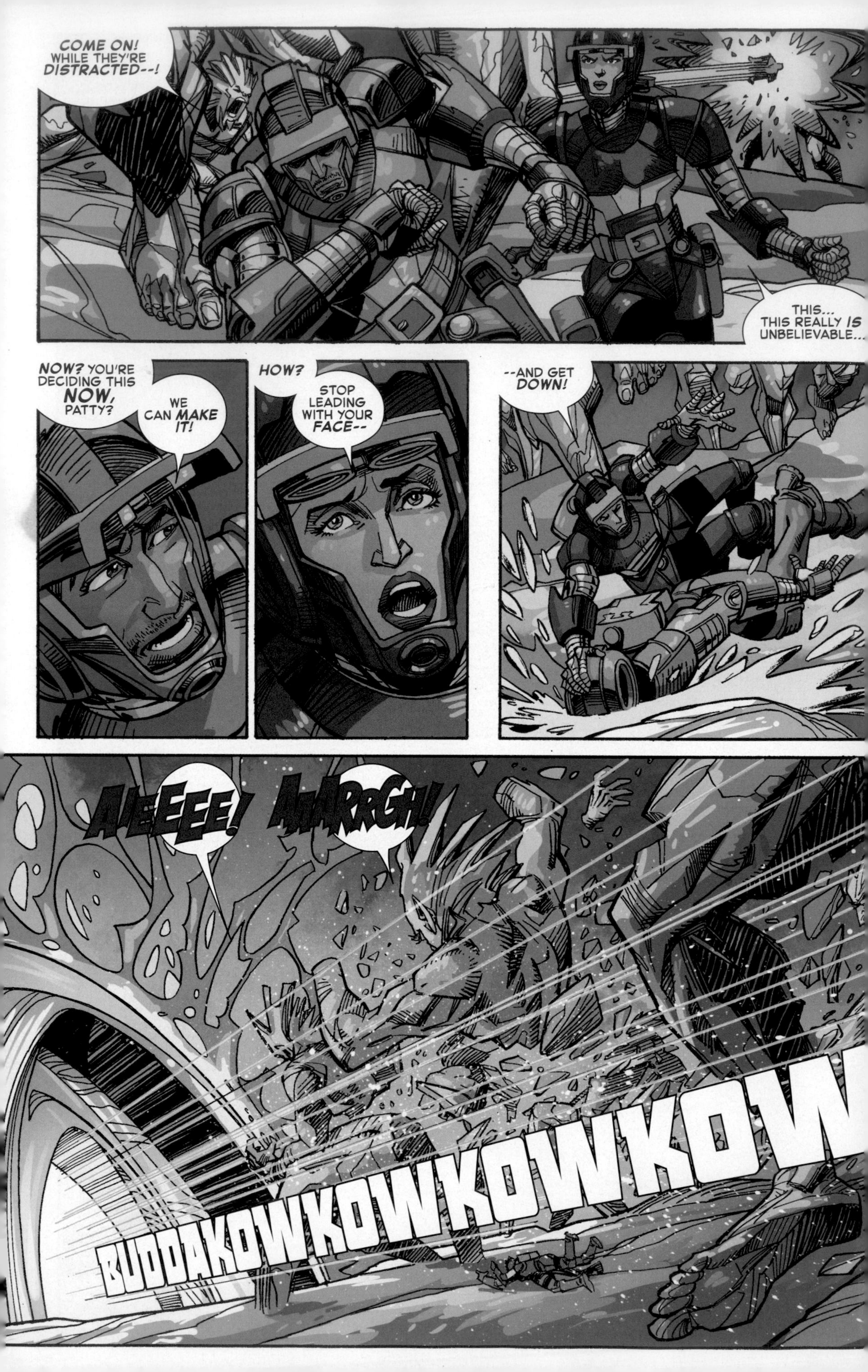
COME ON! WHILE THEY'RE DISTRACTED--!
THIS... THIS REALLY IS UNBELIEVABLE...
NOW? YOU'RE DECIDING THIS NOW, PATTY?
WE CAN MAKE IT!
HOW?
STOP LEADING WITH YOUR FACE--
--AND GET DOWN!
AIEEEE!
AAARRGH!
BUDDAKOWKOWKOWKOWKOW

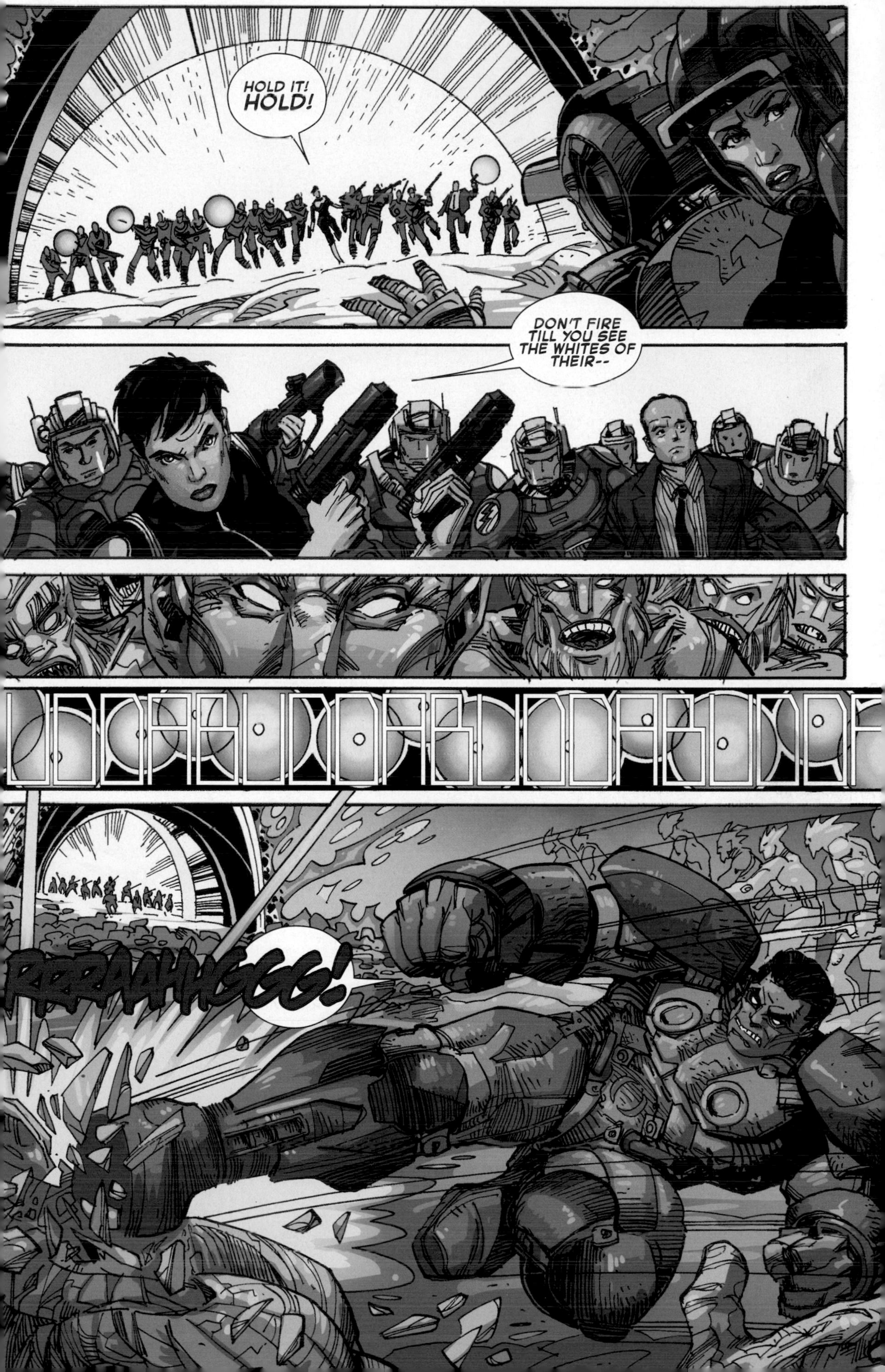
HOLD IT! HOLD!
DON'T FIRE TILL YOU SEE THE WHITES OF THEIR--
RRRAAHHGGG!

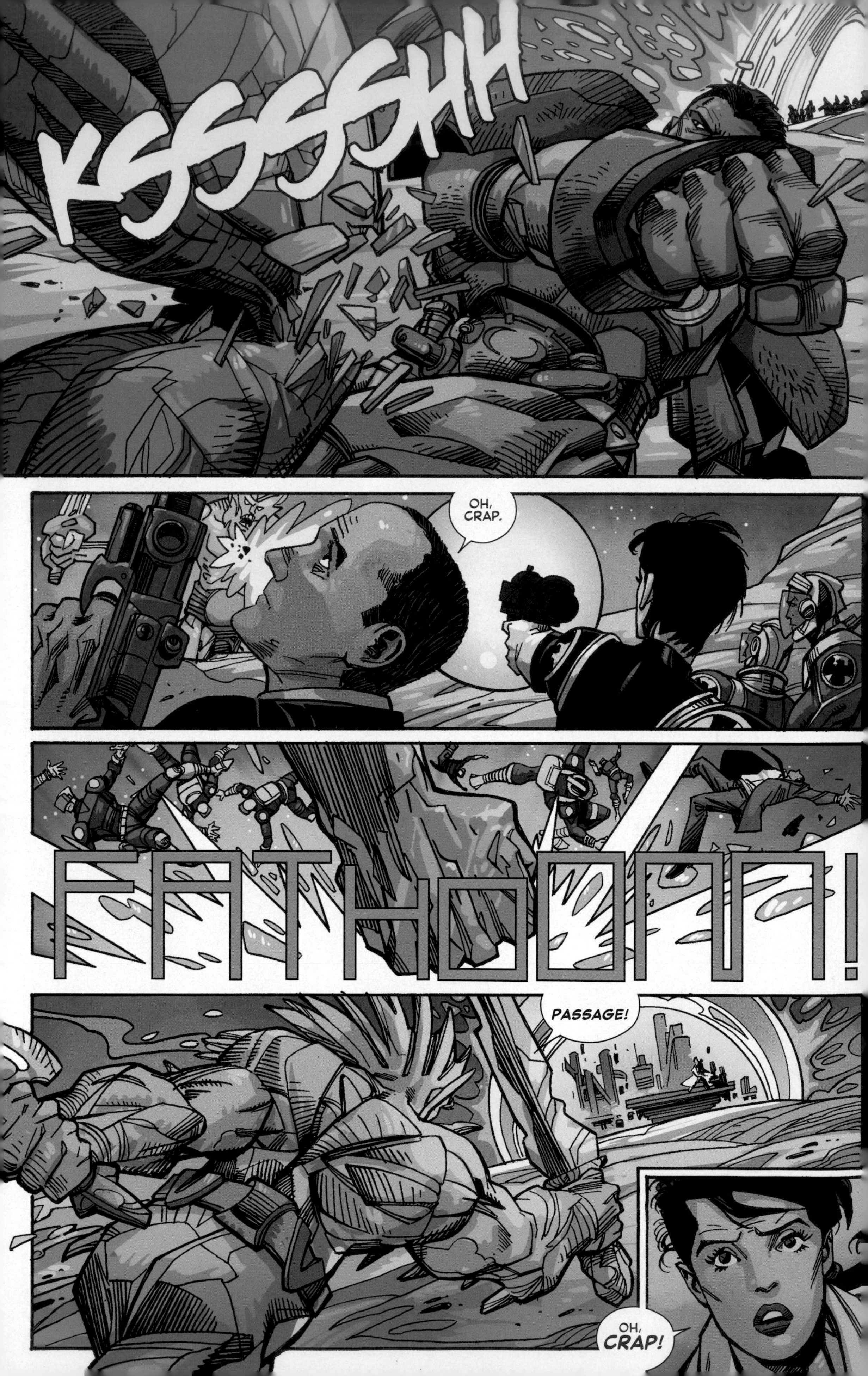
KSSSSHH
OH, CRAP.
FATHOOM!
PASSAGE!
OH, CRAP!

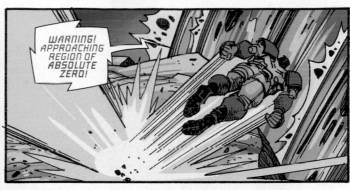

WARNING! APPROACHING REGION OF ABSOLUTE ZERO!

ARMOR THERMAL UNIT TO FULL RADIANT POWER--

SPSHHH

SKSHHHH!

...nnnnnhh...

--REPEAT-- THERMALS ON FULL--

YOU MAY...PUT ME DOWN, FRIEND HULKSMASH. THANKS TO THEE, I ONCE MORE AWAKEN.

MY GRATITUDE IS THINE.

NOW...LET US THRASH GIANTS.

PUNY GIANTS.

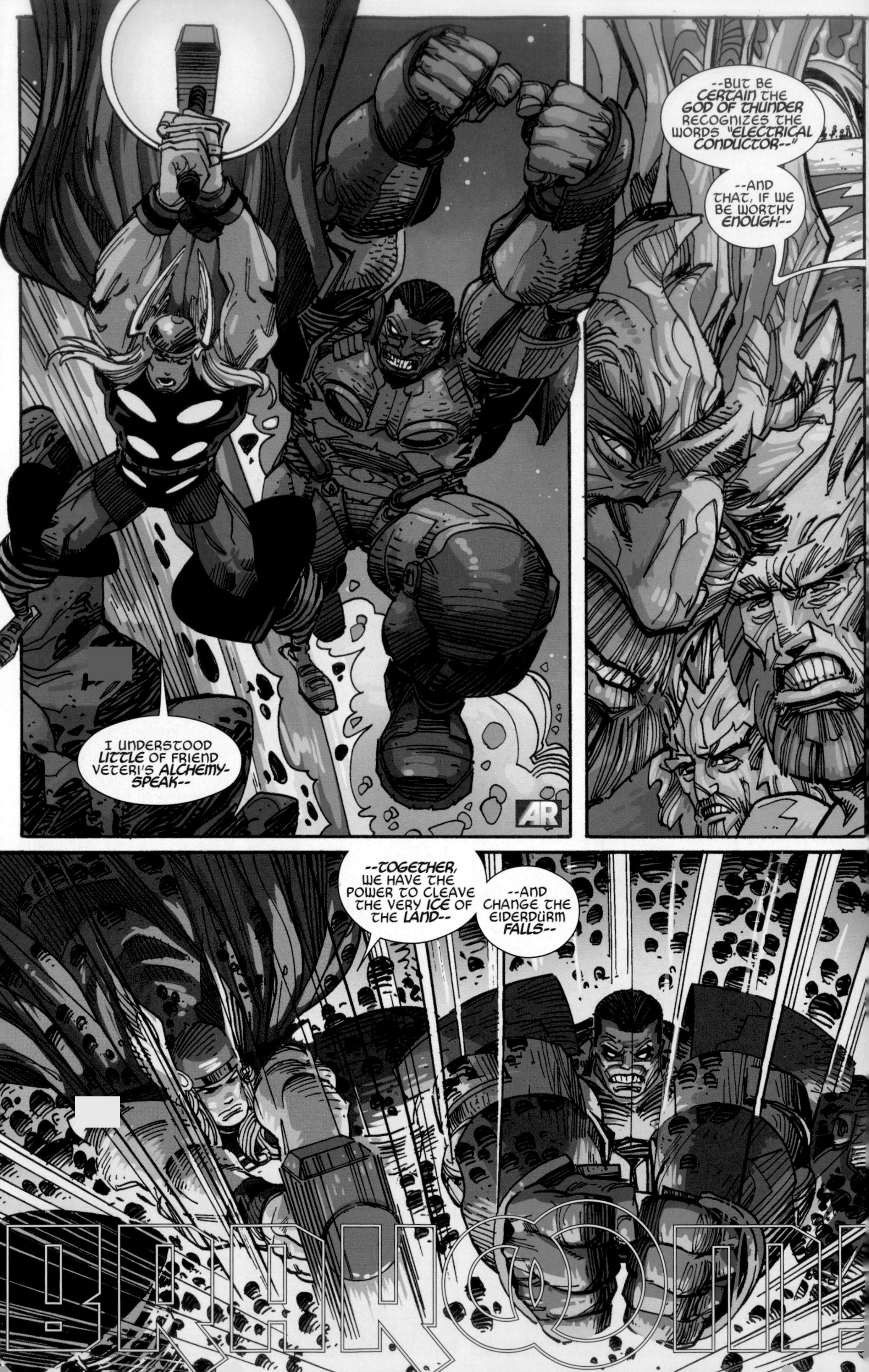
I UNDERSTOOD LITTLE OF FRIEND VETERI'S ALCHEMY-SPEAK--
--BUT BE CERTAIN THE GOD OF THUNDER RECOGNIZES THE WORDS "ELECTRICAL CONDUCTOR--"
--AND THAT, IF WE BE WORTHY ENOUGH--
--TOGETHER, WE HAVE THE POWER TO CLEAVE THE VERY ICE OF THE LAND--
--AND CHANGE THE EIDERDÜRM FALLS--

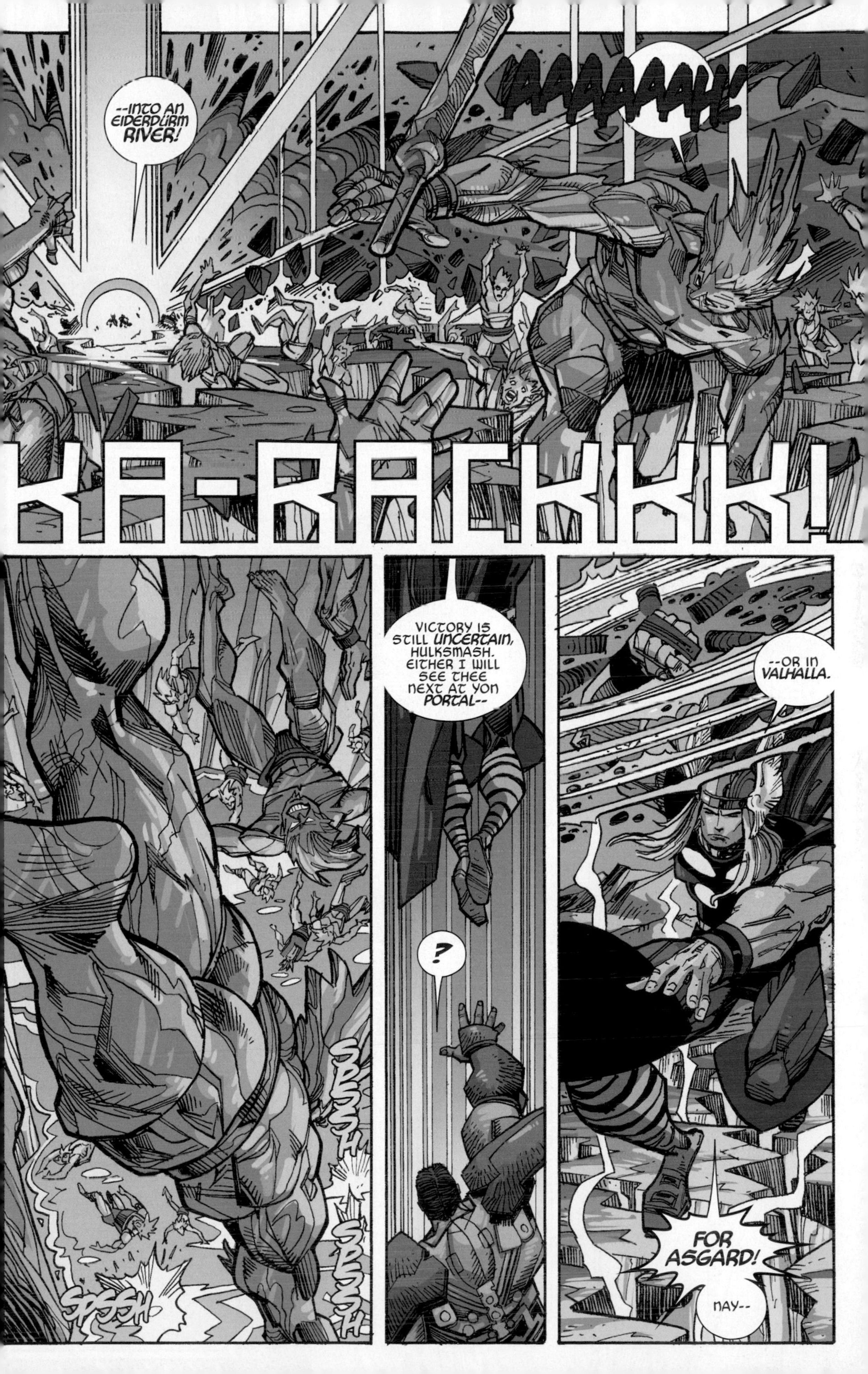
--INTO AN EIDERDÜRM RIVER!
AAAAAAAH!
KA-RACKKK!
VICTORY IS STILL UNCERTAIN, HULKSMASH. EITHER I WILL SEE THEE NEXT AT YON PORTAL--
?
--OR IN VALHALLA.
FOR ASGARD!
NAY--
SPSSH
SPSSH
SPSSH

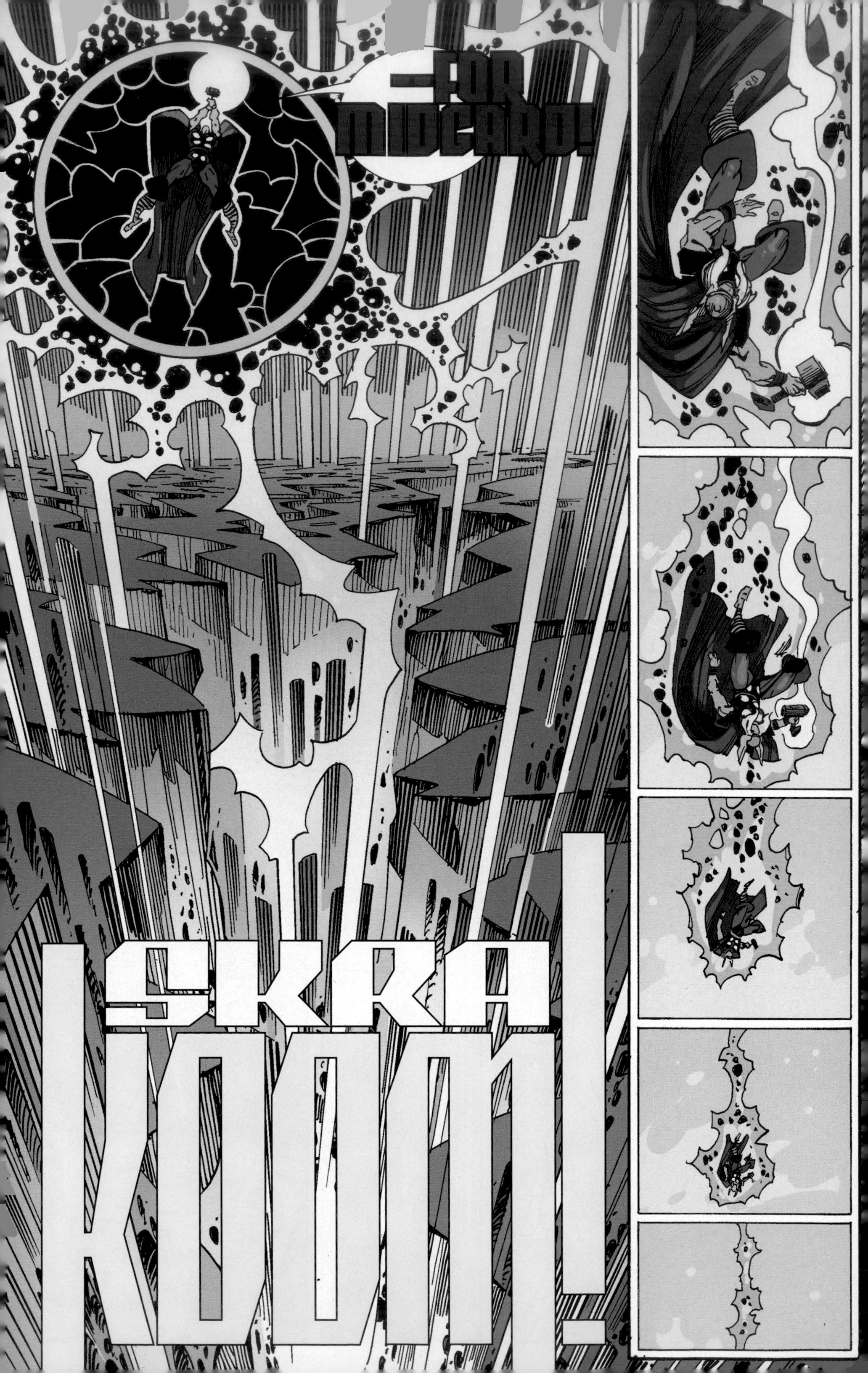
—FOR MIDGARD!
SKRA KOOM!

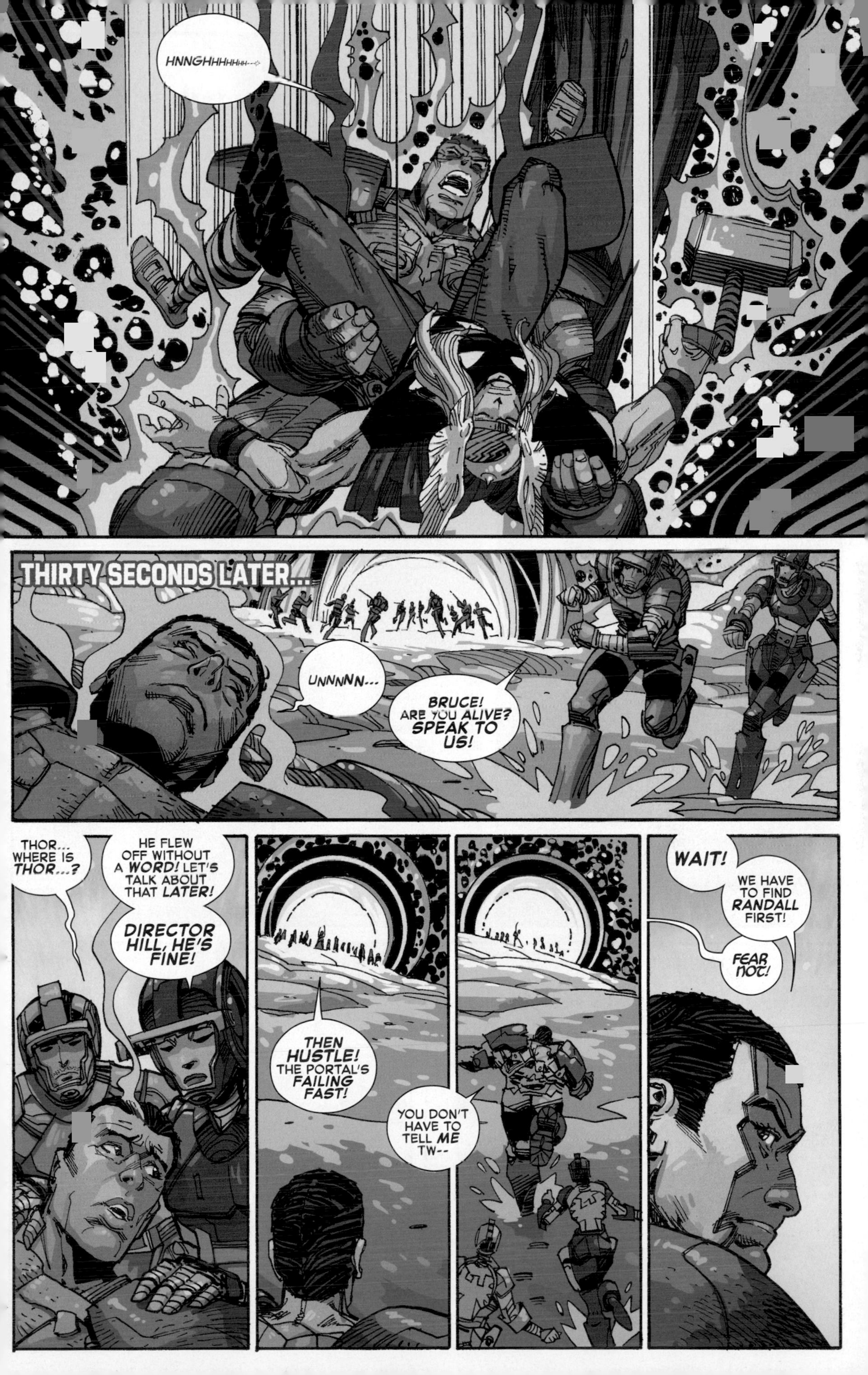
HNNGHHHHhhh--
THIRTY SECONDS LATER...
UNNNNN...
BRUCE! ARE YOU ALIVE? SPEAK TO US!
THOR... WHERE IS THOR...?
HE FLEW OFF WITHOUT A WORD! LET'S TALK ABOUT THAT LATER!
DIRECTOR HILL, HE'S FINE!
THEN HUSTLE! THE PORTAL'S FAILING FAST!
YOU DON'T HAVE TO TELL ME TW--
WAIT!
WE HAVE TO FIND RANDALL FIRST!
FEAR NOT!

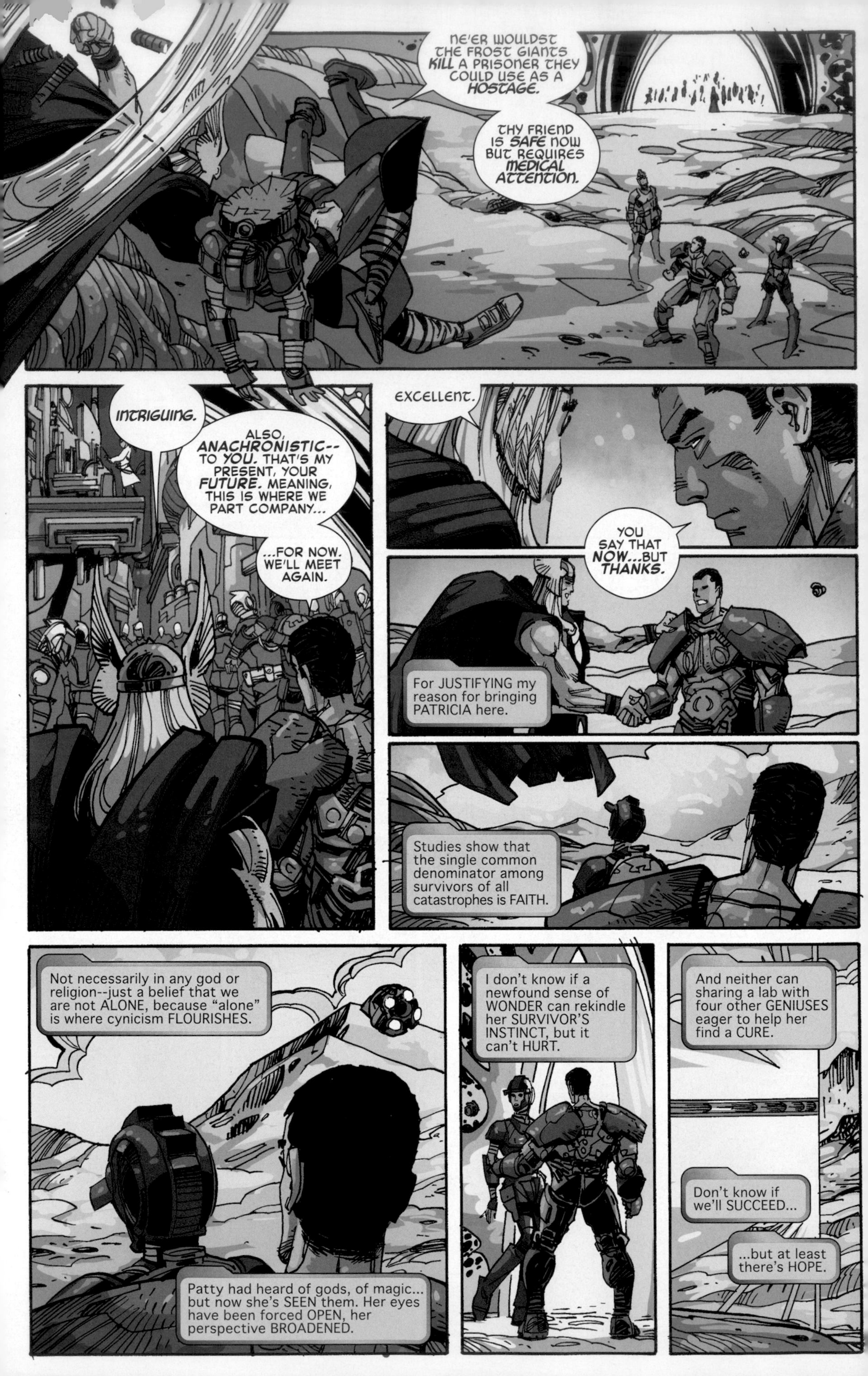
NE'ER WOULDST THE FROST GIANTS KILL A PRISONER THEY COULD USE AS A HOSTAGE.
THY FRIEND IS SAFE NOW BUT REQUIRES MEDICAL ATTENTION.
INTRIGUING.
ALSO, ANACHRONISTIC--TO YOU. THAT'S MY PRESENT, YOUR FUTURE. MEANING, THIS IS WHERE WE PART COMPANY...
...FOR NOW. WE'LL MEET AGAIN.
EXCELLENT.
YOU SAY THAT NOW...BUT THANKS.
For JUSTIFYING my reason for bringing PATRICIA here.
Studies show that the single common denominator among survivors of all catastrophes is FAITH.
Not necessarily in any god or religion--just a belief that we are not ALONE, because "alone" is where cynicism FLOURISHES.
Patty had heard of gods, of magic... but now she's SEEN them. Her eyes have been forced OPEN, her perspective BROADENED.
I don't know if a newfound sense of WONDER can rekindle her SURVIVOR'S INSTINCT, but it can't HURT.
And neither can sharing a lab with four other GENIUSES eager to help her find a CURE.
Don't know if we'll SUCCEED...
...but at least there's HOPE.

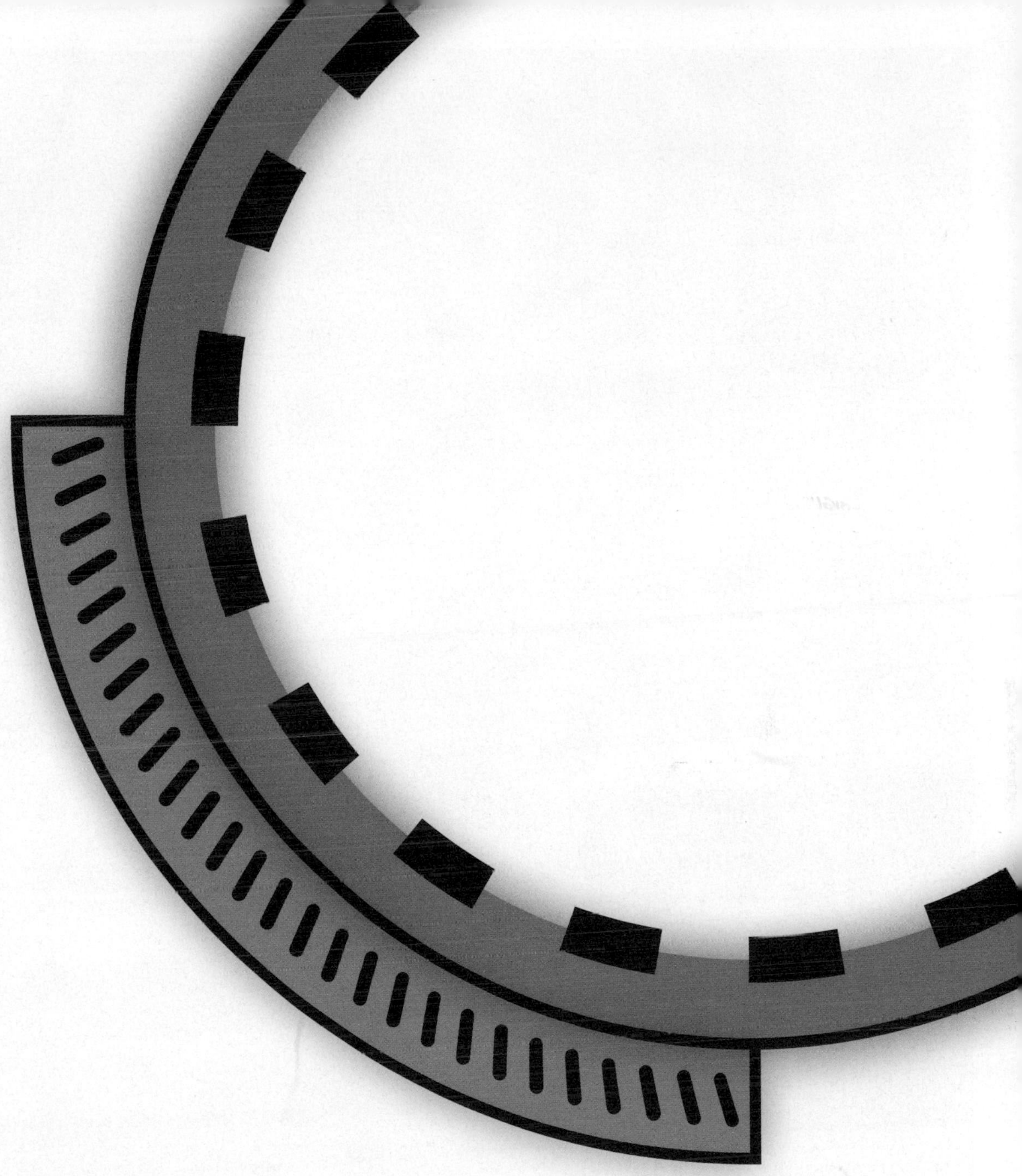

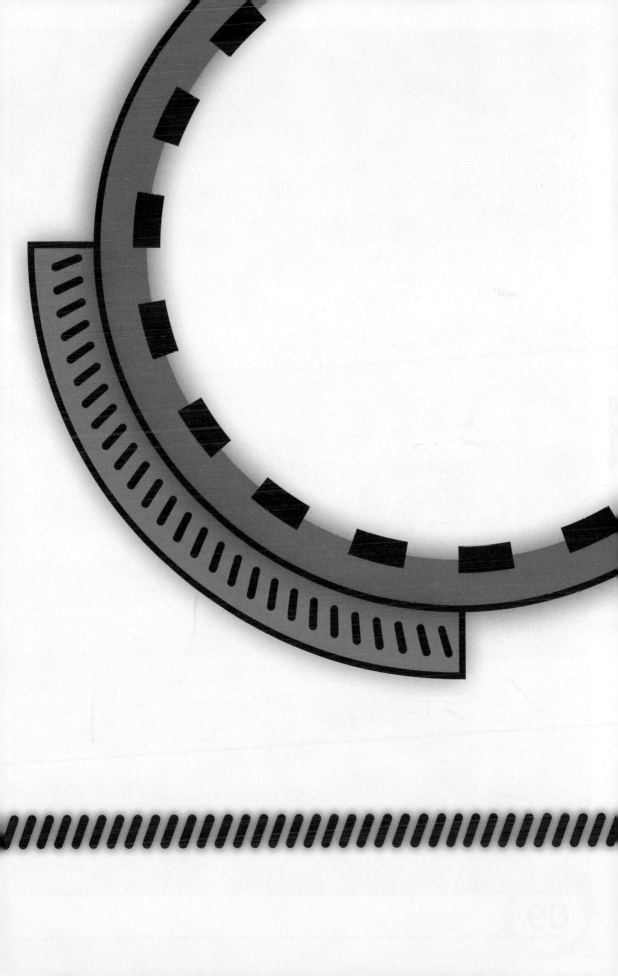

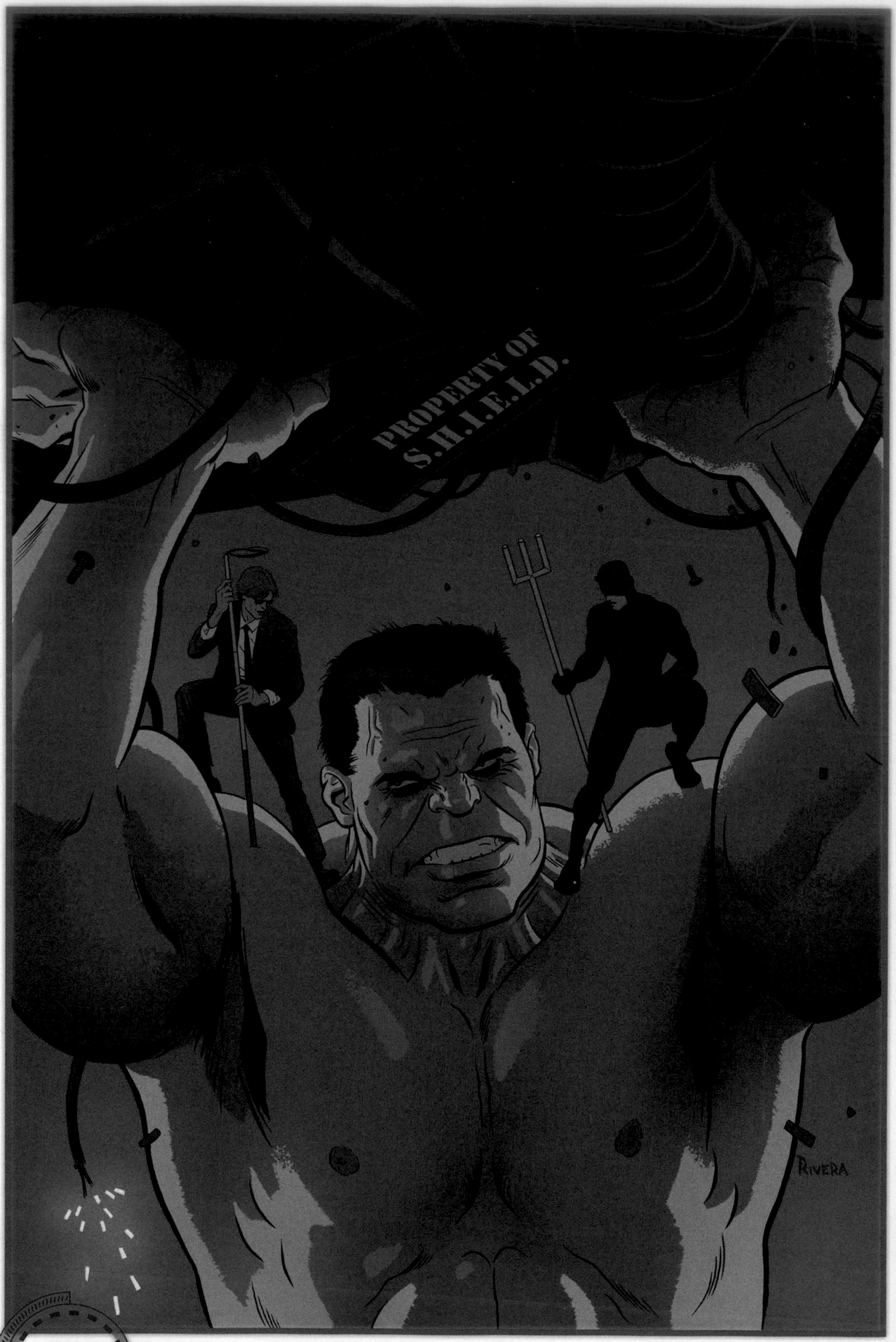
PROPERTY OF
S.H.I.E.L.D.
RIVERA

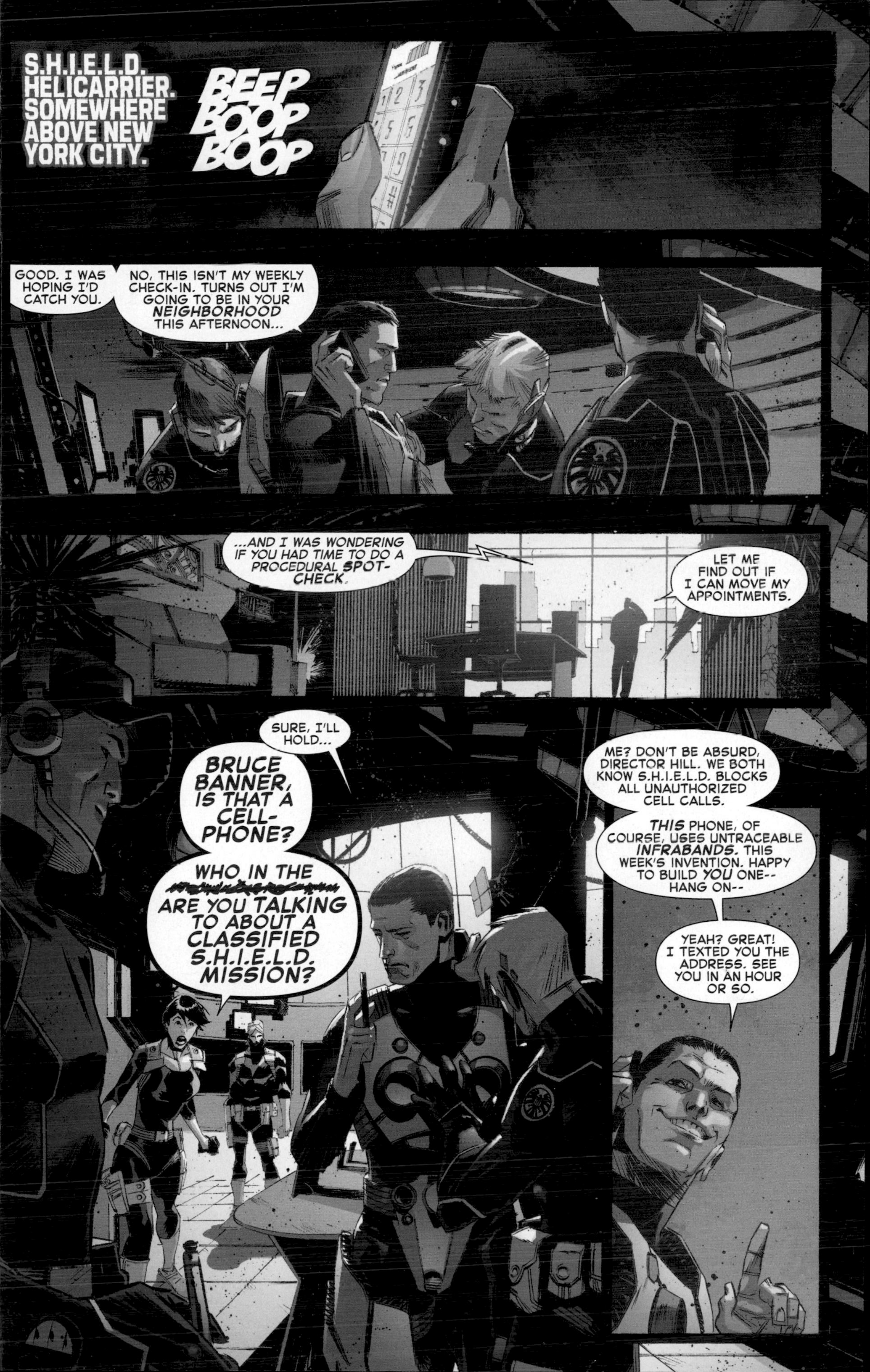
S.H.I.E.L.D. HELICARRIER. SOMEWHERE ABOVE NEW YORK CITY.
BEEP BOOP BOOP
GOOD. I WAS HOPING I'D CATCH YOU.
NO, THIS ISN'T MY WEEKLY CHECK-IN. TURNS OUT I'M GOING TO BE IN YOUR NEIGHBORHOOD THIS AFTERNOON...
...AND I WAS WONDERING IF YOU HAD TIME TO DO A PROCEDURAL SPOT-CHECK.
LET ME FIND OUT IF I CAN MOVE MY APPOINTMENTS.
SURE, I'LL HOLD...
BRUCE BANNER, IS THAT A CELL-PHONE?
WHO IN THE ARE YOU TALKING TO ABOUT A CLASSIFIED S.H.I.E.L.D. MISSION?
ME? DON'T BE ABSURD, DIRECTOR HILL. WE BOTH KNOW S.H.I.E.L.D. BLOCKS ALL UNAUTHORIZED CELL CALLS.
THIS PHONE, OF COURSE, USES UNTRACEABLE INFRABANDS. THIS WEEK'S INVENTION. HAPPY TO BUILD YOU ONE-- HANG ON--
YEAH? GREAT! I TEXTED YOU THE ADDRESS. SEE YOU IN AN HOUR OR SO.

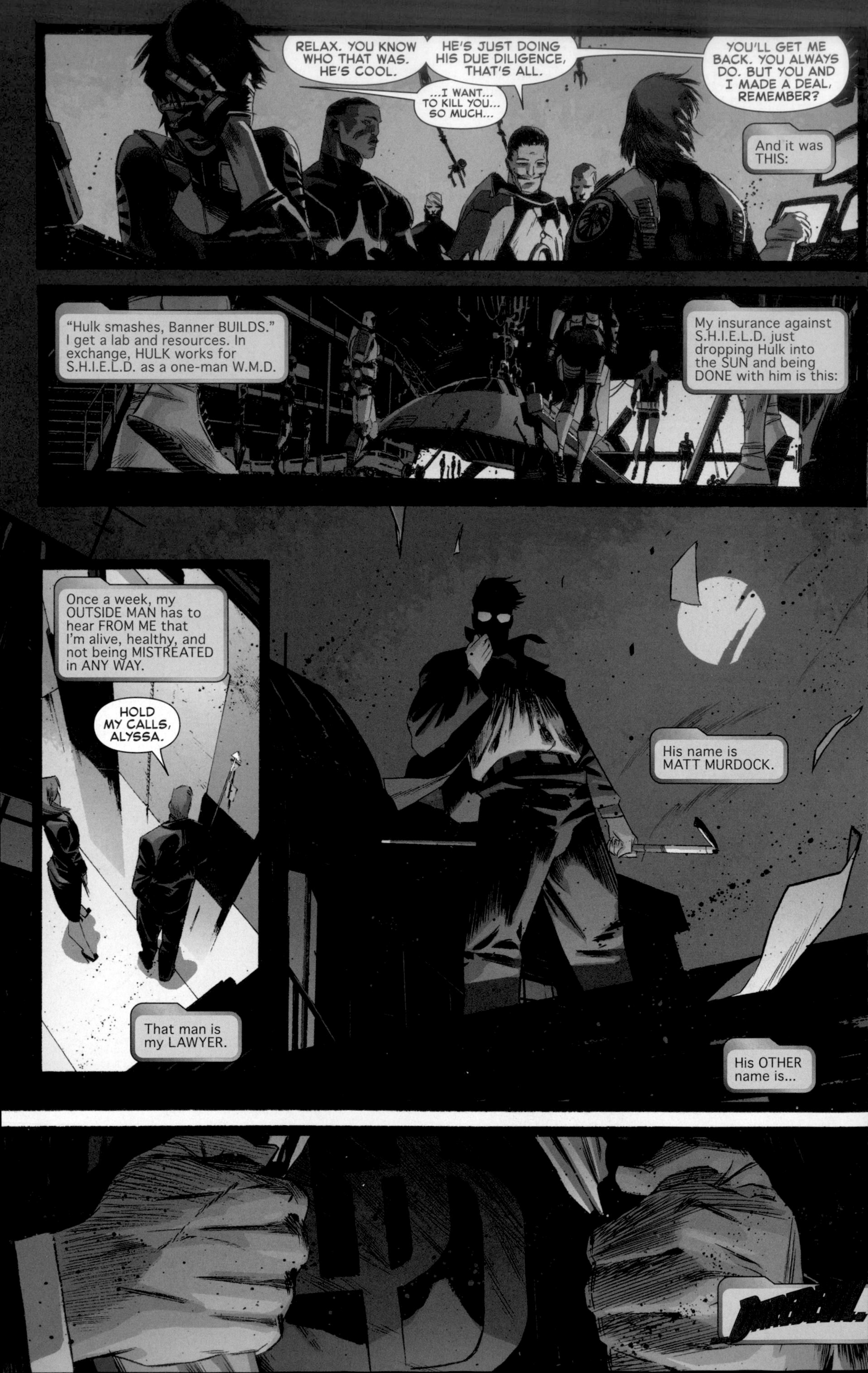
RELAX. YOU KNOW WHO THAT WAS. HE'S COOL.
HE'S JUST DOING HIS DUE DILIGENCE, THAT'S ALL.
...I WANT... TO KILL YOU... SO MUCH...
YOU'LL GET ME BACK. YOU ALWAYS DO. BUT YOU AND I MADE A DEAL, REMEMBER?
And it was THIS:
"Hulk smashes, Banner BUILDS." I get a lab and resources. In exchange, HULK works for S.H.I.E.L.D. as a one-man W.M.D.
My insurance against S.H.I.E.L.D. just dropping Hulk into the SUN and being DONE with him is this:
Once a week, my OUTSIDE MAN has to hear FROM ME that I'm alive, healthy, and not being MISTREATED in ANY WAY.
HOLD MY CALLS, ALYSSA.
That man is my LAWYER.
His name is MATT MURDOCK.
His OTHER name is...
DAREDEVIL..

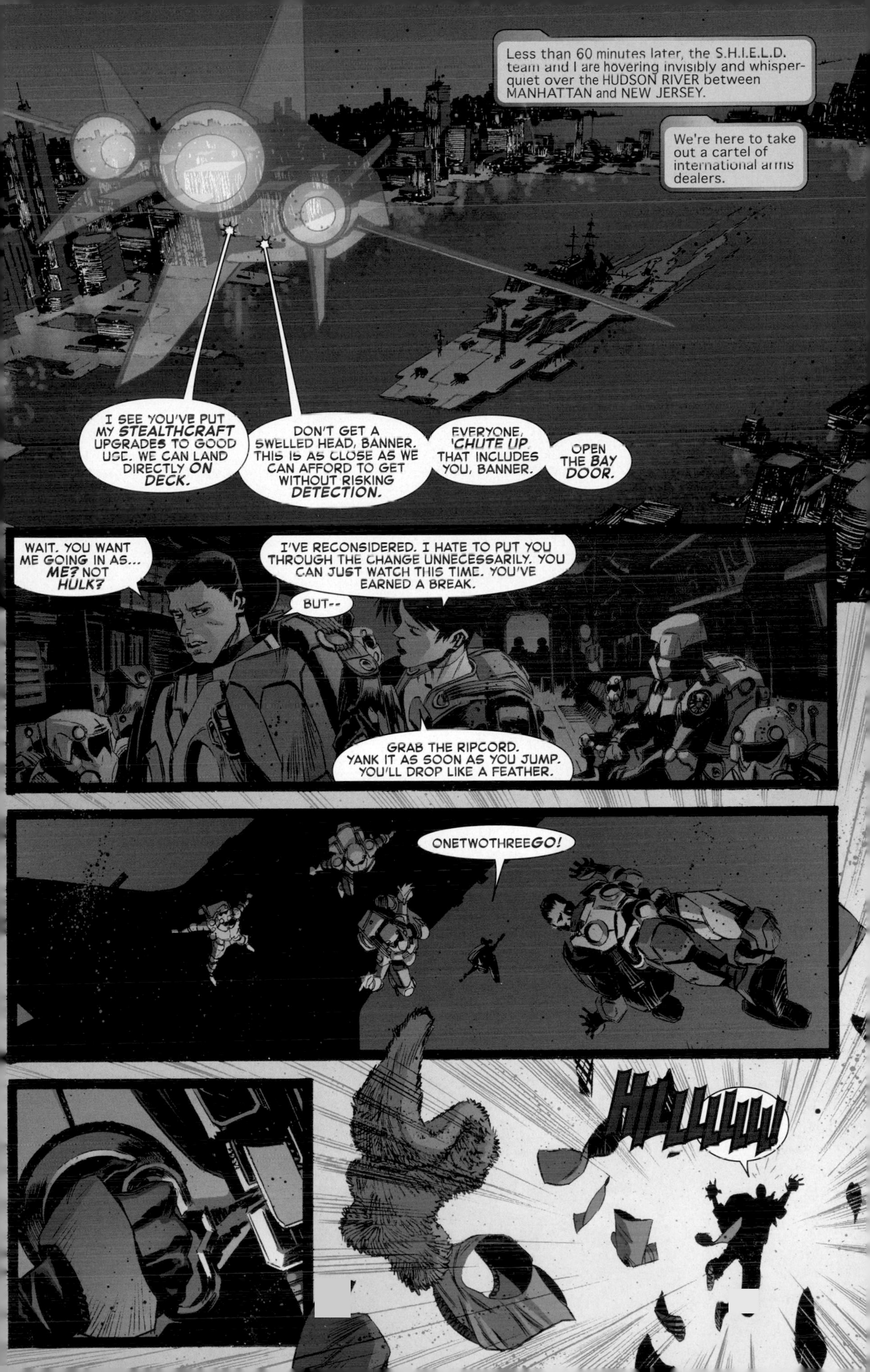
Less than 60 minutes later, the S.H.I.E.L.D. team and I are hovering invisibly and whisper-quiet over the HUDSON RIVER between MANHATTAN and NEW JERSEY.
We're here to take out a cartel of international arms dealers.
I SEE YOU'VE PUT MY STEALTHCRAFT UPGRADES TO GOOD USE. WE CAN LAND DIRECTLY ON DECK.
DON'T GET A SWELLED HEAD, BANNER. THIS IS AS CLOSE AS WE CAN AFFORD TO GET WITHOUT RISKING DETECTION.
EVERYONE, 'CHUTE UP. THAT INCLUDES YOU, BANNER.
OPEN THE BAY DOOR.
WAIT. YOU WANT ME GOING IN AS... ME? NOT HULK?
I'VE RECONSIDERED. I HATE TO PUT YOU THROUGH THE CHANGE UNNECESSARILY. YOU CAN JUST WATCH THIS TIME. YOU'VE EARNED A BREAK.
BUT--
GRAB THE RIPCORD. YANK IT AS SOON AS YOU JUMP. YOU'LL DROP LIKE A FEATHER.
ONETWOTHREEGO!
HILLLLLL!

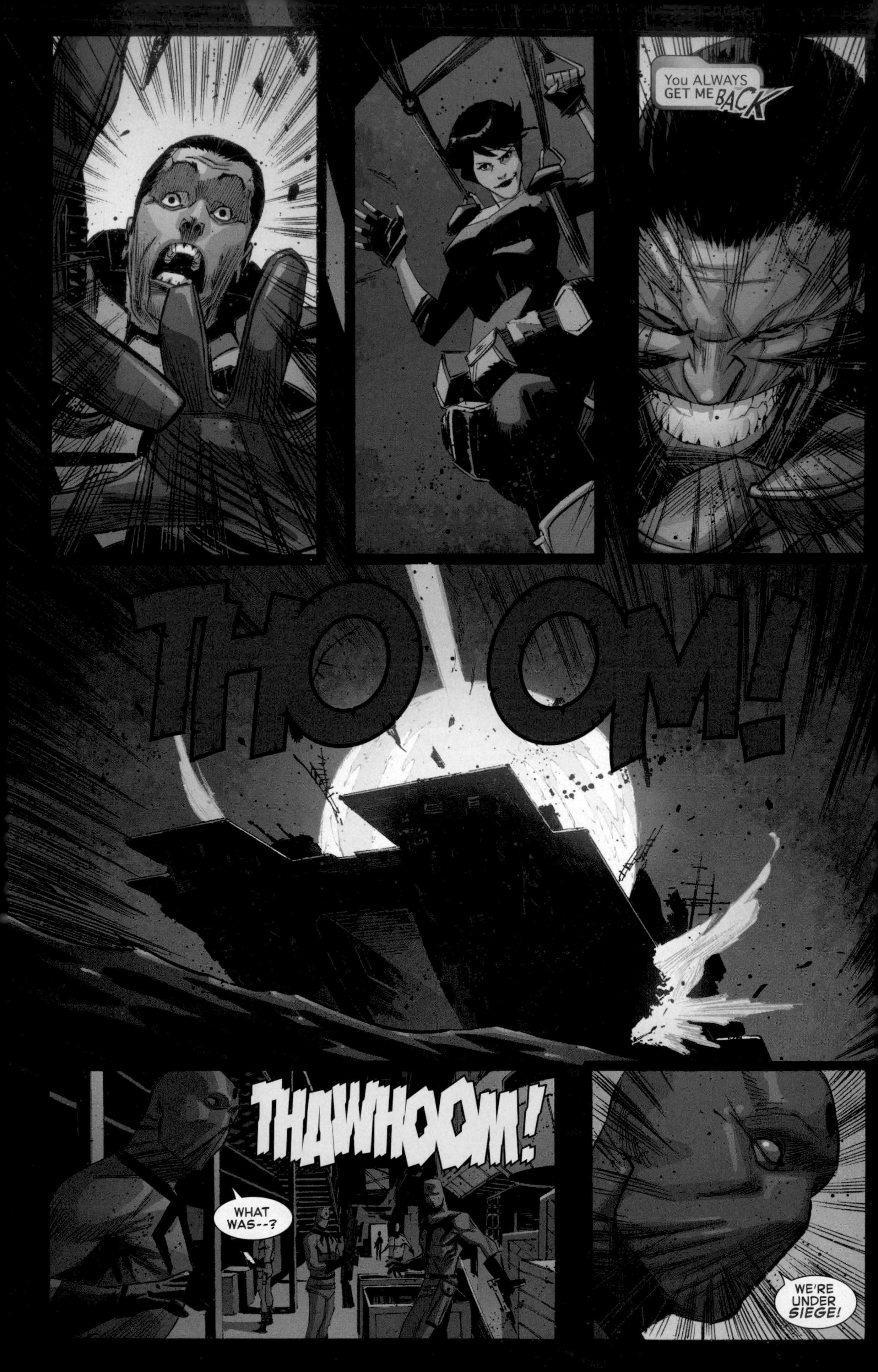

You ALWAYS GET ME BACK
THOOOM!
THAWHOOM!
WHAT WAS--?
WE'RE UNDER SIEGE!

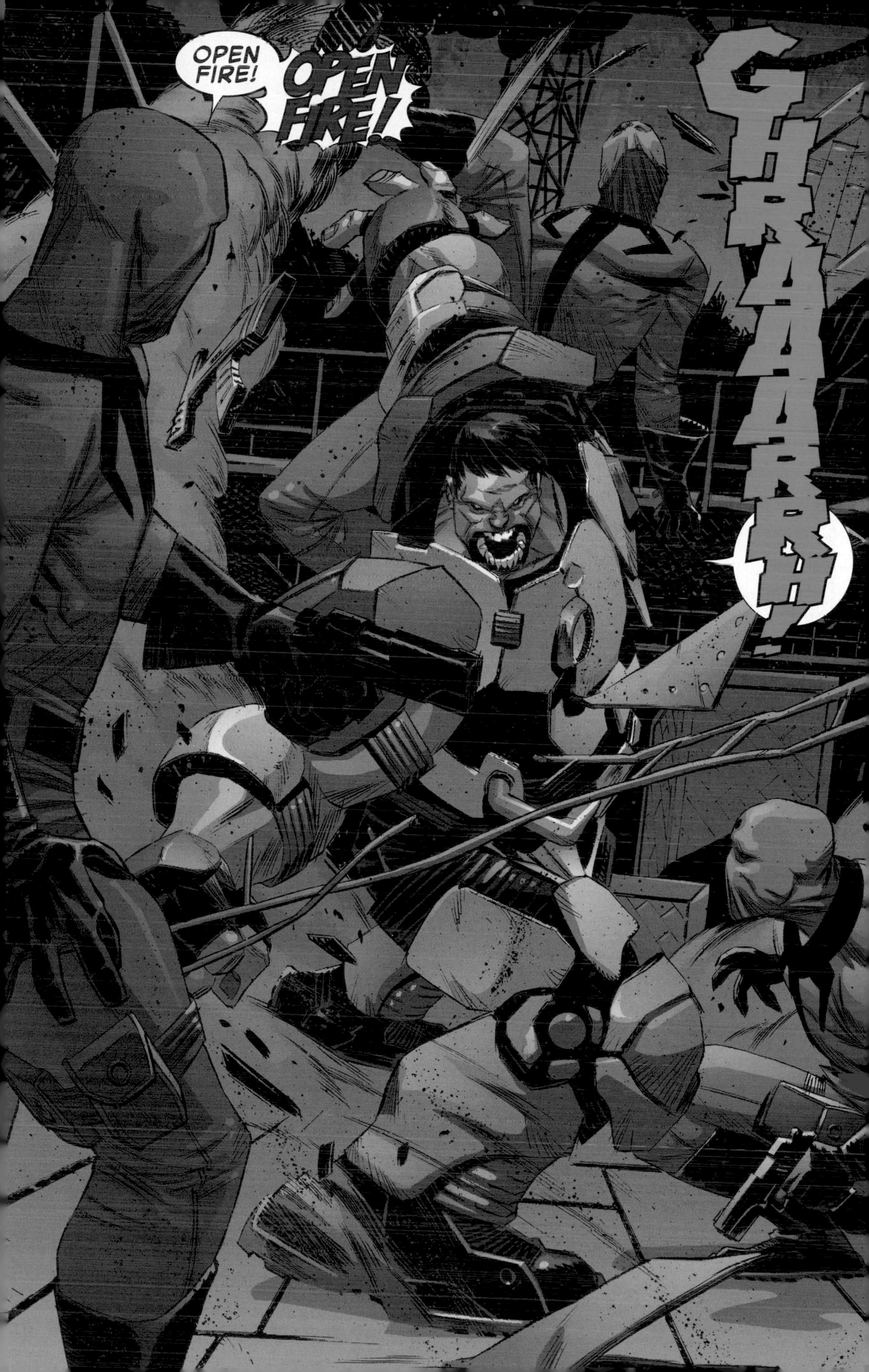
OPEN FIRE!
OPEN FIRE!
GHRAARRH!

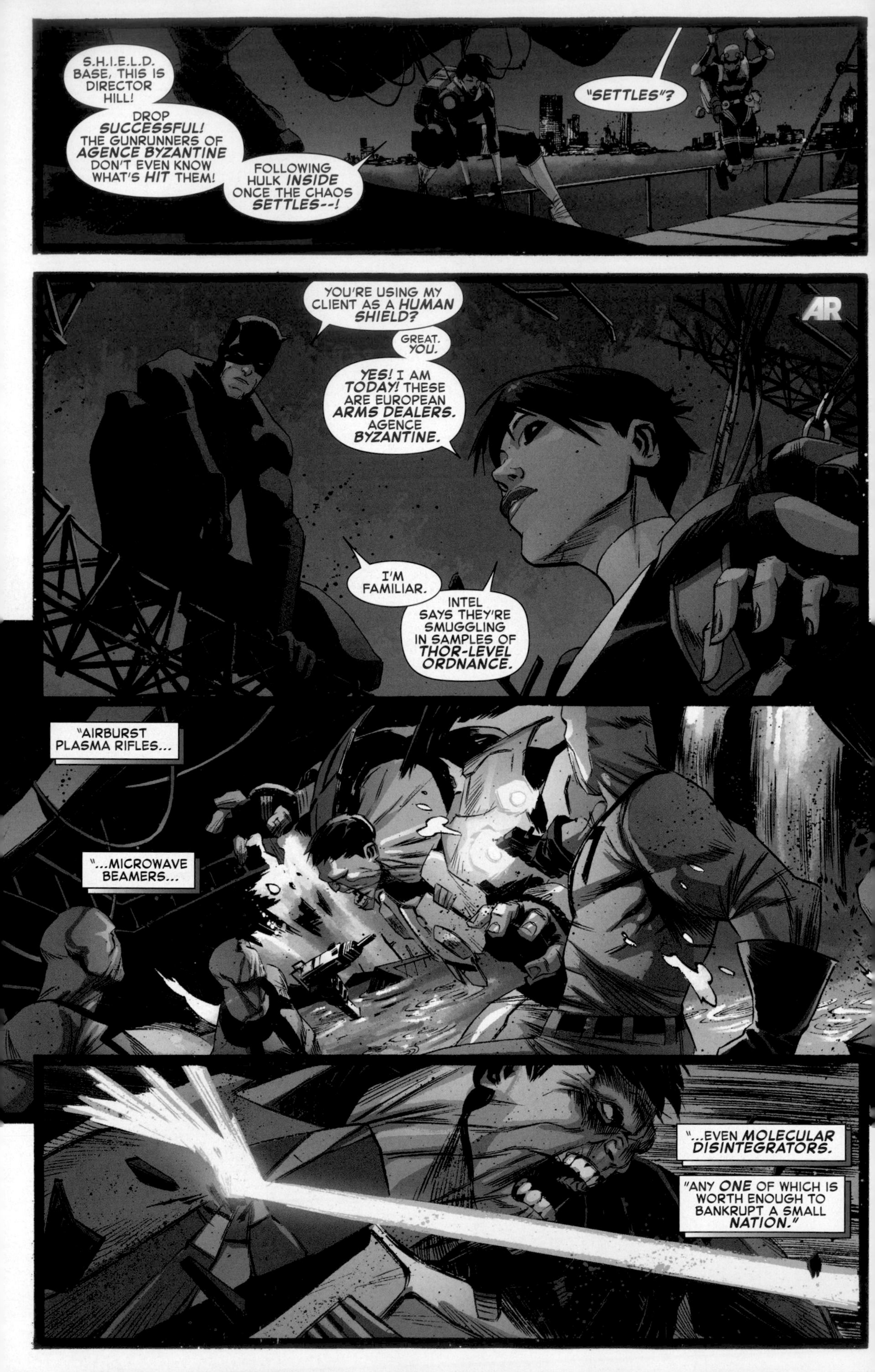
S.H.I.E.L.D. BASE, THIS IS DIRECTOR HILL!
DROP SUCCESSFUL! THE GUNRUNNERS OF AGENCE BYZANTINE DON'T EVEN KNOW WHAT'S HIT THEM!
FOLLOWING HULK INSIDE ONCE THE CHAOS SETTLES--!
"SETTLES"?
YOU'RE USING MY CLIENT AS A HUMAN SHIELD?
GREAT. YOU.
YES! I AM TODAY! THESE ARE EUROPEAN ARMS DEALERS. AGENCE BYZANTINE.
I'M FAMILIAR.
INTEL SAYS THEY'RE SMUGGLING IN SAMPLES OF THOR-LEVEL ORDNANCE.
"AIRBURST PLASMA RIFLES...
"...MICROWAVE BEAMERS...
"...EVEN MOLECULAR DISINTEGRATORS.
"ANY ONE OF WHICH IS WORTH ENOUGH TO BANKRUPT A SMALL NATION."

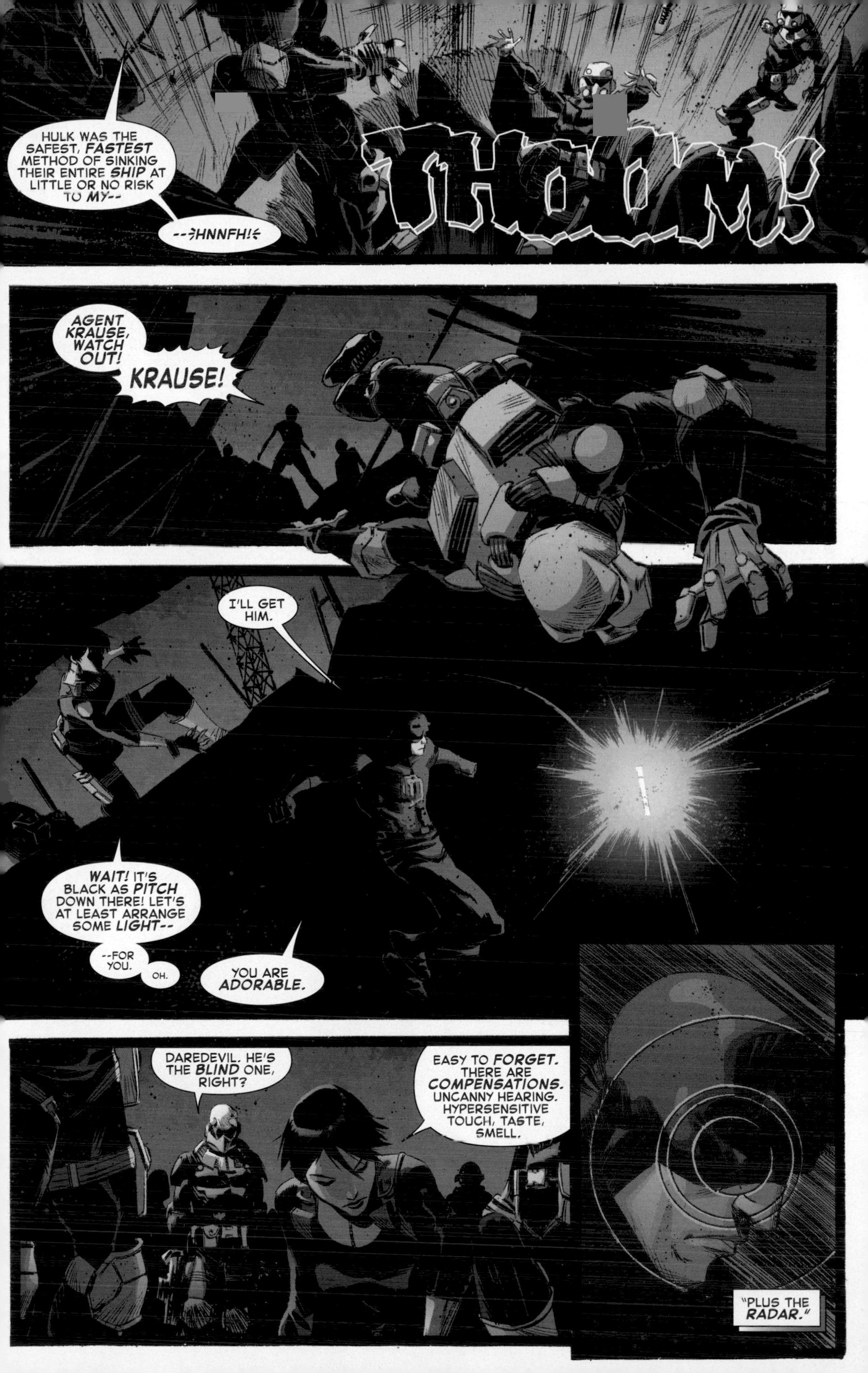
HULK WAS THE SAFEST, FASTEST METHOD OF SINKING THEIR ENTIRE SHIP AT LITTLE OR NO RISK TO MY--
--HNNFH!--
THOOM!
AGENT KRAUSE, WATCH OUT!
KRAUSE!
I'LL GET HIM.
WAIT! IT'S BLACK AS PITCH DOWN THERE! LET'S AT LEAST ARRANGE SOME LIGHT--
--FOR YOU.
OH.
YOU ARE ADORABLE.
DAREDEVIL. HE'S THE BLIND ONE, RIGHT?
EASY TO FORGET. THERE ARE COMPENSATIONS. UNCANNY HEARING. HYPERSENSITIVE TOUCH, TASTE, SMELL.
"PLUS THE RADAR."

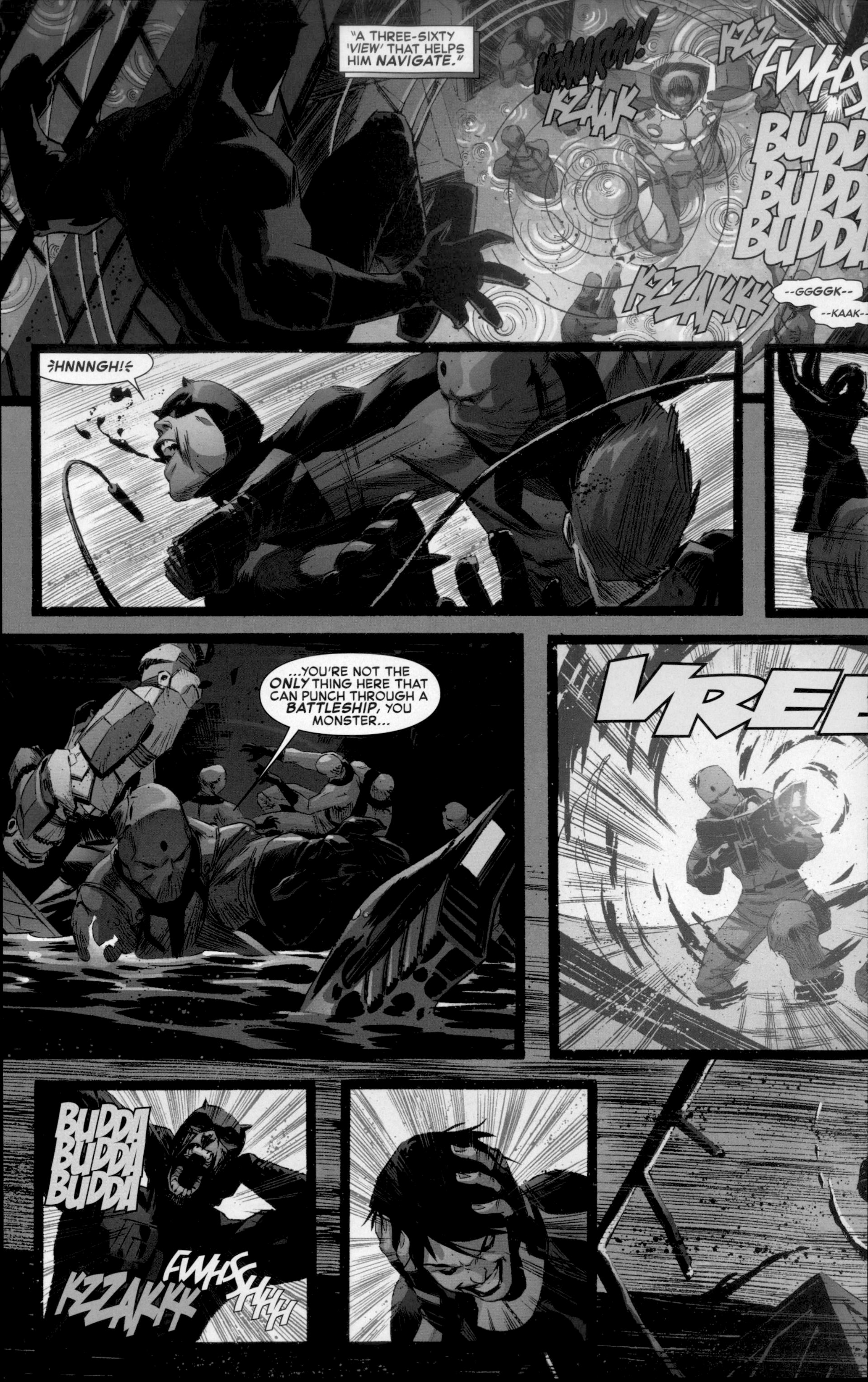
"A THREE-SIXTY 'VIEW' THAT HELPS HIM NAVIGATE."
KZAAK
KZZ
BUDD
BUDD
BUDDA
KZZAKKK
--GGGGK--
--KAAK--
HNNNGH!
...YOU'RE NOT THE ONLY THING HERE THAT CAN PUNCH THROUGH A BATTLESHIP, YOU MONSTER...
VREE
BUDDA
BUDDA
BUDDA
FWHOSHHH
KZZAKKK

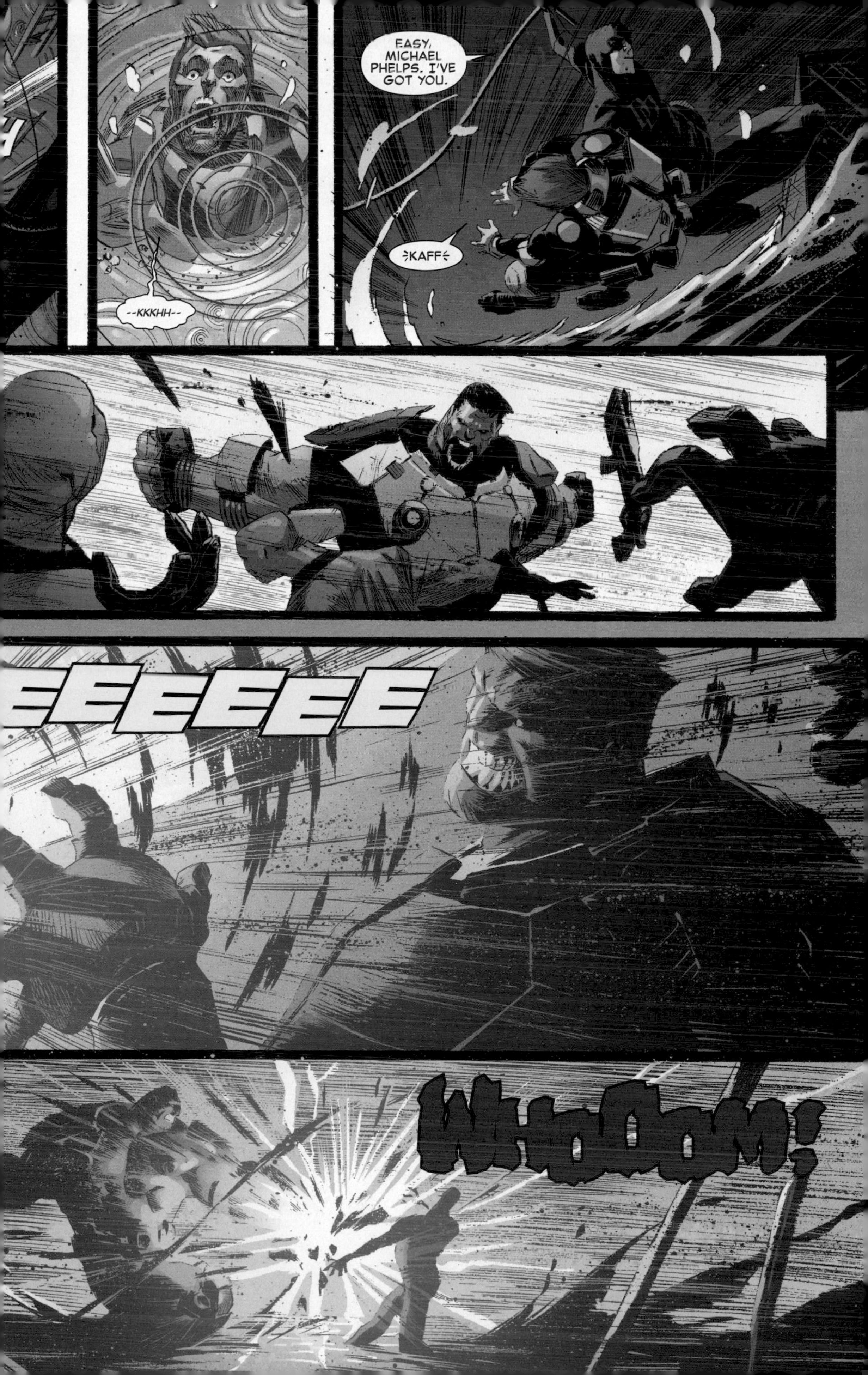
--KKKHH--
EASY, MICHAEL PHELPS. I'VE GOT YOU.
KAFF
EEEEEE
WHOOOM!

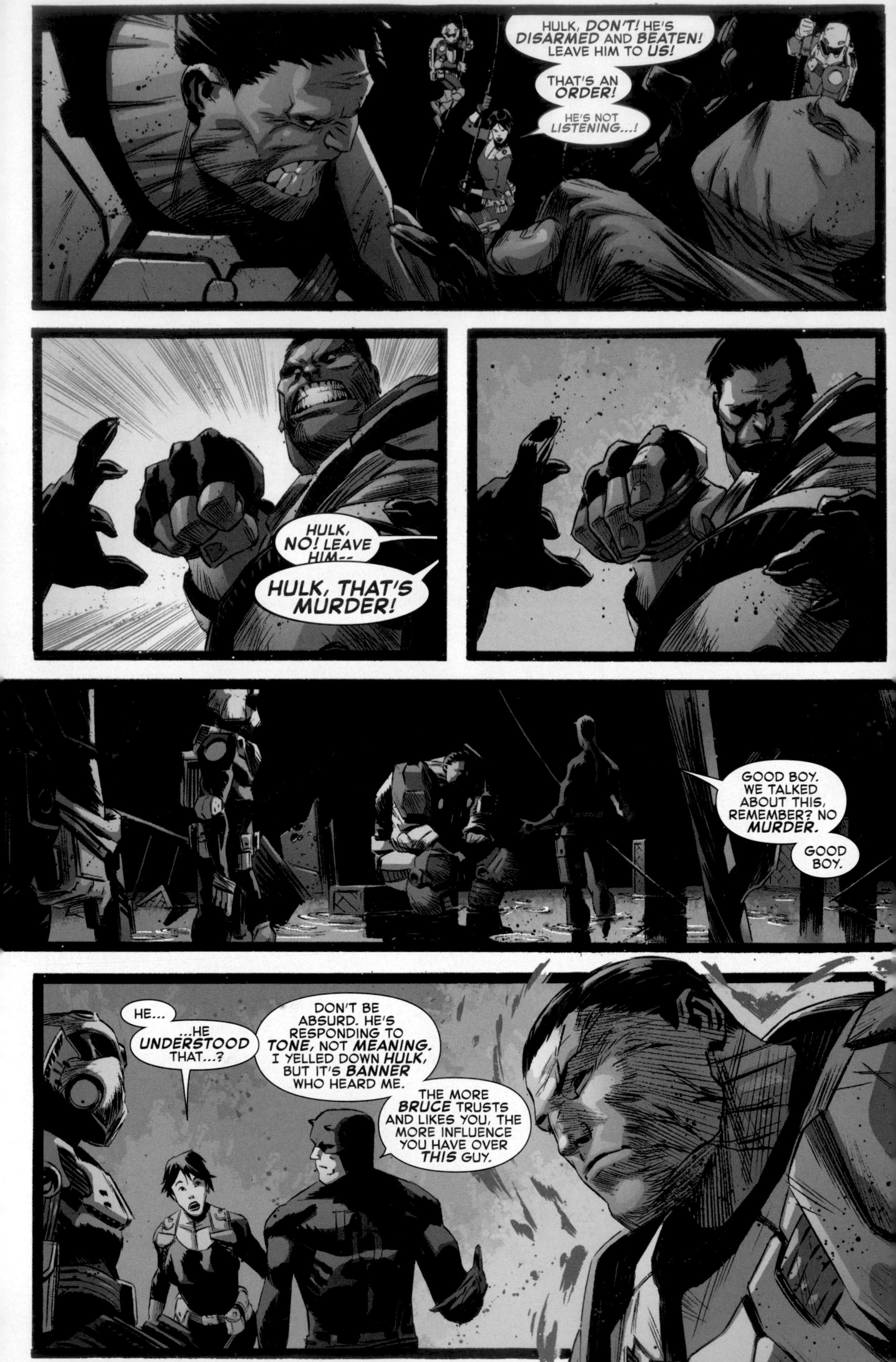
HULK, DON'T! HE'S DISARMED AND BEATEN! LEAVE HIM TO US!
THAT'S AN ORDER!
HE'S NOT LISTENING...!
HULK, NO! LEAVE HIM--
HULK, THAT'S MURDER!
GOOD BOY. WE TALKED ABOUT THIS, REMEMBER? NO MURDER.
GOOD BOY.
HE...
...HE UNDERSTOOD THAT...?
DON'T BE ABSURD. HE'S RESPONDING TO TONE, NOT MEANING. I YELLED DOWN HULK, BUT IT'S BANNER WHO HEARD ME.
THE MORE BRUCE TRUSTS AND LIKES YOU, THE MORE INFLUENCE YOU HAVE OVER THIS GUY.

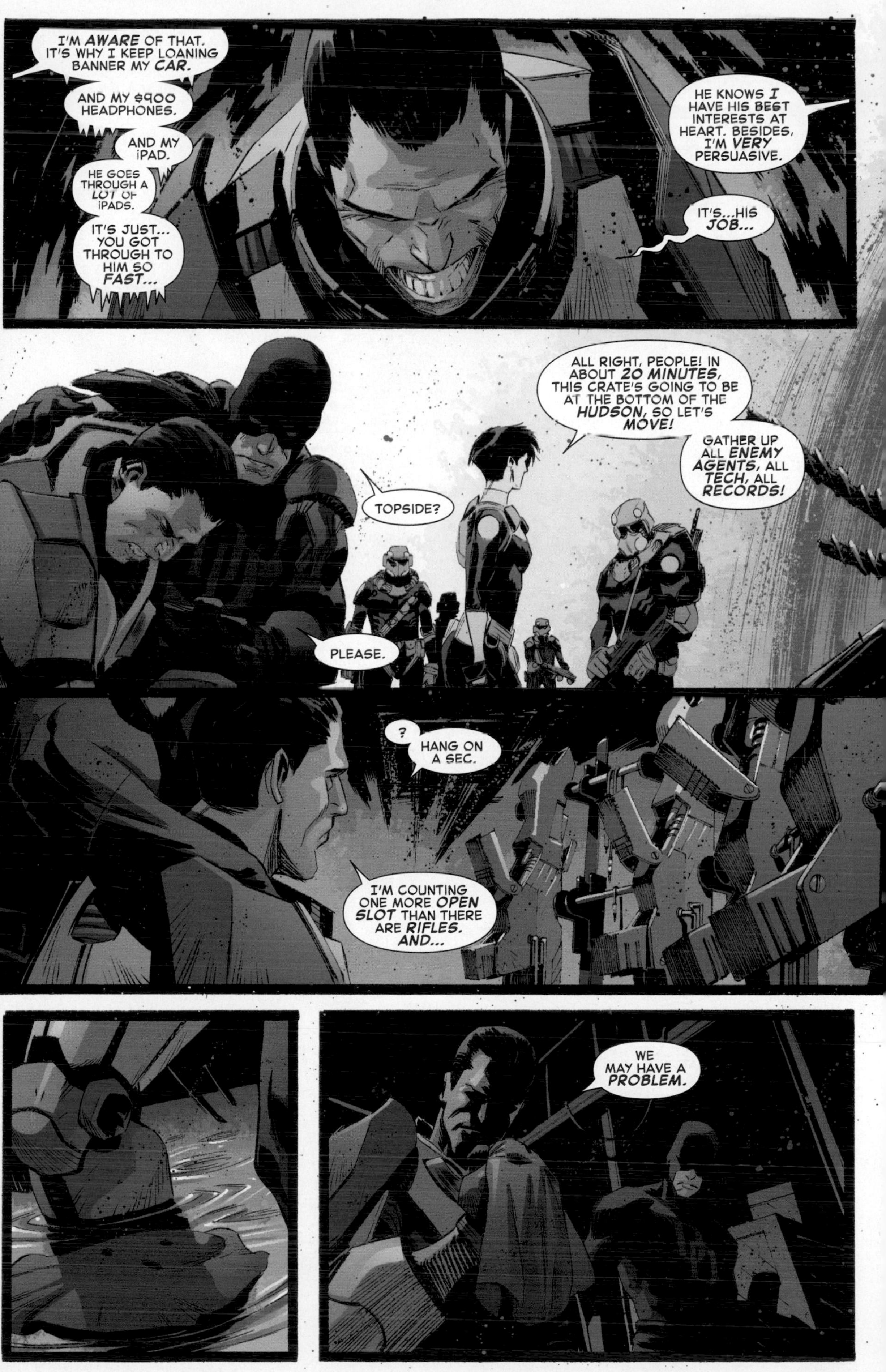
I'M AWARE OF THAT. IT'S WHY I KEEP LOANING BANNER MY CAR.
AND MY $900 HEADPHONES.
AND MY iPAD.
HE GOES THROUGH A LOT OF iPADS.
IT'S JUST... YOU GOT THROUGH TO HIM SO FAST...
HE KNOWS I HAVE HIS BEST INTERESTS AT HEART. BESIDES, I'M VERY PERSUASIVE.
IT'S...HIS JOB...
ALL RIGHT, PEOPLE! IN ABOUT 20 MINUTES, THIS CRATE'S GOING TO BE AT THE BOTTOM OF THE HUDSON, SO LET'S MOVE!
GATHER UP ALL ENEMY AGENTS, ALL TECH, ALL RECORDS!
TOPSIDE?
PLEASE.
?
HANG ON A SEC.
I'M COUNTING ONE MORE OPEN SLOT THAN THERE ARE RIFLES. AND...
WE MAY HAVE A PROBLEM.

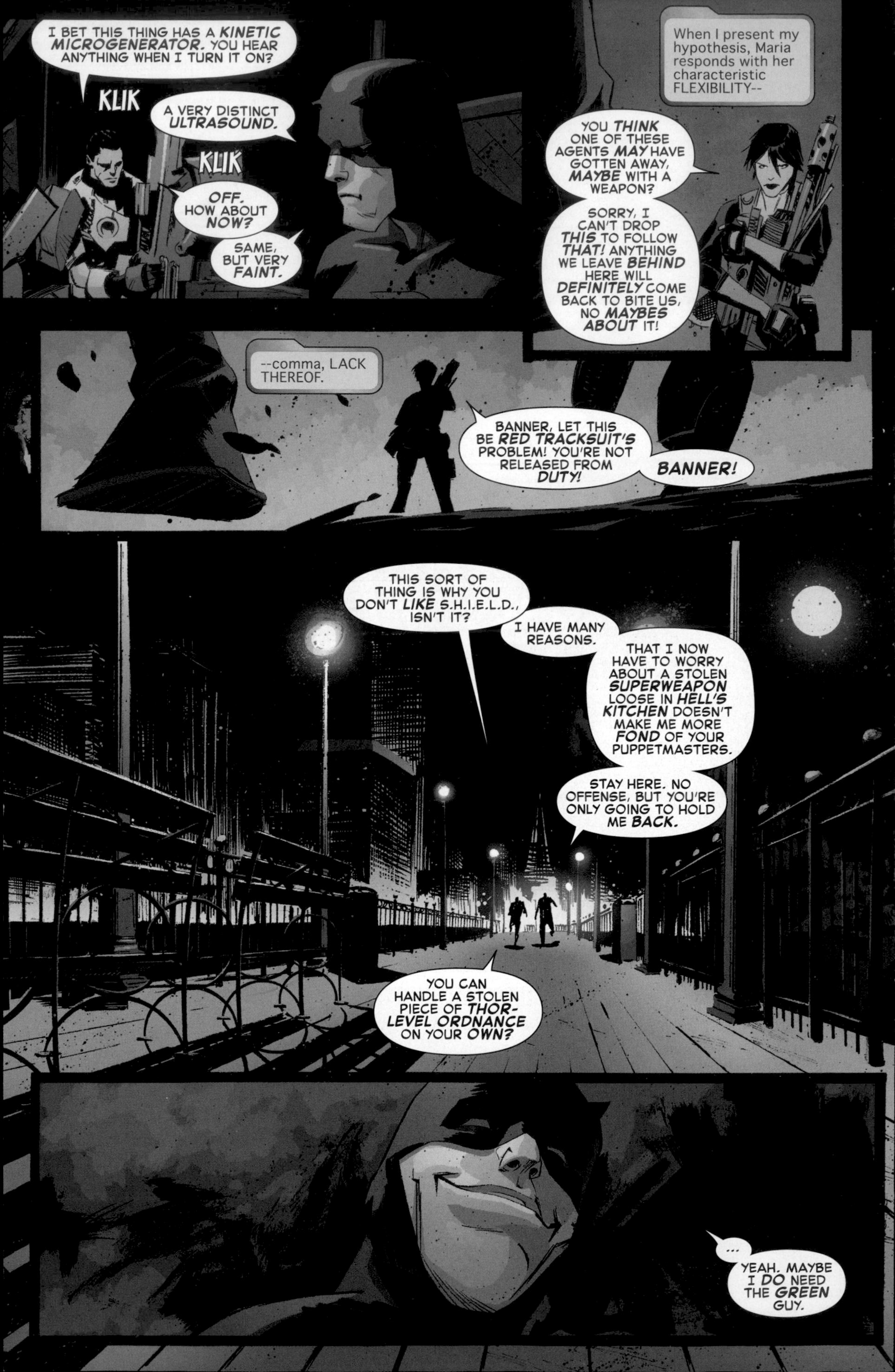
I BET THIS THING HAS A KINETIC MICROGENERATOR. YOU HEAR ANYTHING WHEN I TURN IT ON?
KLIK
A VERY DISTINCT ULTRASOUND.
KLIK
OFF. HOW ABOUT NOW?
SAME, BUT VERY FAINT.
When I present my hypothesis, Maria responds with her characteristic FLEXIBILITY--
YOU THINK ONE OF THESE AGENTS MAY HAVE GOTTEN AWAY, MAYBE WITH A WEAPON?
SORRY, I CAN'T DROP THIS TO FOLLOW THAT! ANYTHING WE LEAVE BEHIND HERE WILL DEFINITELY COME BACK TO BITE US, NO MAYBES ABOUT IT!
--comma, LACK THEREOF.
BANNER, LET THIS BE RED TRACKSUIT'S PROBLEM! YOU'RE NOT RELEASED FROM DUTY!
BANNER!
THIS SORT OF THING IS WHY YOU DON'T LIKE S.H.I.E.L.D., ISN'T IT?
I HAVE MANY REASONS.
THAT I NOW HAVE TO WORRY ABOUT A STOLEN SUPERWEAPON LOOSE IN HELL'S KITCHEN DOESN'T MAKE ME MORE FOND OF YOUR PUPPETMASTERS.
STAY HERE. NO OFFENSE, BUT YOU'RE ONLY GOING TO HOLD ME BACK.
YOU CAN HANDLE A STOLEN PIECE OF THOR-LEVEL ORDNANCE ON YOUR OWN?
...
YEAH. MAYBE I DO NEED THE GREEN GUY.

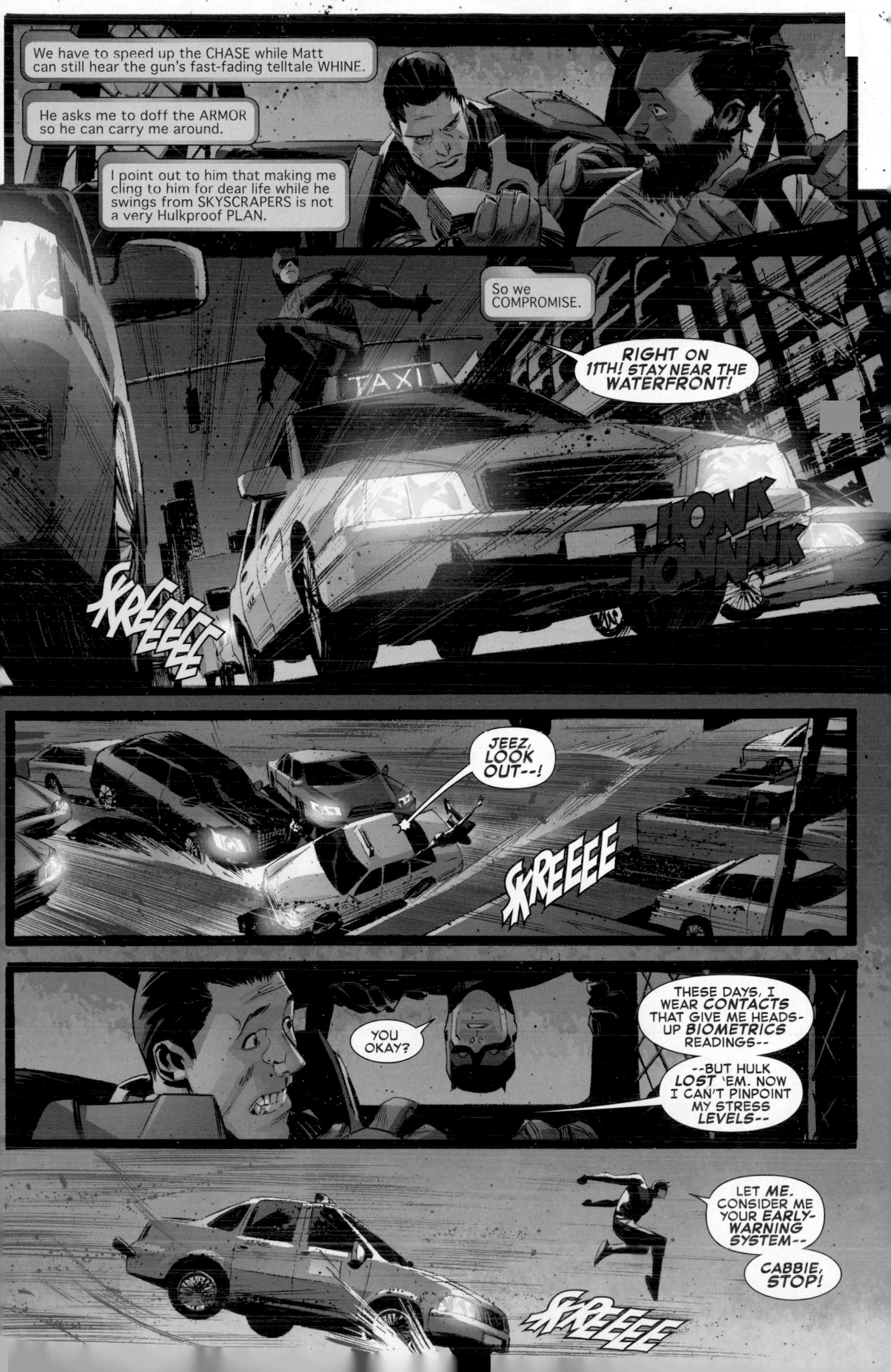
We have to speed up the CHASE while Matt can still hear the gun's fast-fading telltale WHINE.
He asks me to doff the ARMOR so he can carry me around.
I point out to him that making me cling to him for dear life while he swings from SKYSCRAPERS is not a very Hulkproof PLAN.
So we COMPROMISE.
RIGHT ON 11TH! STAY NEAR THE WATERFRONT!
TAXI
HONK HONNNK
SKREEEEE
JEEZ, LOOK OUT--!
SKREEEE
YOU OKAY?
THESE DAYS, I WEAR CONTACTS THAT GIVE ME HEADS-UP BIOMETRICS READINGS--
--BUT HULK LOST 'EM. NOW I CAN'T PINPOINT MY STRESS LEVELS--
LET ME. CONSIDER ME YOUR EARLY-WARNING SYSTEM--
CABBIE, STOP!
SKREEEE

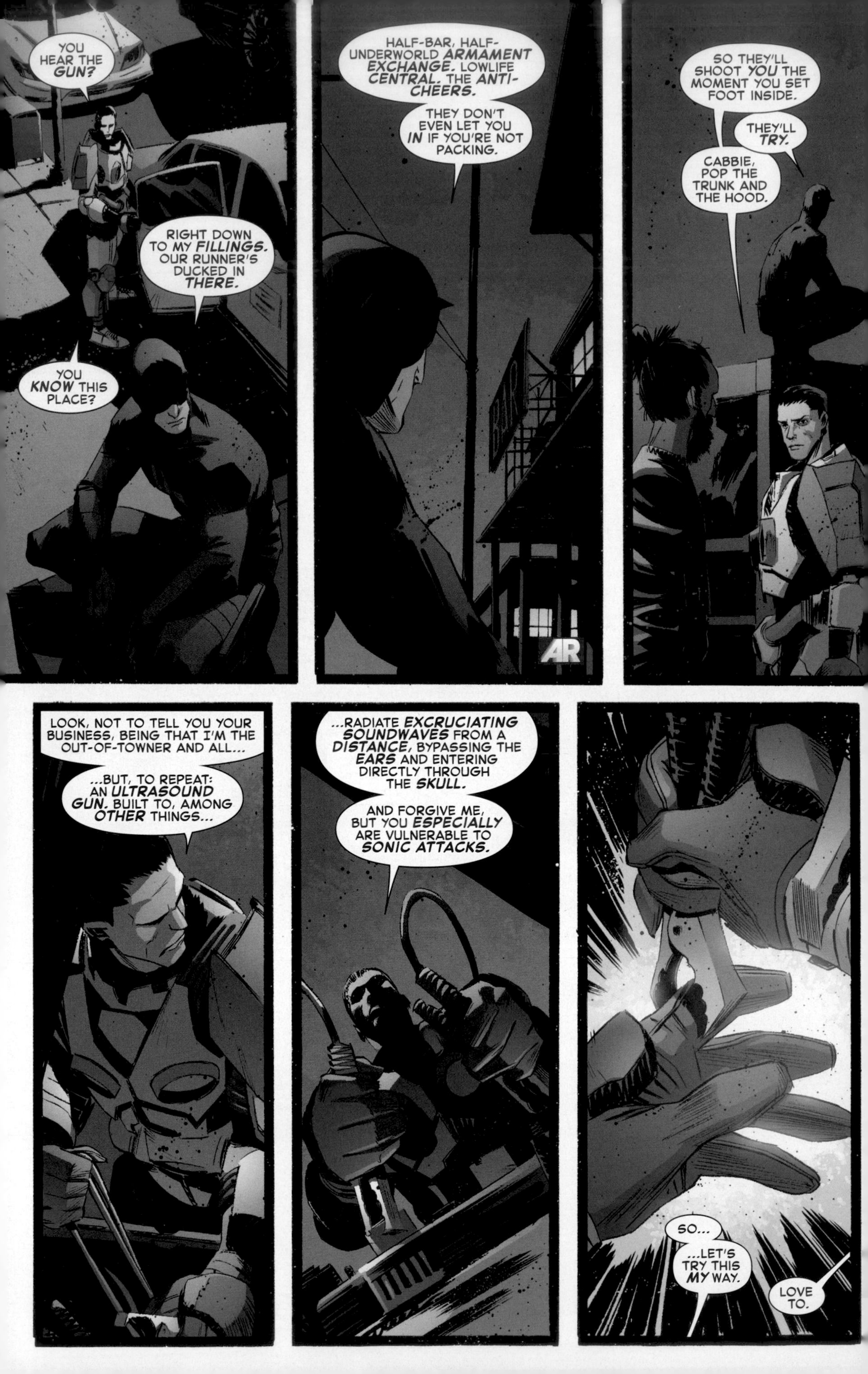

YOU HEAR THE GUN?
RIGHT DOWN TO MY FILLINGS. OUR RUNNER'S DUCKED IN THERE.
YOU KNOW THIS PLACE?
HALF-BAR, HALF-UNDERWORLD ARMAMENT EXCHANGE. LOWLIFE CENTRAL. THE ANTI-CHEERS.
THEY DON'T EVEN LET YOU IN IF YOU'RE NOT PACKING.
BAR
SO THEY'LL SHOOT YOU THE MOMENT YOU SET FOOT INSIDE.
THEY'LL TRY.
CABBIE, POP THE TRUNK AND THE HOOD.
LOOK, NOT TO TELL YOU YOUR BUSINESS, BEING THAT I'M THE OUT-OF-TOWNER AND ALL...
...BUT, TO REPEAT: AN ULTRASOUND GUN. BUILT TO, AMONG OTHER THINGS...
...RADIATE EXCRUCIATING SOUNDWAVES FROM A DISTANCE, BYPASSING THE EARS AND ENTERING DIRECTLY THROUGH THE SKULL.
AND FORGIVE ME, BUT YOU ESPECIALLY ARE VULNERABLE TO SONIC ATTACKS.
SO...
...LET'S TRY THIS MY WAY.
LOVE TO.

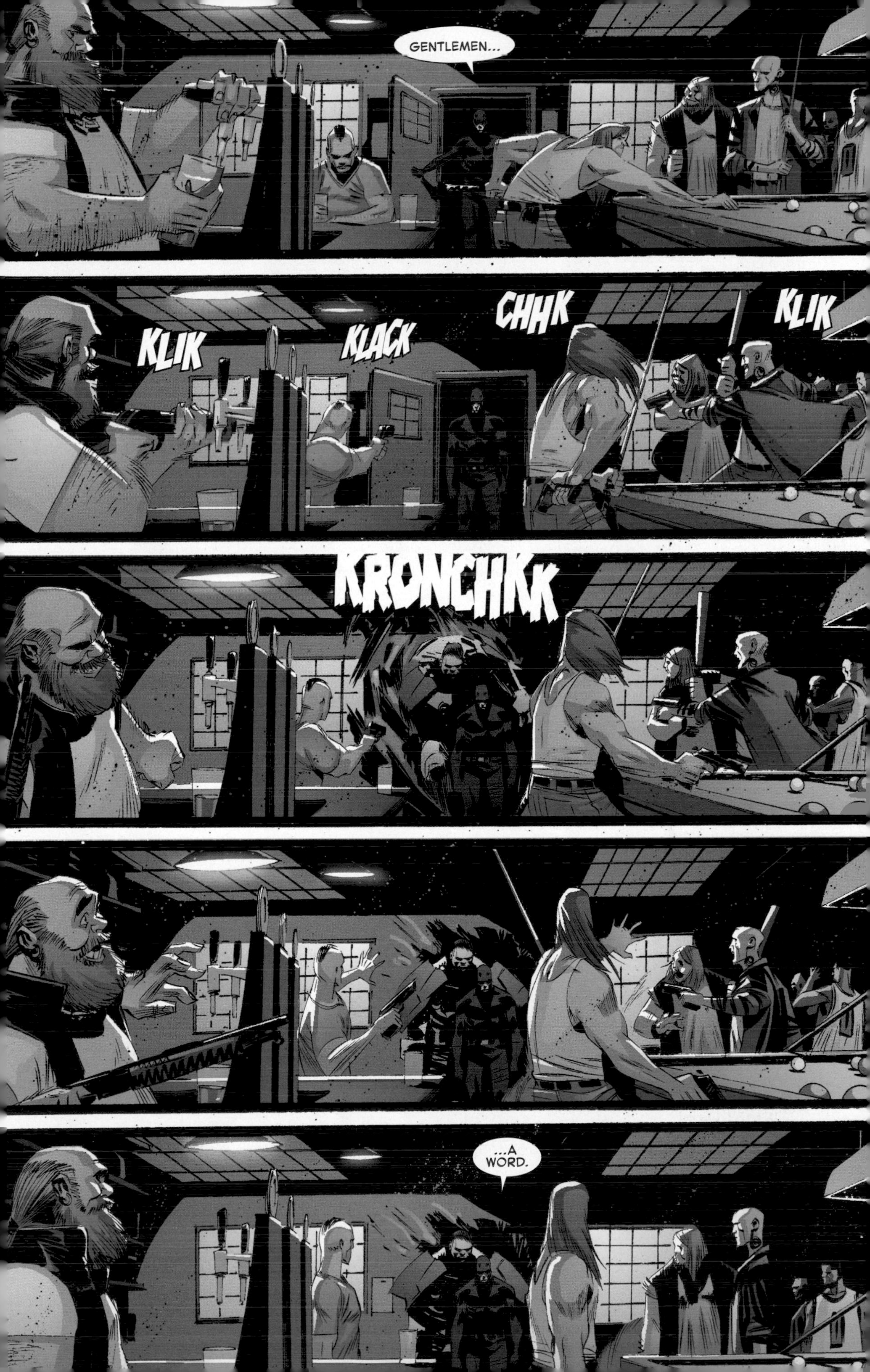
GENTLEMEN...
KLIK
KLACK
CHHK
KLIK
KRONCHKK
...A WORD.

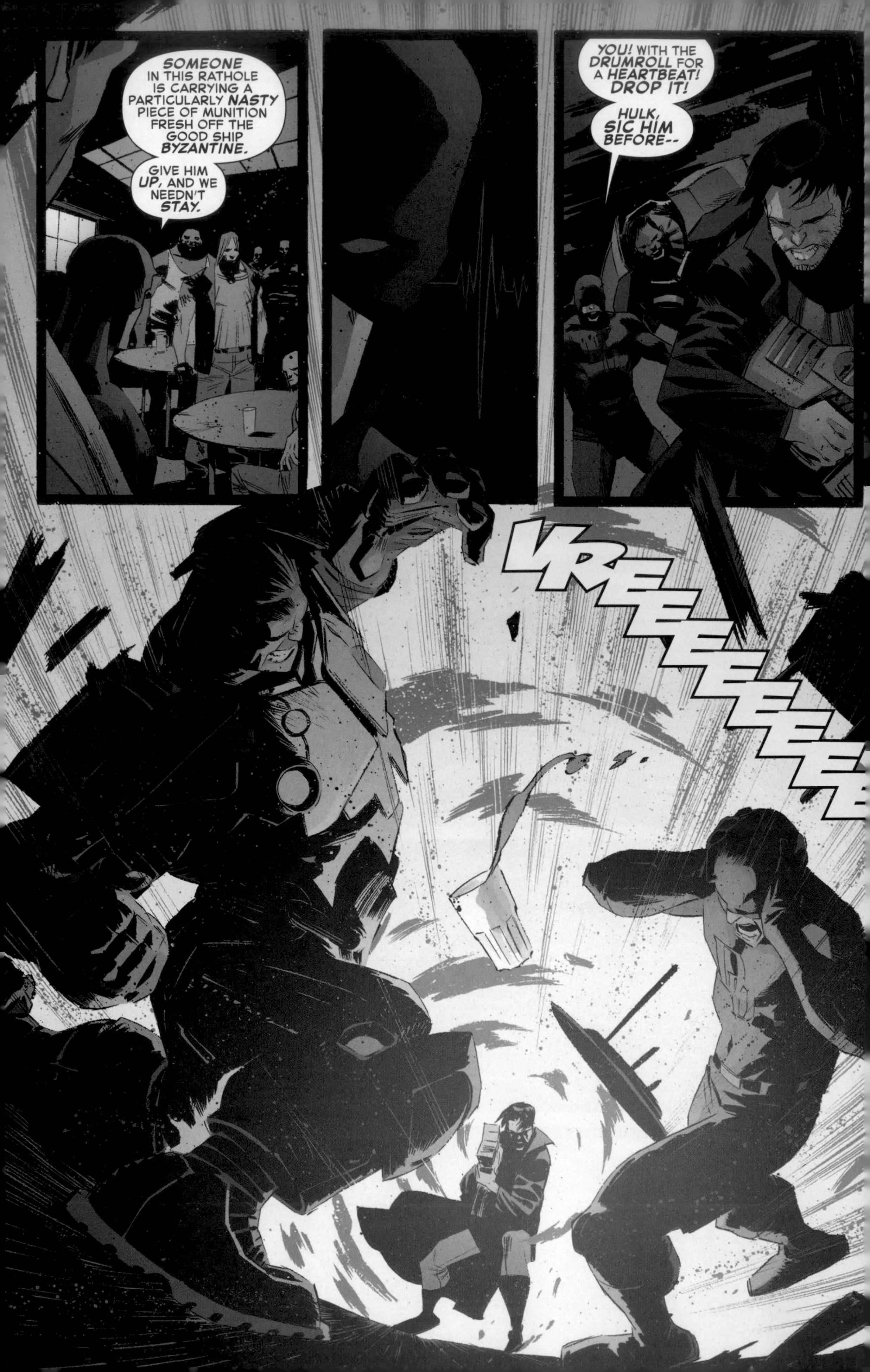
SOMEONE IN THIS RATHOLE IS CARRYING A PARTICULARLY NASTY PIECE OF MUNITION FRESH OFF THE GOOD SHIP BYZANTINE.
GIVE HIM UP, AND WE NEEDN'T STAY.
YOU! WITH THE DRUMROLL FOR A HEARTBEAT! DROP IT!
HULK, SIC HIM BEFORE--
VREEEEEEEEEEEEE

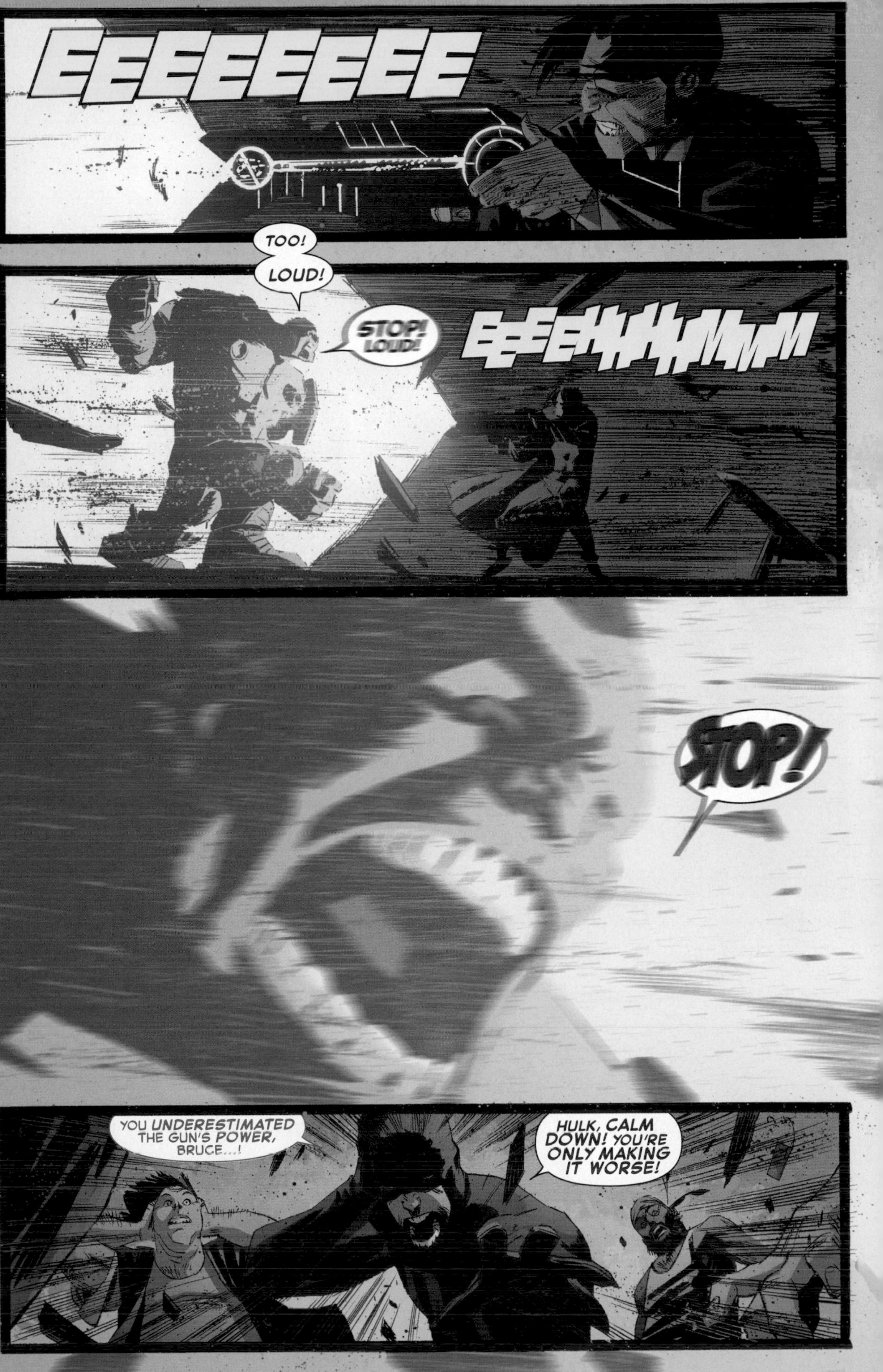
EEEEEEEEE
TOO!
LOUD!
STOP! LOUD!
EEEEHHHHMMMM
STOP!
YOU UNDERESTIMATED THE GUN'S POWER, BRUCE...!
HULK, CALM DOWN! YOU'RE ONLY MAKING IT WORSE!

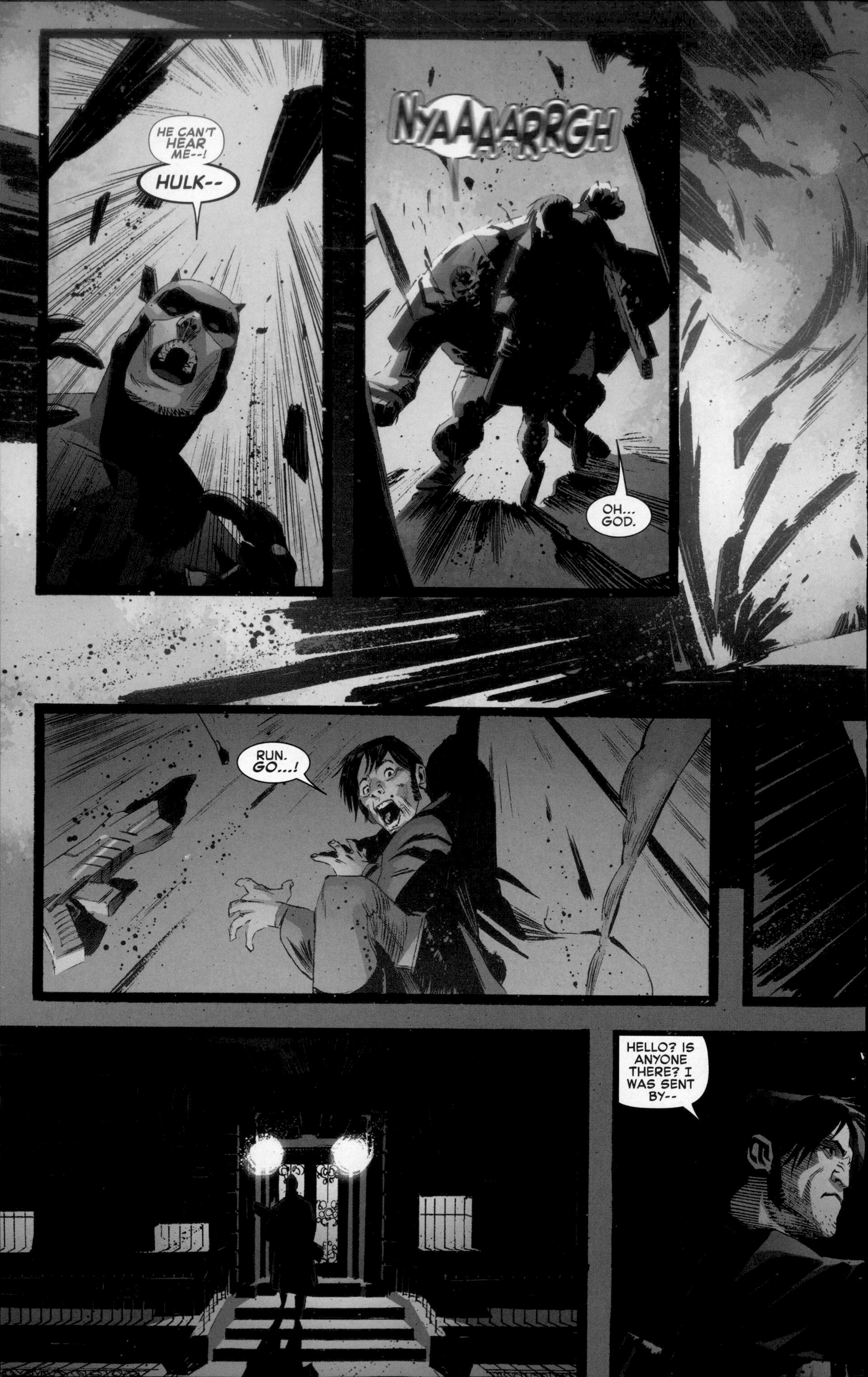
HE CAN'T HEAR ME--!
HULK--
NYAAAARRRGH
OH... GOD.
RUN. GO...!
HELLO? IS ANYONE THERE? I WAS SENT BY--

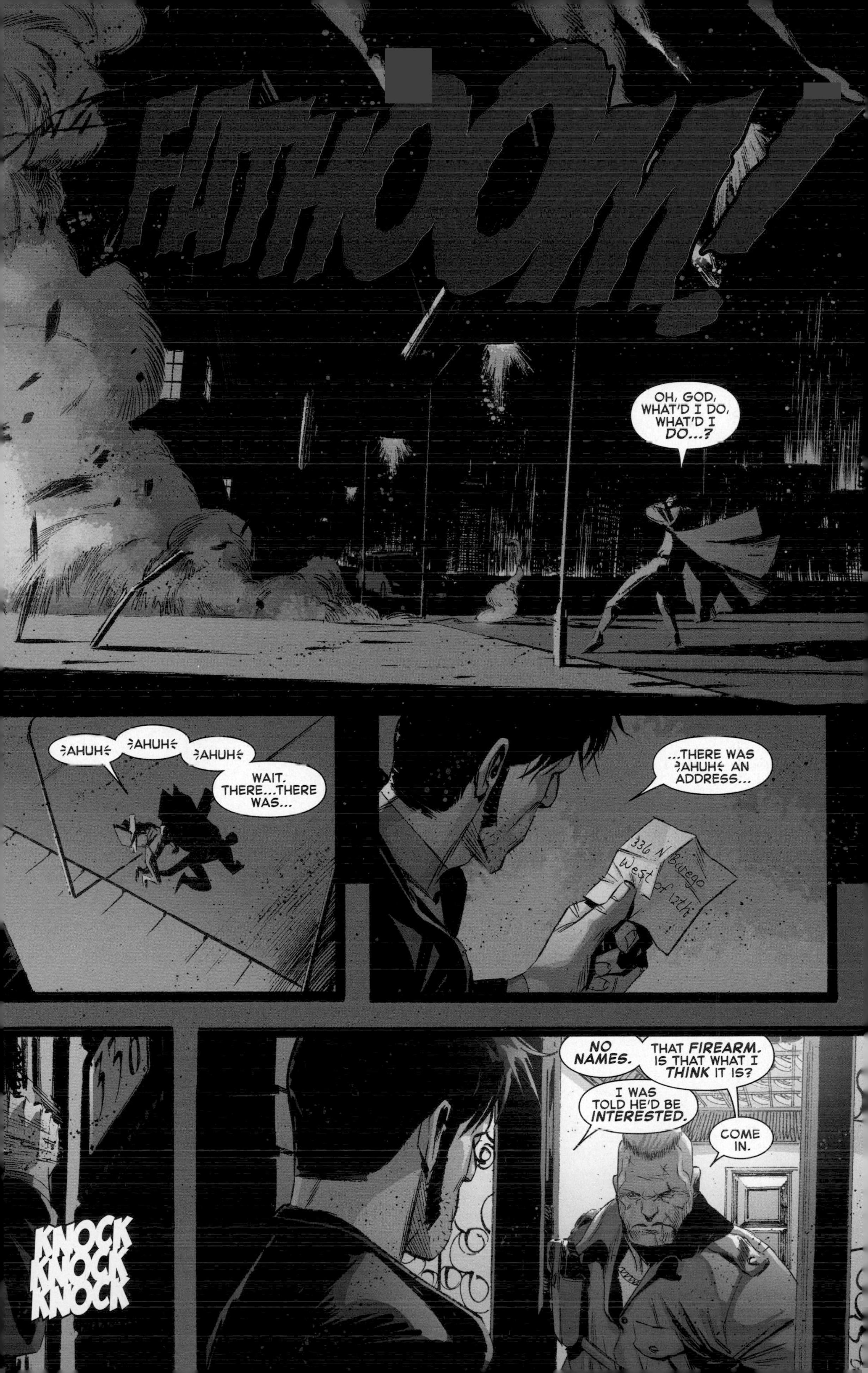
FATHOOM!
OH, GOD, WHAT'D I DO, WHAT'D I DO...?
AHUH
AHUH
AHUH
WAIT. THERE...THERE WAS...
...THERE WAS AHUH AN ADDRESS...
336 N Barego West of 12th
KNOCK KNOCK KNOCK
NO NAMES.
THAT FIREARM. IS THAT WHAT I THINK IT IS?
I WAS TOLD HE'D BE INTERESTED.
COME IN.

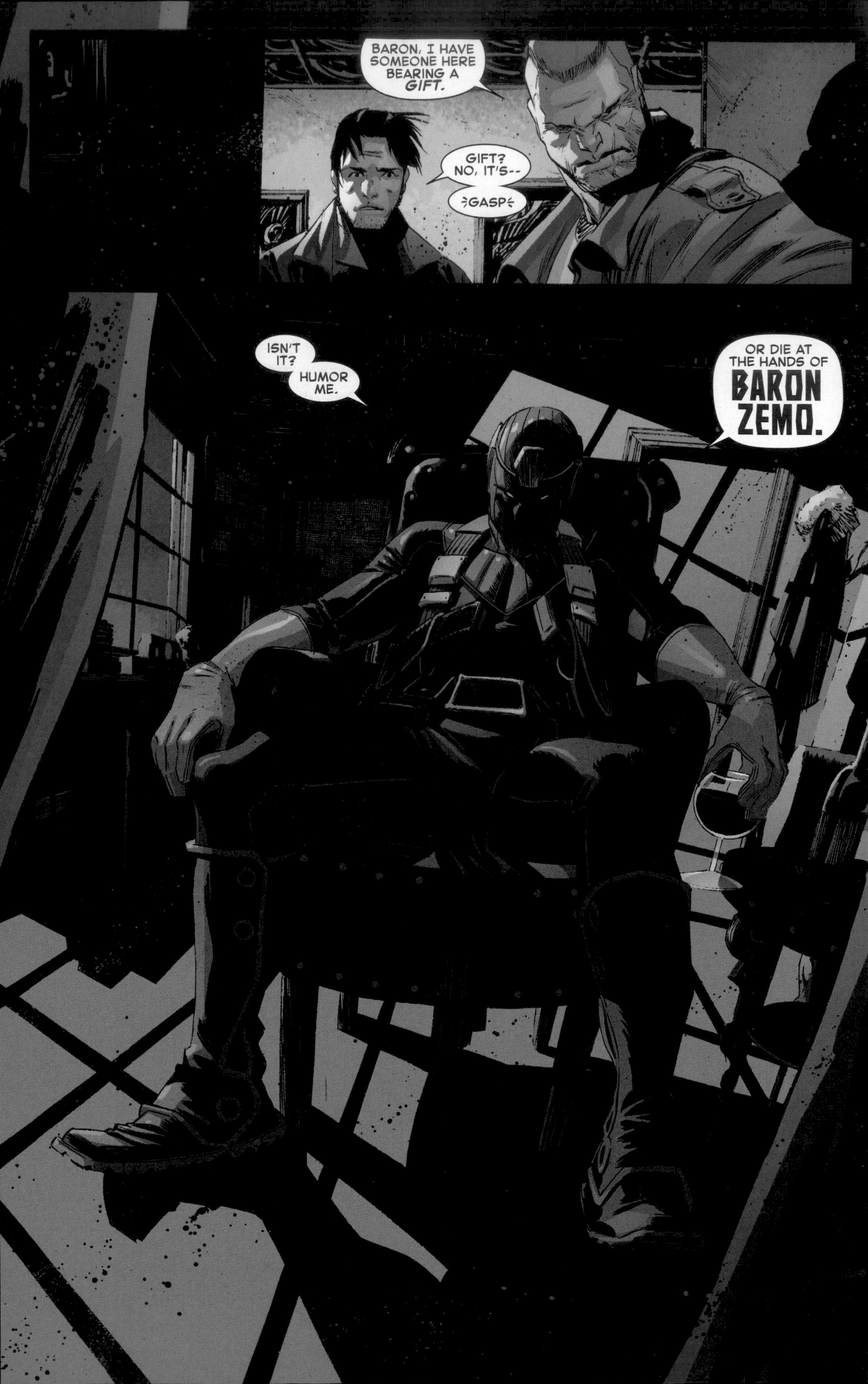

BARON, I HAVE SOMEONE HERE BEARING A GIFT.
GIFT? NO, IT'S--
GASP
ISN'T IT?
HUMOR ME.
OR DIE AT THE HANDS OF BARON ZEMO.

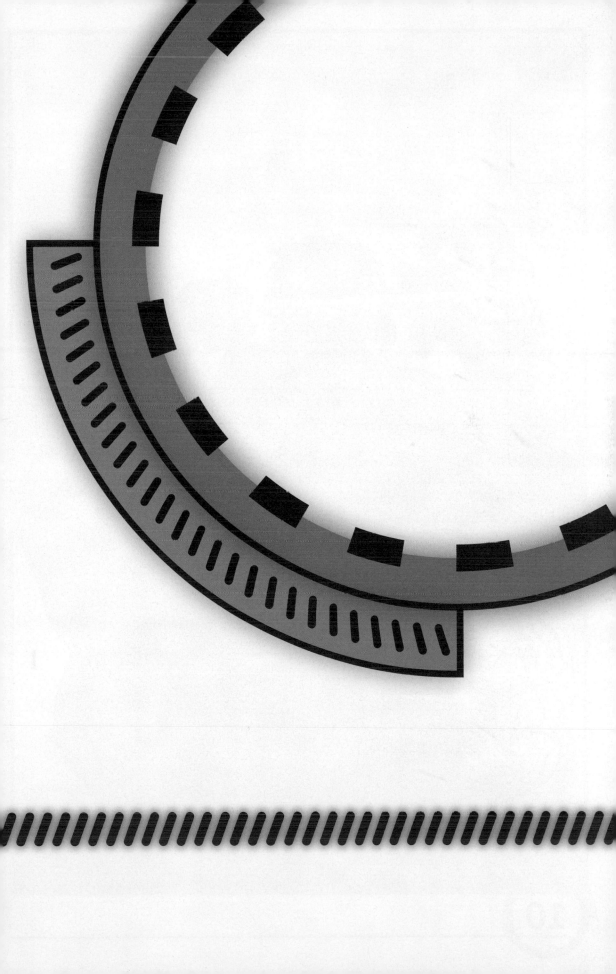

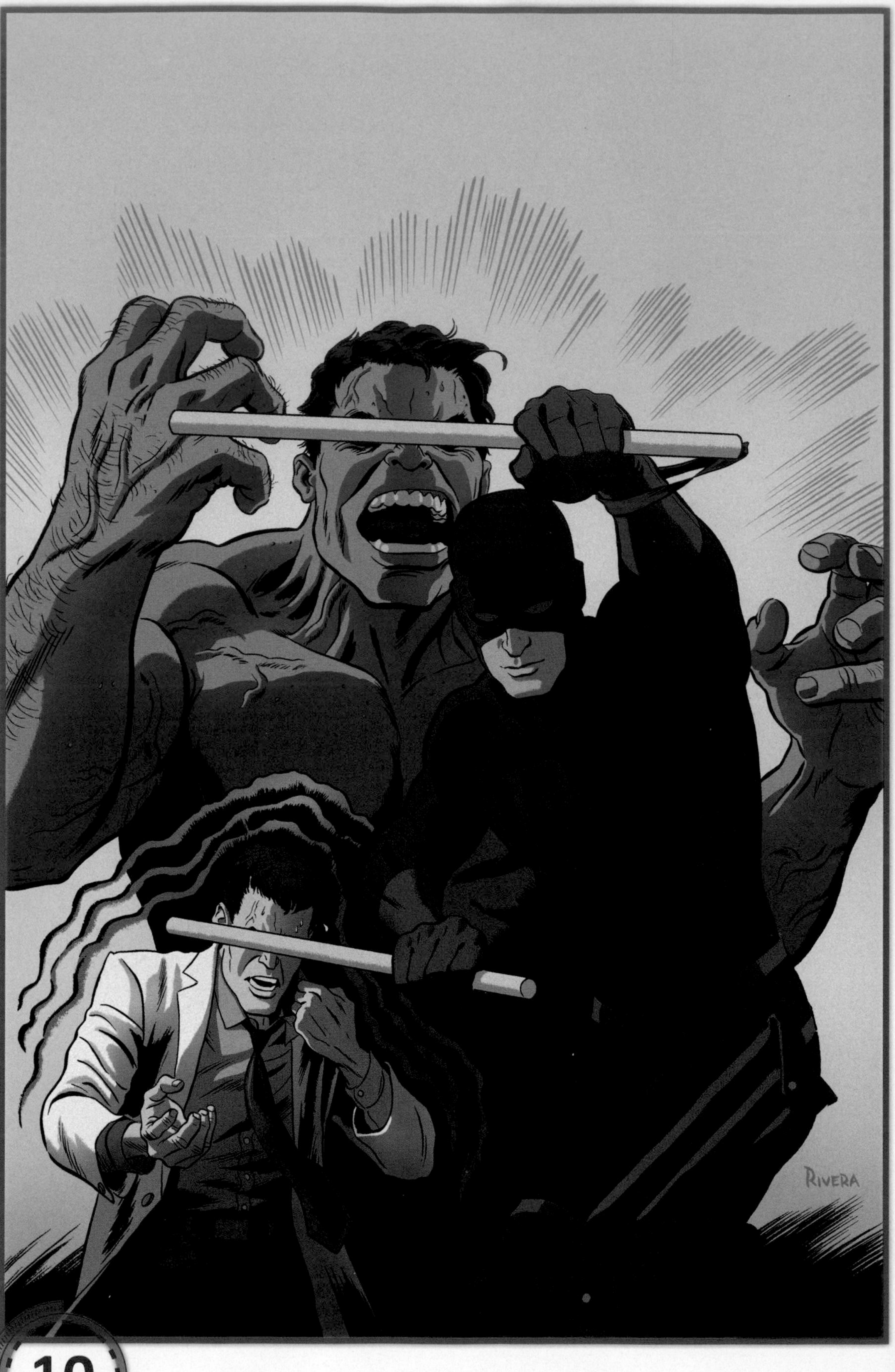
RIVERA

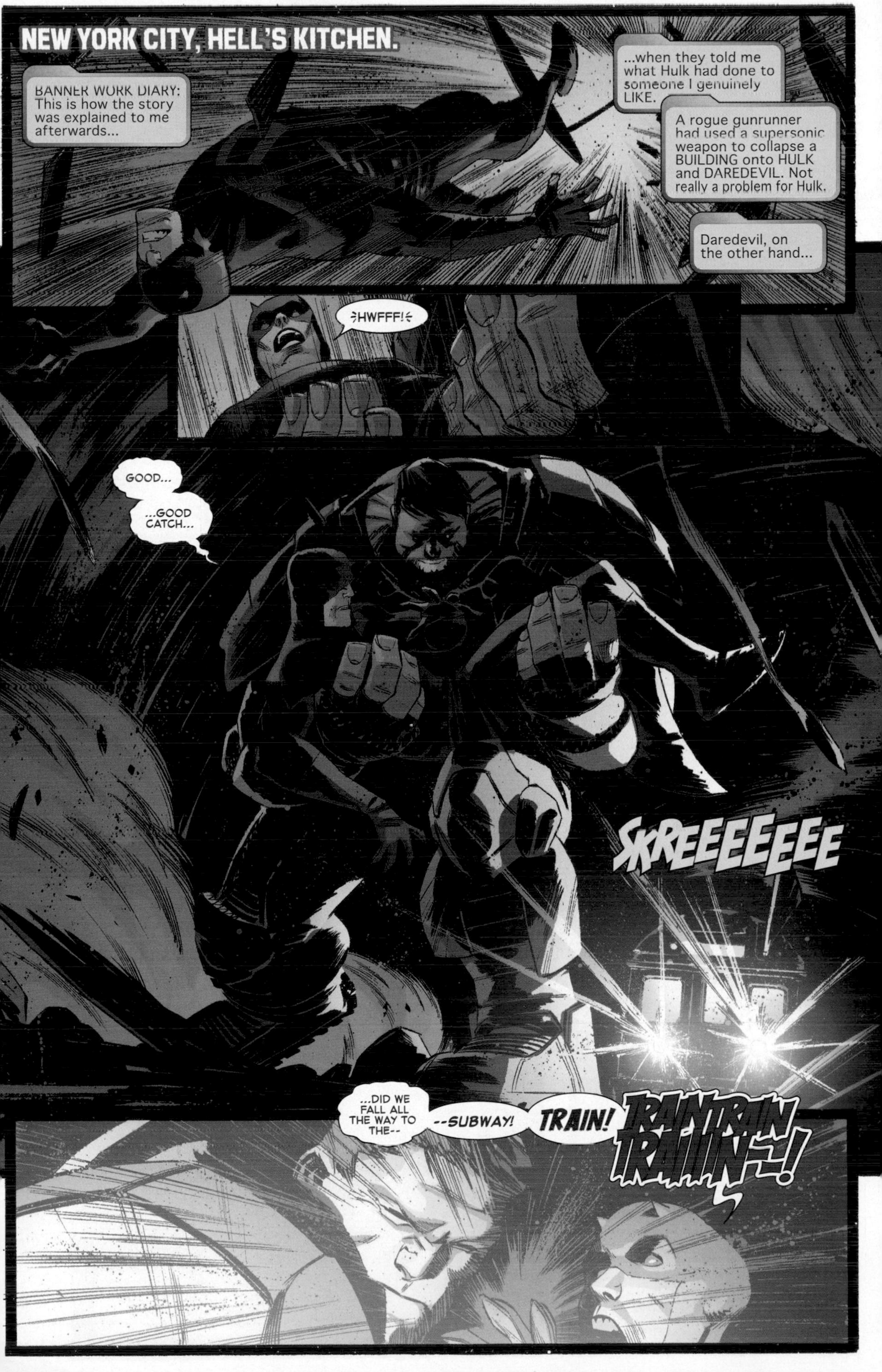
NEW YORK CITY, HELL'S KITCHEN.
BANNER WORK DIARY: This is how the story was explained to me afterwards...
...when they told me what Hulk had done to someone I genuinely LIKE.
A rogue gunrunner had used a supersonic weapon to collapse a BUILDING onto HULK and DAREDEVIL. Not really a problem for Hulk.
Daredevil, on the other hand...
HWFFF!
GOOD...
...GOOD CATCH...
SKREEEEEEEE
...DID WE FALL ALL THE WAY TO THE--
--SUBWAY!
TRAIN!
TRAINTRAIN TRAIIIN--!

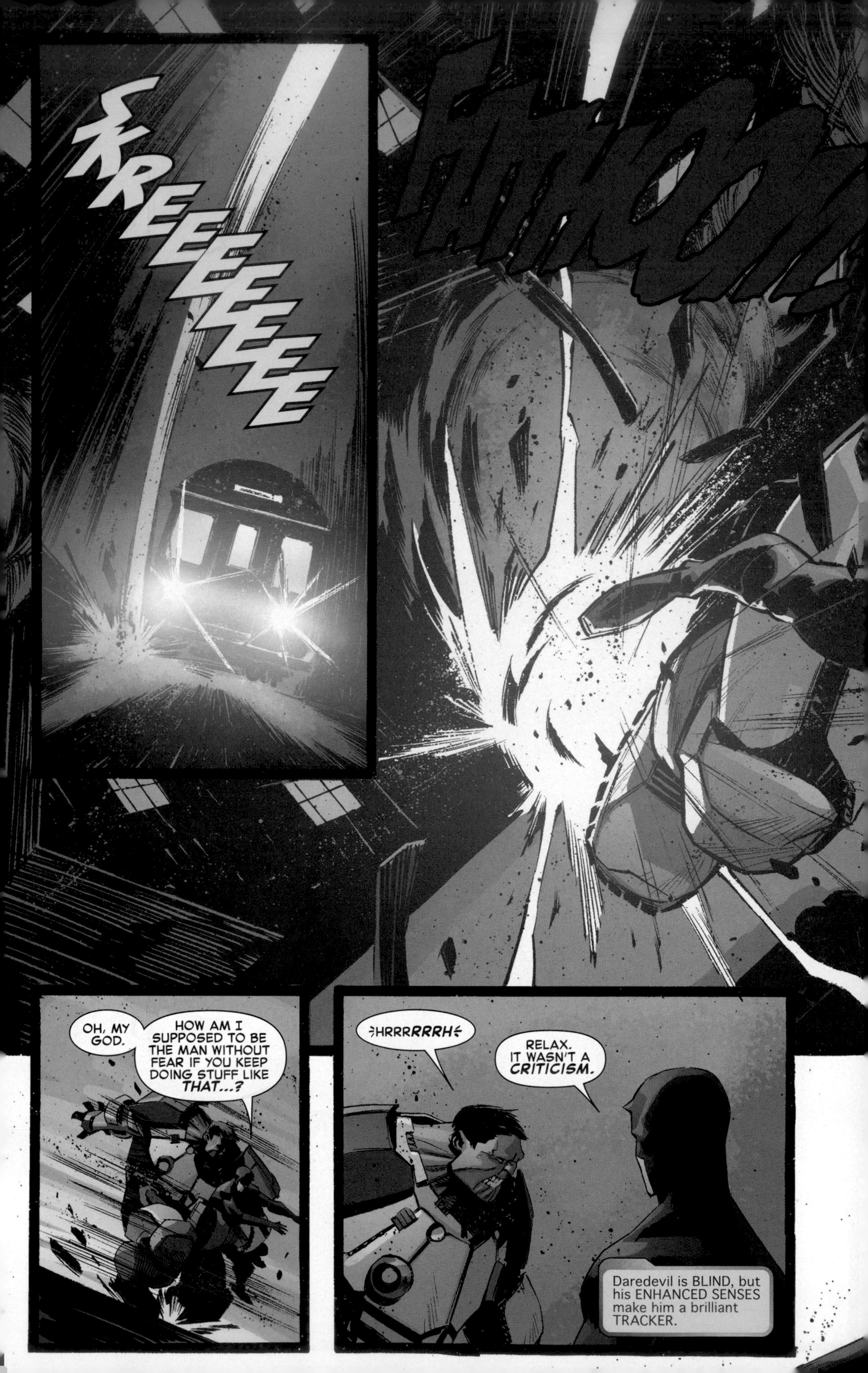
SKREEEEEEEEE
OH, MY GOD.
HOW AM I SUPPOSED TO BE THE MAN WITHOUT FEAR IF YOU KEEP DOING STUFF LIKE THAT...?
HRRRRRRH
RELAX. IT WASN'T A CRITICISM.
Daredevil is BLIND, but his ENHANCED SENSES make him a brilliant TRACKER.

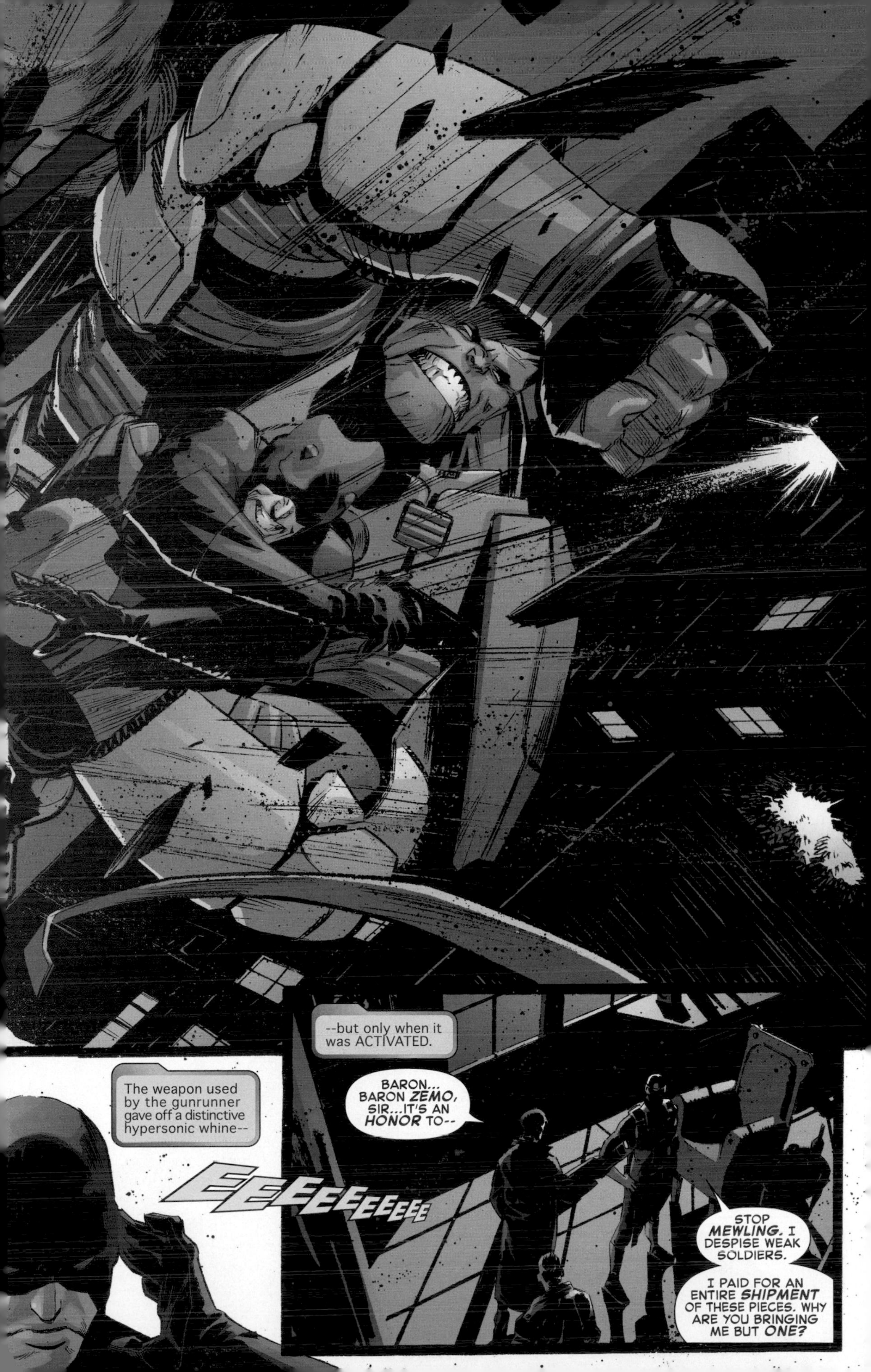

The weapon used by the gunrunner gave off a distinctive hypersonic whine--
EEEEEEEEEEE
--but only when it was ACTIVATED.
BARON... BARON ZEMO, SIR...IT'S AN HONOR TO--
STOP MEWLING. I DESPISE WEAK SOLDIERS.
I PAID FOR AN ENTIRE SHIPMENT OF THESE PIECES. WHY ARE YOU BRINGING ME BUT ONE?

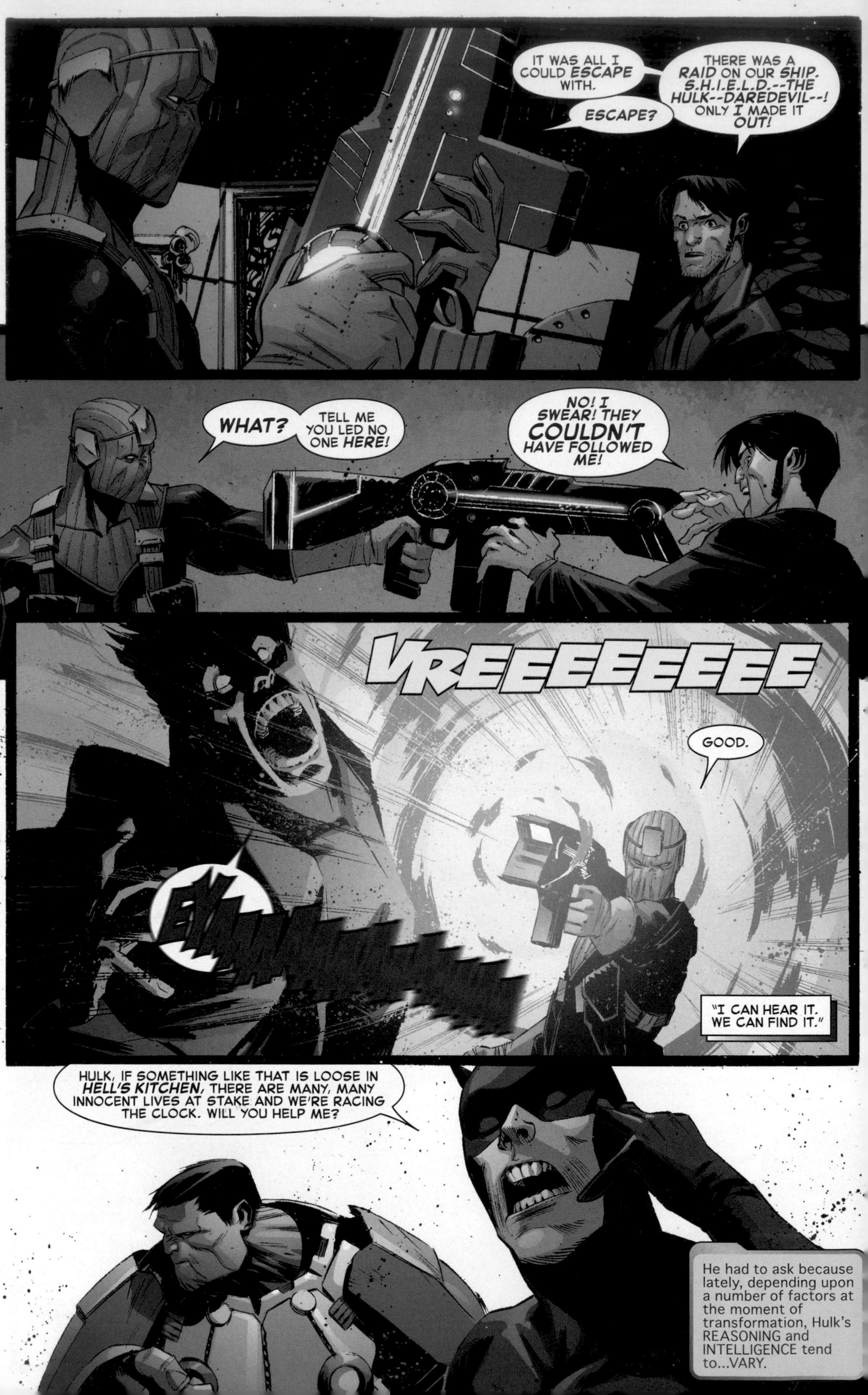
IT WAS ALL I COULD ESCAPE WITH.
ESCAPE?
THERE WAS A RAID ON OUR SHIP. S.H.I.E.L.D.--THE HULK--DAREDEVIL--! ONLY I MADE IT OUT!
WHAT?
TELL ME YOU LED NO ONE HERE!
NO! I SWEAR! THEY COULDN'T HAVE FOLLOWED ME!
VREEEEEEEE
GOOD.
"I CAN HEAR IT. WE CAN FIND IT."
HULK, IF SOMETHING LIKE THAT IS LOOSE IN HELL'S KITCHEN, THERE ARE MANY, MANY INNOCENT LIVES AT STAKE AND WE'RE RACING THE CLOCK. WILL YOU HELP ME?
He had to ask because lately, depending upon a number of factors at the moment of transformation, Hulk's REASONING and INTELLIGENCE tend to...VARY.

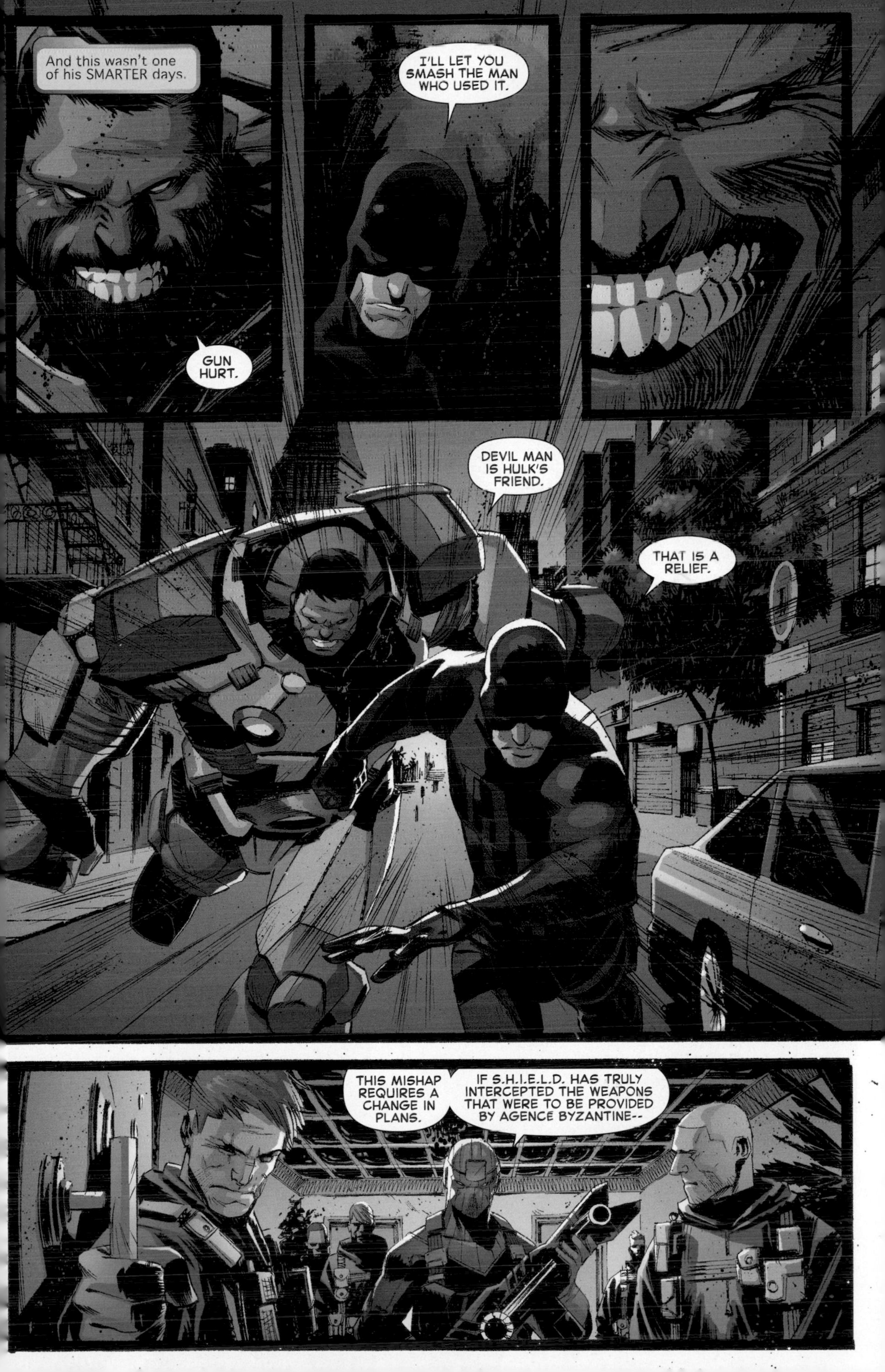
And this wasn't one of his SMARTER days.
GUN HURT.
I'LL LET YOU SMASH THE MAN WHO USED IT.
DEVIL MAN IS HULK'S FRIEND.
THAT IS A RELIEF.
THIS MISHAP REQUIRES A CHANGE IN PLANS.
IF S.H.I.E.L.D. HAS TRULY INTERCEPTED THE WEAPONS THAT WERE TO BE PROVIDED BY AGENCE BYZANTINE--

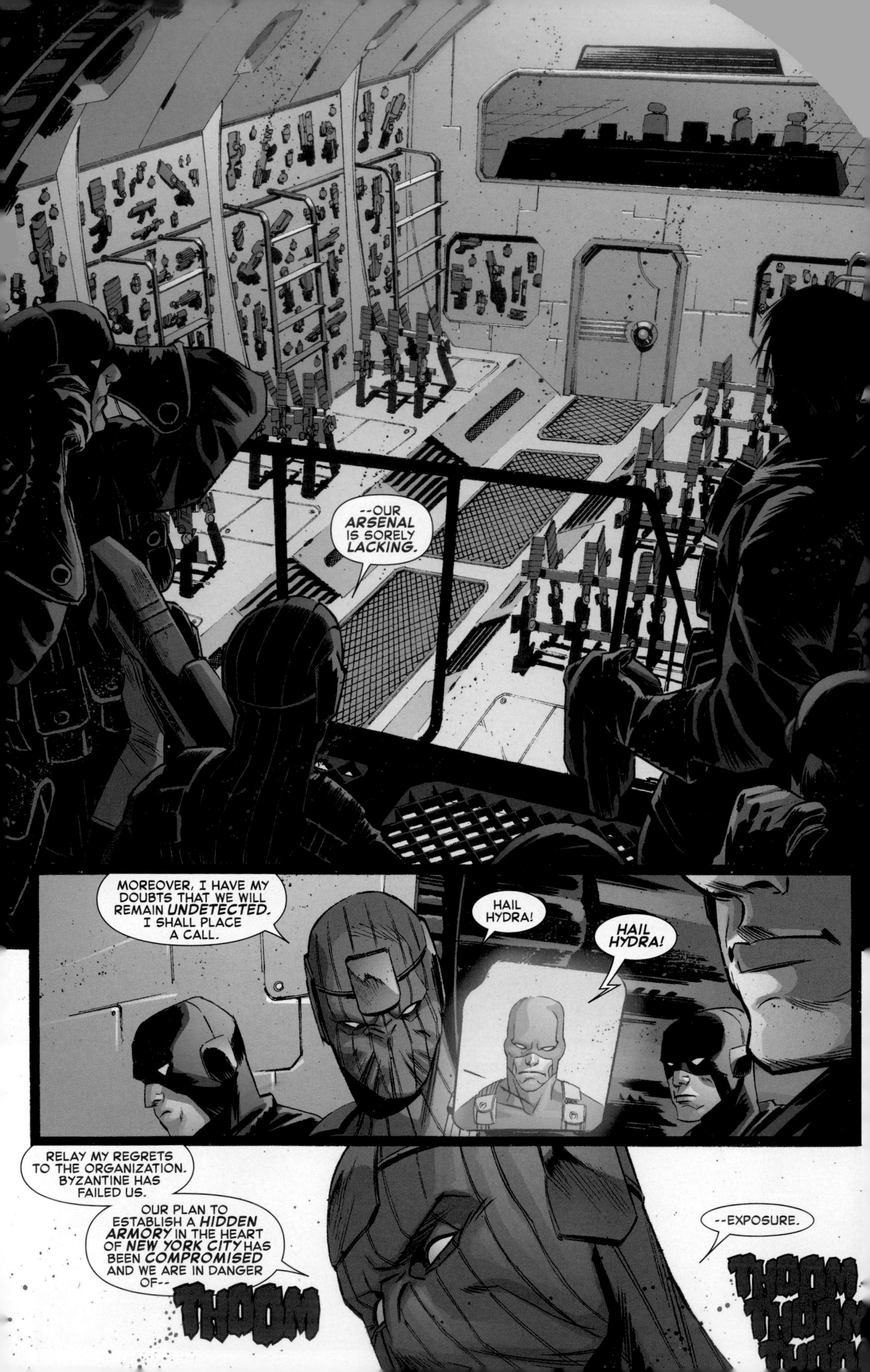
--OUR ARSENAL IS SORELY LACKING.
MOREOVER, I HAVE MY DOUBTS THAT WE WILL REMAIN UNDETECTED. I SHALL PLACE A CALL.
HAIL HYDRA!
HAIL HYDRA!
RELAY MY REGRETS TO THE ORGANIZATION. BYZANTINE HAS FAILED US.
OUR PLAN TO ESTABLISH A HIDDEN ARMORY IN THE HEART OF NEW YORK CITY HAS BEEN COMPROMISED AND WE ARE IN DANGER OF--
THOOM
--EXPOSURE.
THOOM

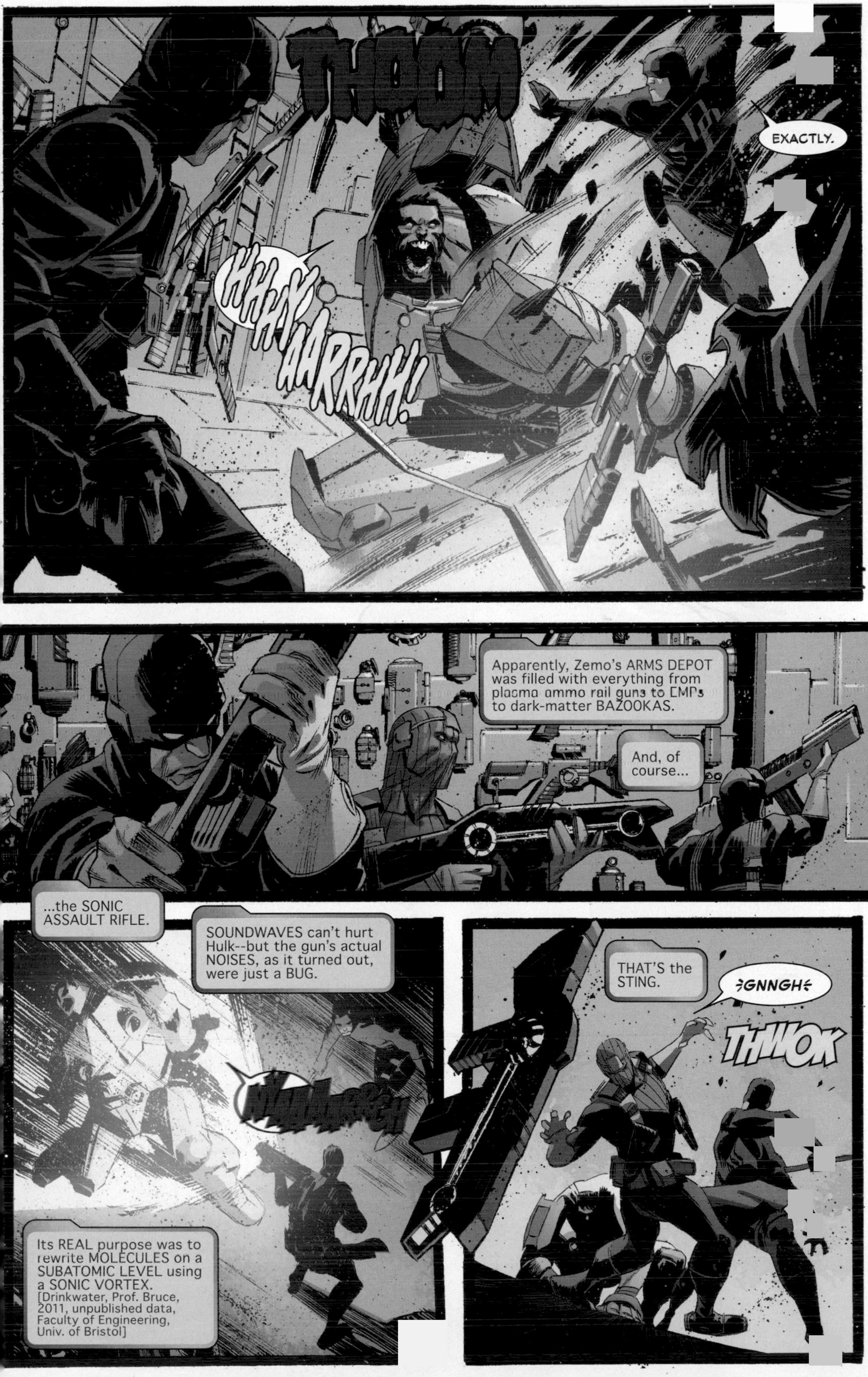
THOOM
EXACTLY.
HHHYAARRHH!
Apparently, Zemo's ARMS DEPOT was filled with everything from plasma ammo rail guns to EMPs to dark-matter BAZOOKAS.
And, of course...
...the SONIC ASSAULT RIFLE.
SOUNDWAVES can't hurt Hulk--but the gun's actual NOISES, as it turned out, were just a BUG.
Its REAL purpose was to rewrite MOLECULES on a SUBATOMIC LEVEL using a SONIC VORTEX. [Drinkwater, Prof. Bruce, 2011, unpublished data, Faculty of Engineering, Univ. of Bristol]
THAT'S the STING.
GNNGH
THWOK

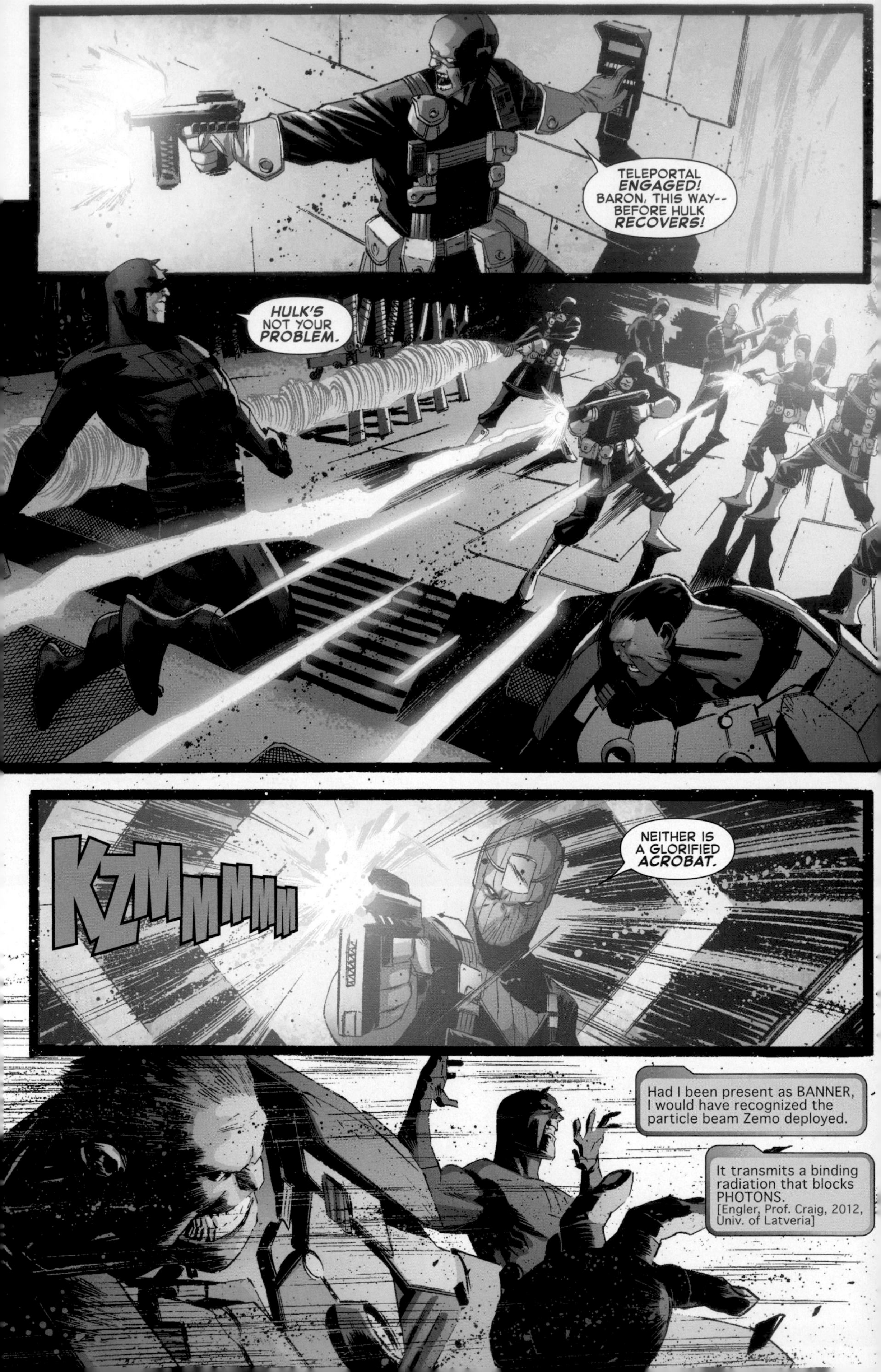
TELEPORTAL ENGAGED! BARON, THIS WAY-- BEFORE HULK RECOVERS!
HULK'S NOT YOUR PROBLEM.
KZMMMMMM
NEITHER IS A GLORIFIED ACROBAT.
Had I been present as BANNER, I would have recognized the particle beam Zemo deployed.
It transmits a binding radiation that blocks PHOTONS.
[Engler, Prof. Craig, 2012, Univ. of Latveria]

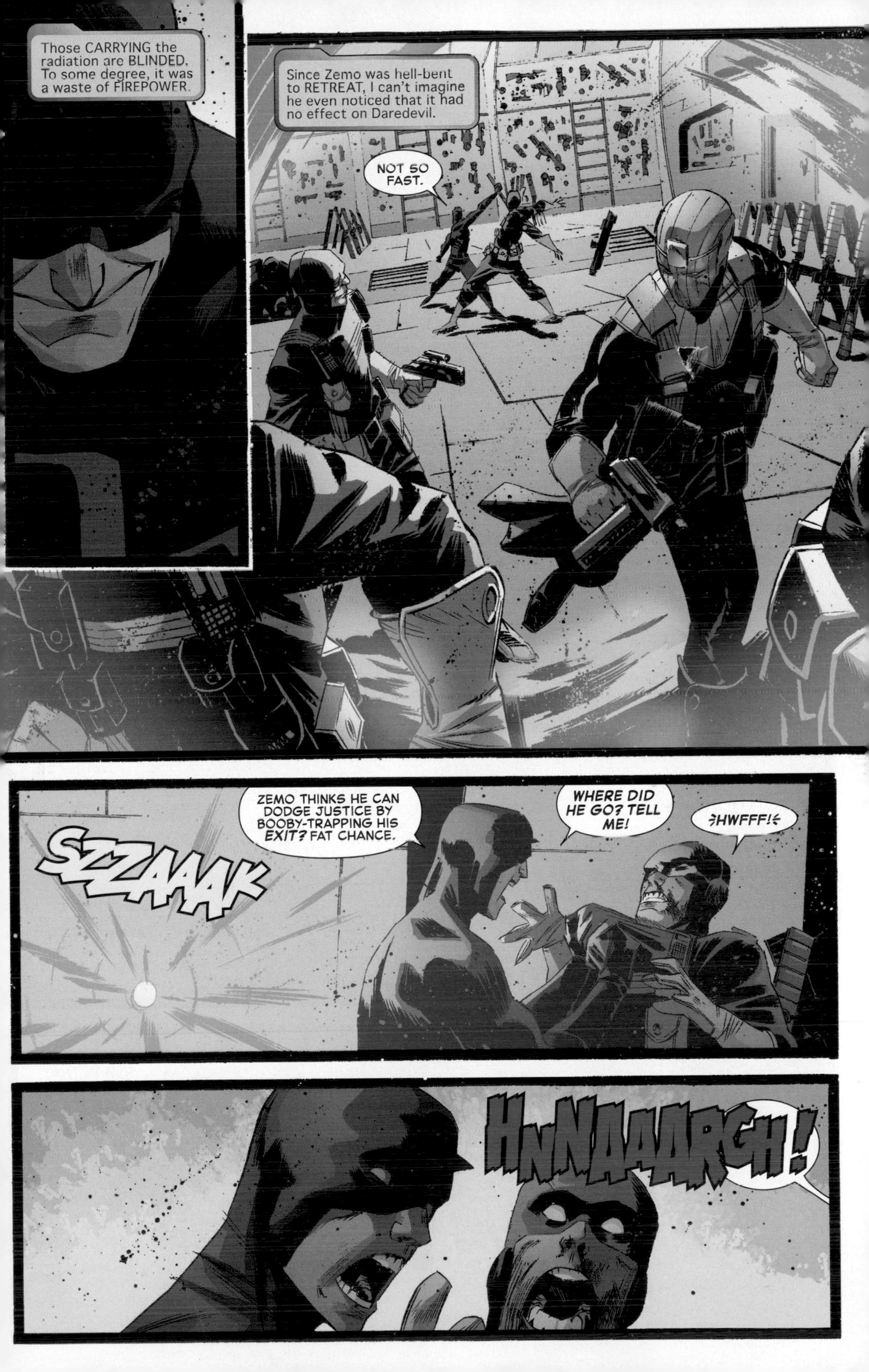
Those CARRYING the radiation are BLINDED. To some degree, it was a waste of FIREPOWER.
Since Zemo was hell-bent to RETREAT, I can't imagine he even noticed that it had no effect on Daredevil.
NOT SO FAST.
SZZAAAK
ZEMO THINKS HE CAN DODGE JUSTICE BY BOOBY-TRAPPING HIS EXIT? FAT CHANCE.
WHERE DID HE GO? TELL ME!
HWFFF!
HNNAAARGH!

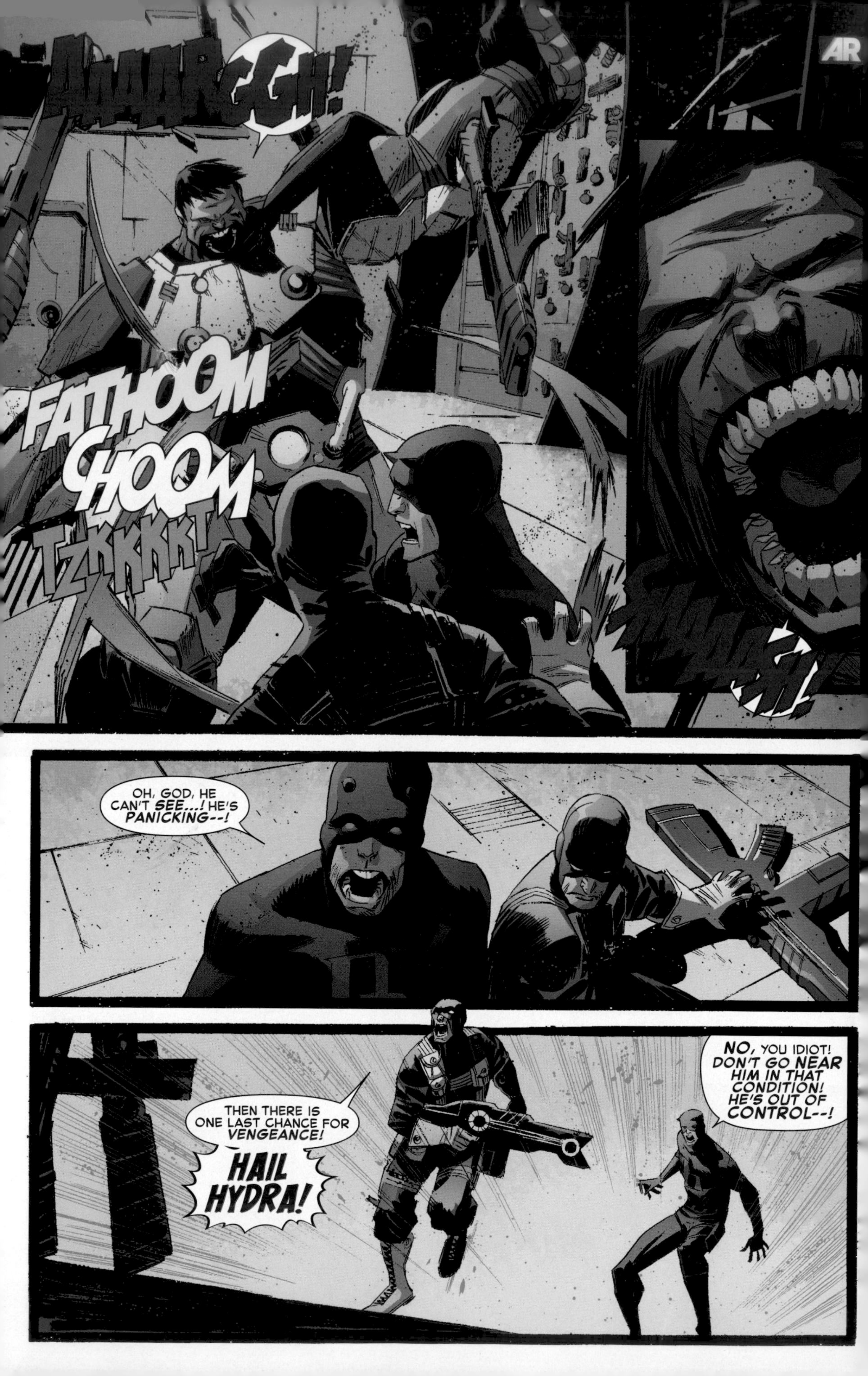
AAAARGGH!
FATHOOM
CHOOM
TZKKKT
OH, GOD, HE CAN'T SEE...! HE'S PANICKING--!
THEN THERE IS ONE LAST CHANCE FOR VENGEANCE!
HAIL HYDRA!
NO, YOU IDIOT! DON'T GO NEAR HIM IN THAT CONDITION! HE'S OUT OF CONTROL--!

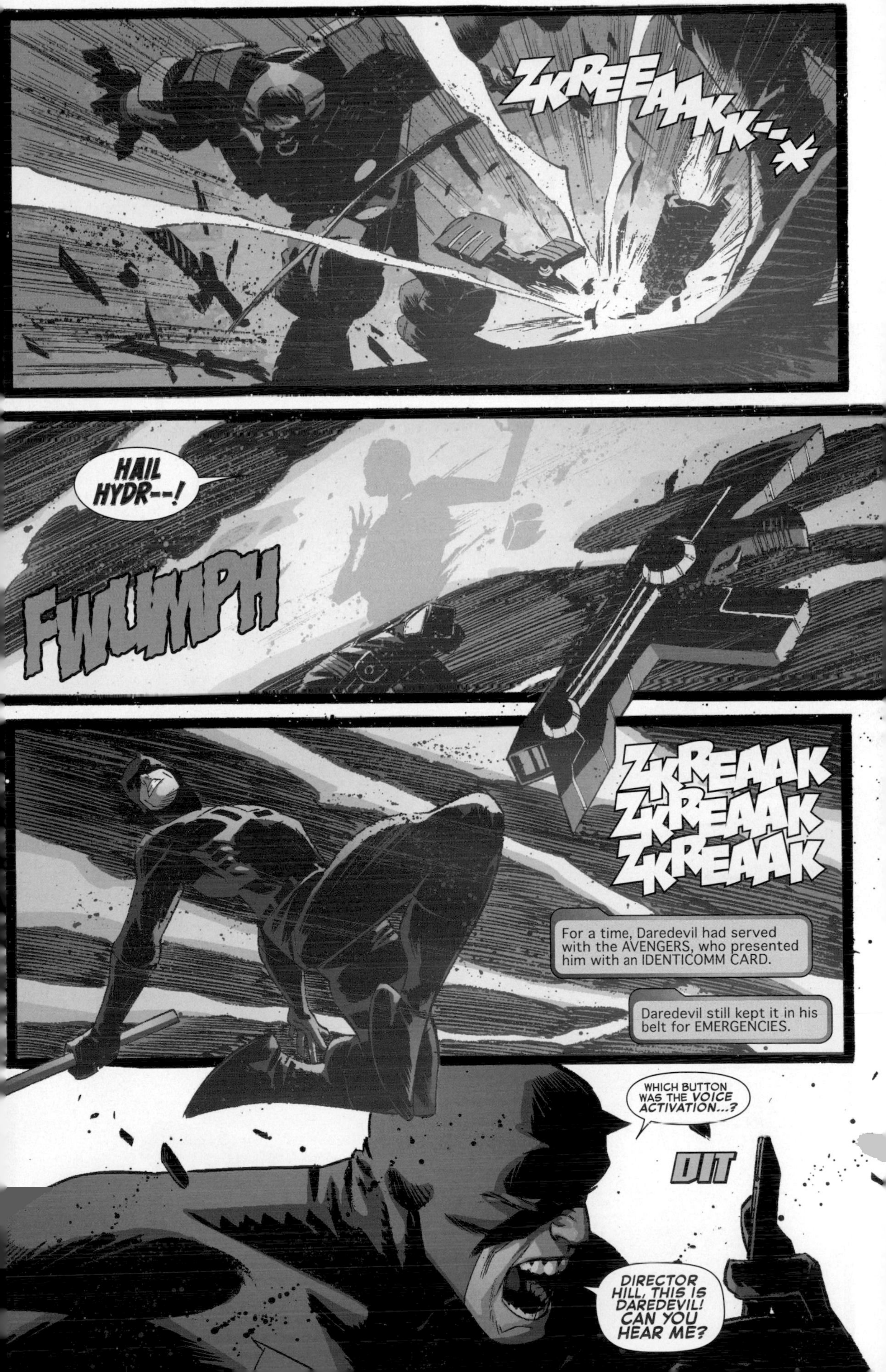
ZKREEAAKK--*
HAIL HYDR--!
FWUMPH
ZKREAAK
ZKREAAK
ZKREAAK
For a time, Daredevil had served with the AVENGERS, who presented him with an IDENTICOMM CARD.
Daredevil still kept it in his belt for EMERGENCIES.
WHICH BUTTON WAS THE VOICE ACTIVATION...?
DIT
DIRECTOR HILL, THIS IS DAREDEVIL! CAN YOU HEAR ME?

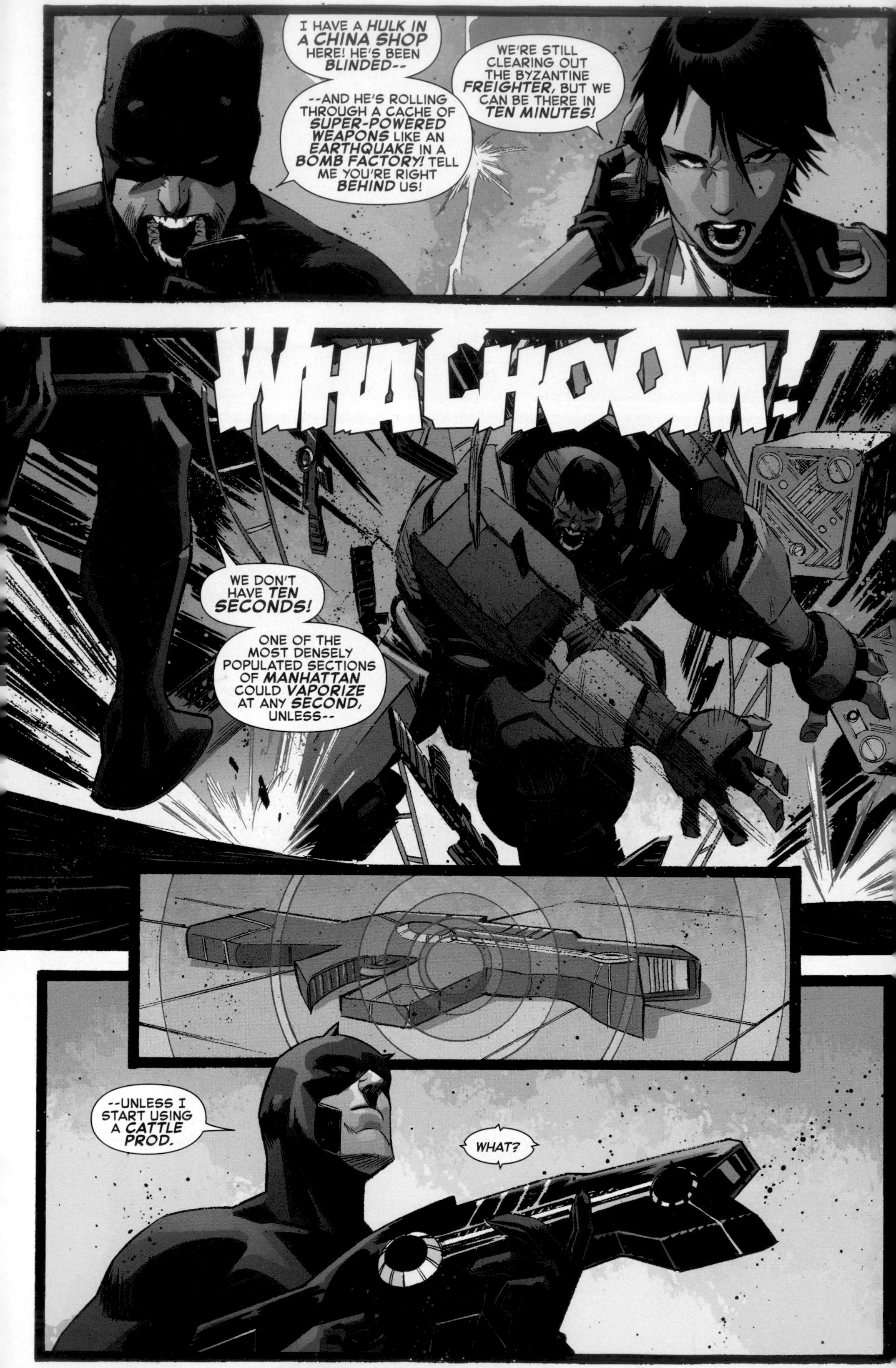
I HAVE A HULK IN A CHINA SHOP HERE! HE'S BEEN BLINDED--
--AND HE'S ROLLING THROUGH A CACHE OF SUPER-POWERED WEAPONS LIKE AN EARTHQUAKE IN A BOMB FACTORY! TELL ME YOU'RE RIGHT BEHIND US!
WE'RE STILL CLEARING OUT THE BYZANTINE FREIGHTER, BUT WE CAN BE THERE IN TEN MINUTES!
WHACHOOM!
WE DON'T HAVE TEN SECONDS!
ONE OF THE MOST DENSELY POPULATED SECTIONS OF MANHATTAN COULD VAPORIZE AT ANY SECOND, UNLESS--
--UNLESS I START USING A CATTLE PROD.
WHAT?

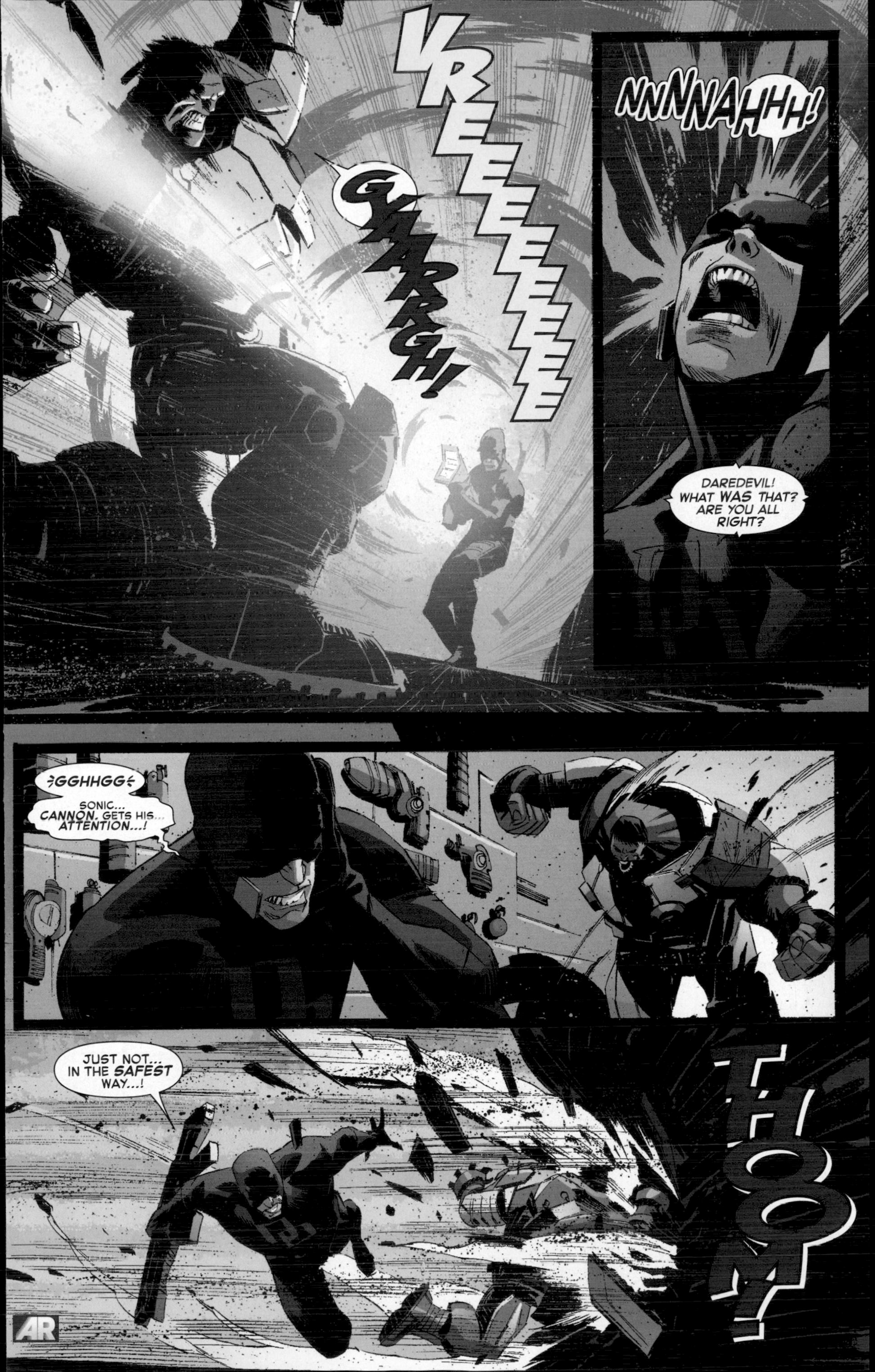
VREEEEEEEEEEE
GYAARGH!
NNNNAHHH!
DAREDEVIL! WHAT WAS THAT? ARE YOU ALL RIGHT?
GGHHGG
SONIC... CANNON. GETS HIS... ATTENTION...!
JUST NOT... IN THE SAFEST WAY...!
THOOM!
AR

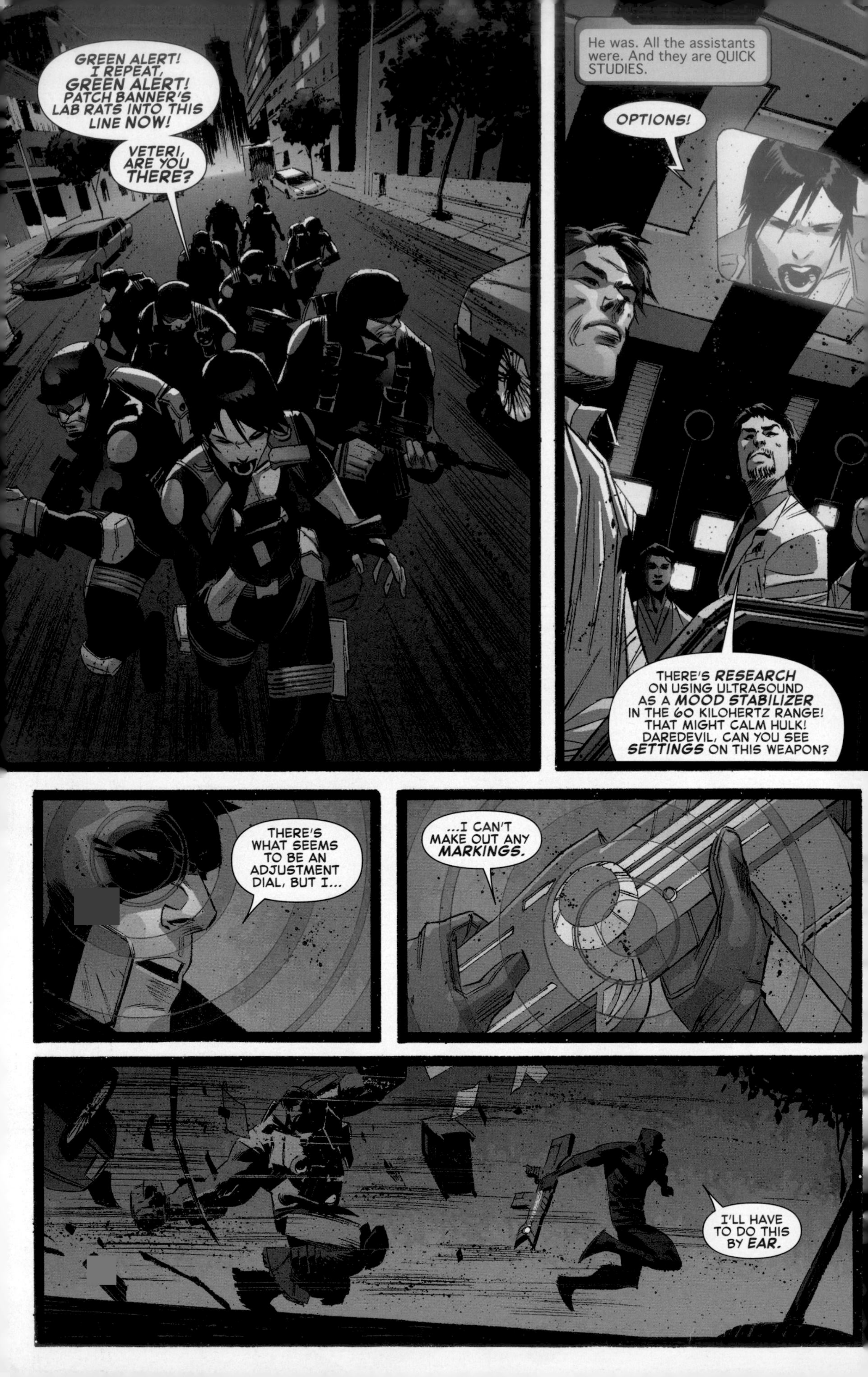
GREEN ALERT! I REPEAT, GREEN ALERT! PATCH BANNER'S LAB RATS INTO THIS LINE NOW!
VETERI, ARE YOU THERE?
He was. All the assistants were. And they are QUICK STUDIES.
OPTIONS!
THERE'S RESEARCH ON USING ULTRASOUND AS A MOOD STABILIZER IN THE 60 KILOHERTZ RANGE! THAT MIGHT CALM HULK! DAREDEVIL, CAN YOU SEE SETTINGS ON THIS WEAPON?
THERE'S WHAT SEEMS TO BE AN ADJUSTMENT DIAL, BUT I...
...I CAN'T MAKE OUT ANY MARKINGS.
I'LL HAVE TO DO THIS BY EAR.

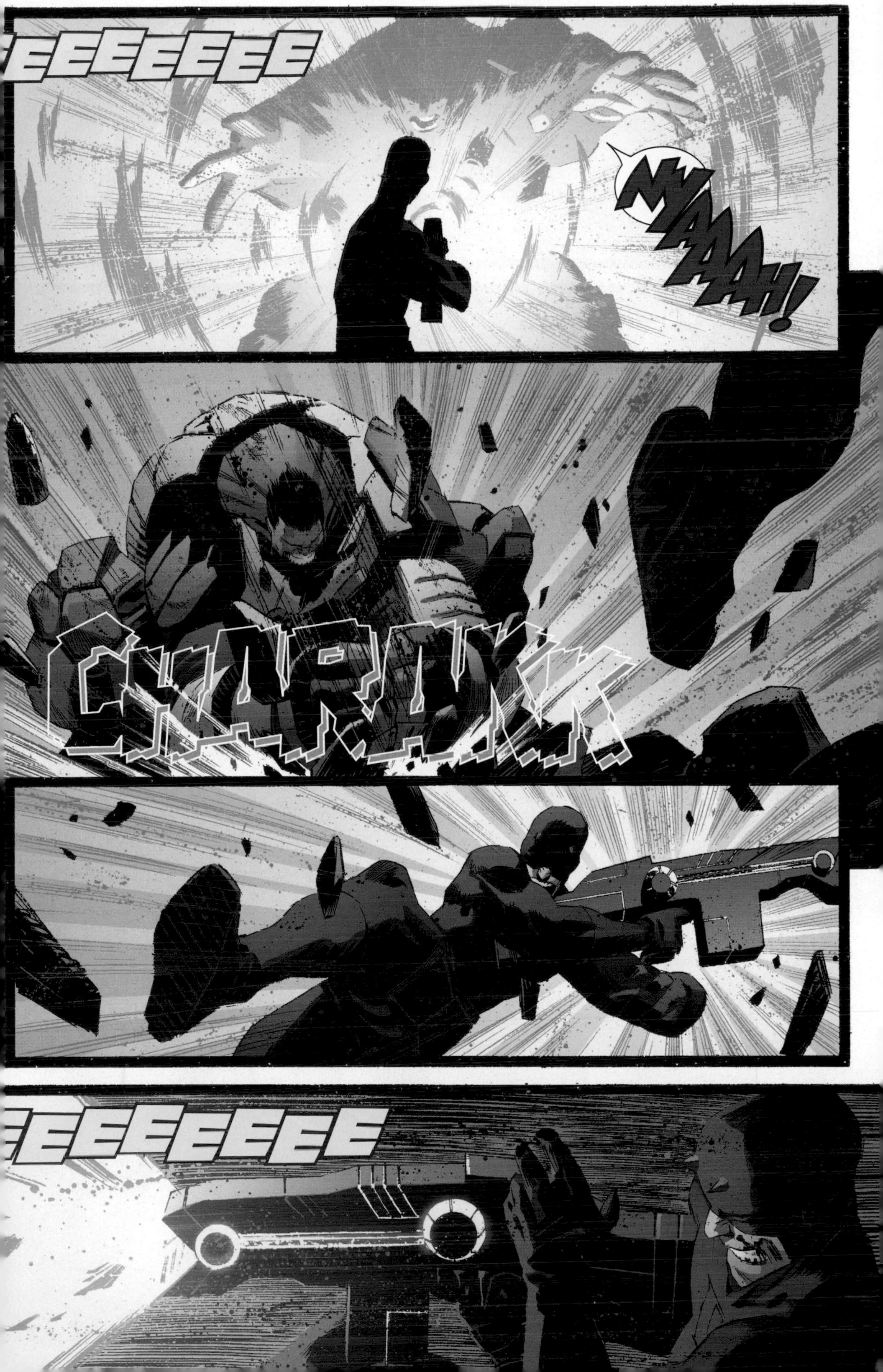
EEEEEEEE
NYAAAH!
EEEEEEEE

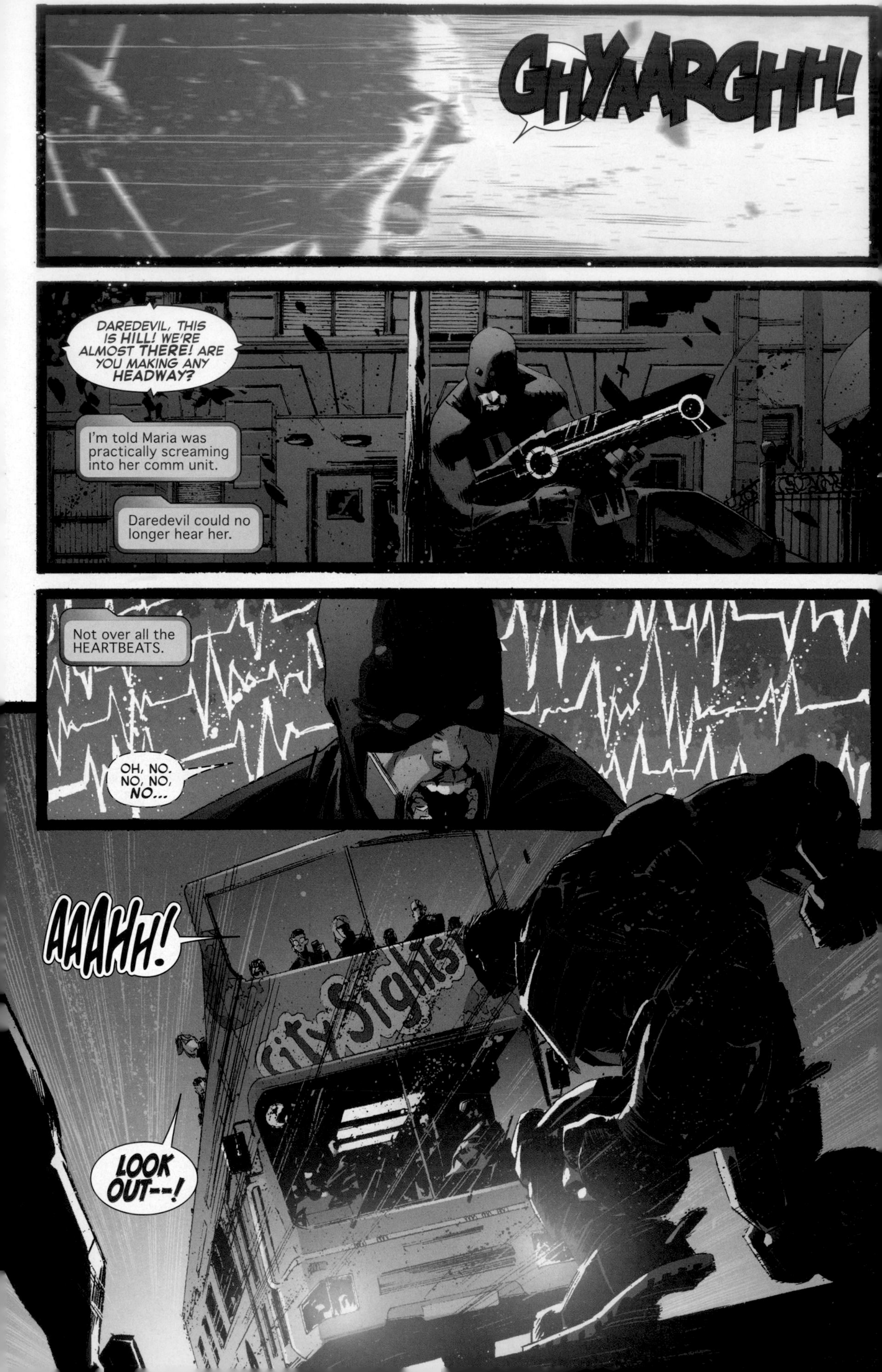
GHYAARGHH!
DAREDEVIL, THIS IS HILL! WE'RE ALMOST THERE! ARE YOU MAKING ANY HEADWAY?
I'm told Maria was practically screaming into her comm unit.
Daredevil could no longer hear her.
Not over all the HEARTBEATS.
OH, NO. NO, NO, NO...
AAAHH!
City Sights
LOOK OUT--!

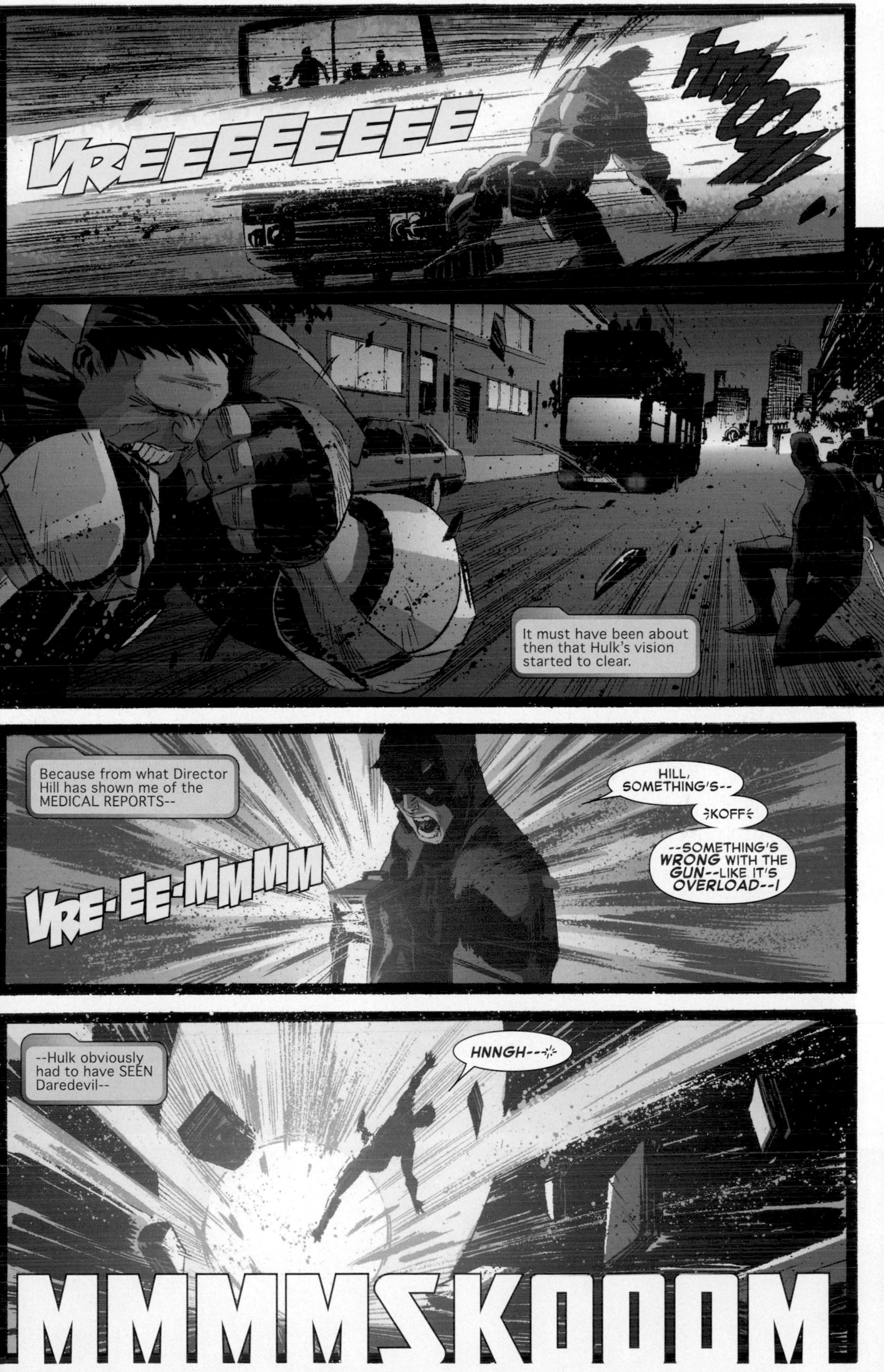
VREEEEEEEEE
It must have been about then that Hulk's vision started to clear.
Because from what Director Hill has shown me of the MEDICAL REPORTS--
HILL, SOMETHING'S--
KOFF
--SOMETHING'S WRONG WITH THE GUN--LIKE IT'S OVERLOAD--I
VRE-EE-MMMM
--Hulk obviously had to have SEEN Daredevil--
HNNGH--
MMMMSKOOOM

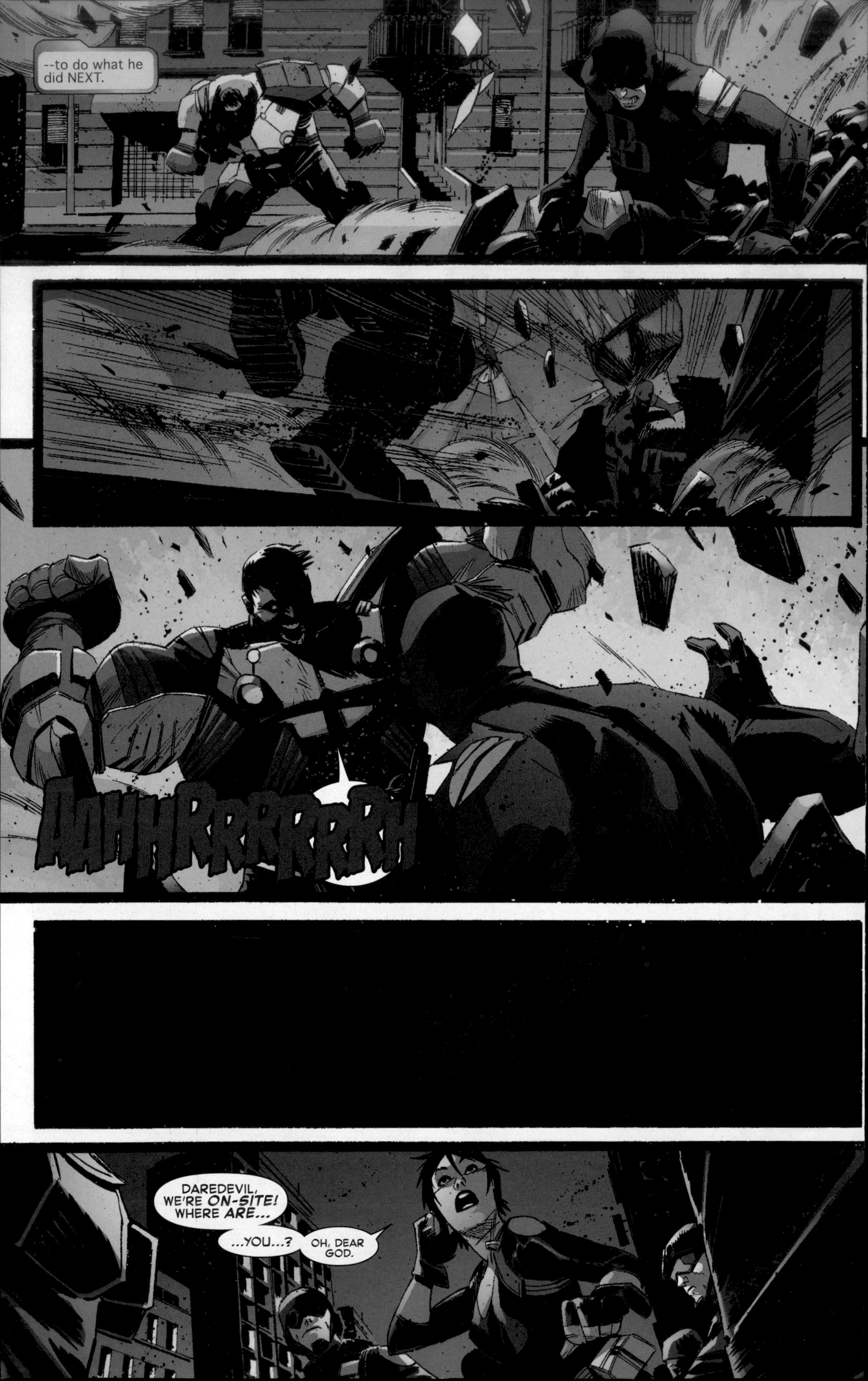
--to do what he did NEXT.
DAREDEVIL, WE'RE ON-SITE! WHERE ARE...
...YOU...?
OH, DEAR GOD.

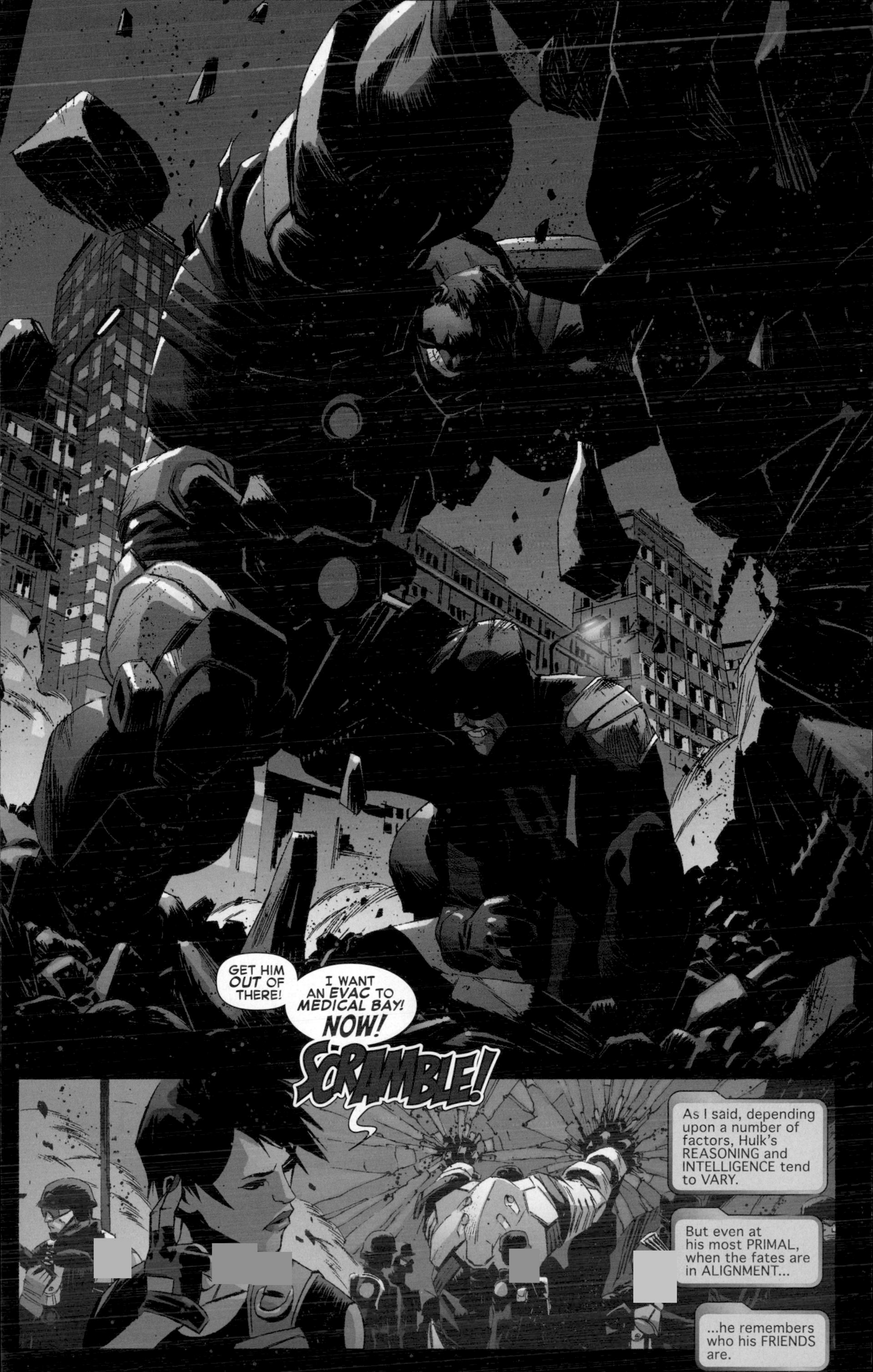
GET HIM OUT OF THERE!
I WANT AN EVAC TO MEDICAL BAY! NOW!
SCRAMBLE!
As I said, depending upon a number of factors, Hulk's REASONING and INTELLIGENCE tend to VARY.
But even at his most PRIMAL, when the fates are in ALIGNMENT...
...he remembers who his FRIENDS are.

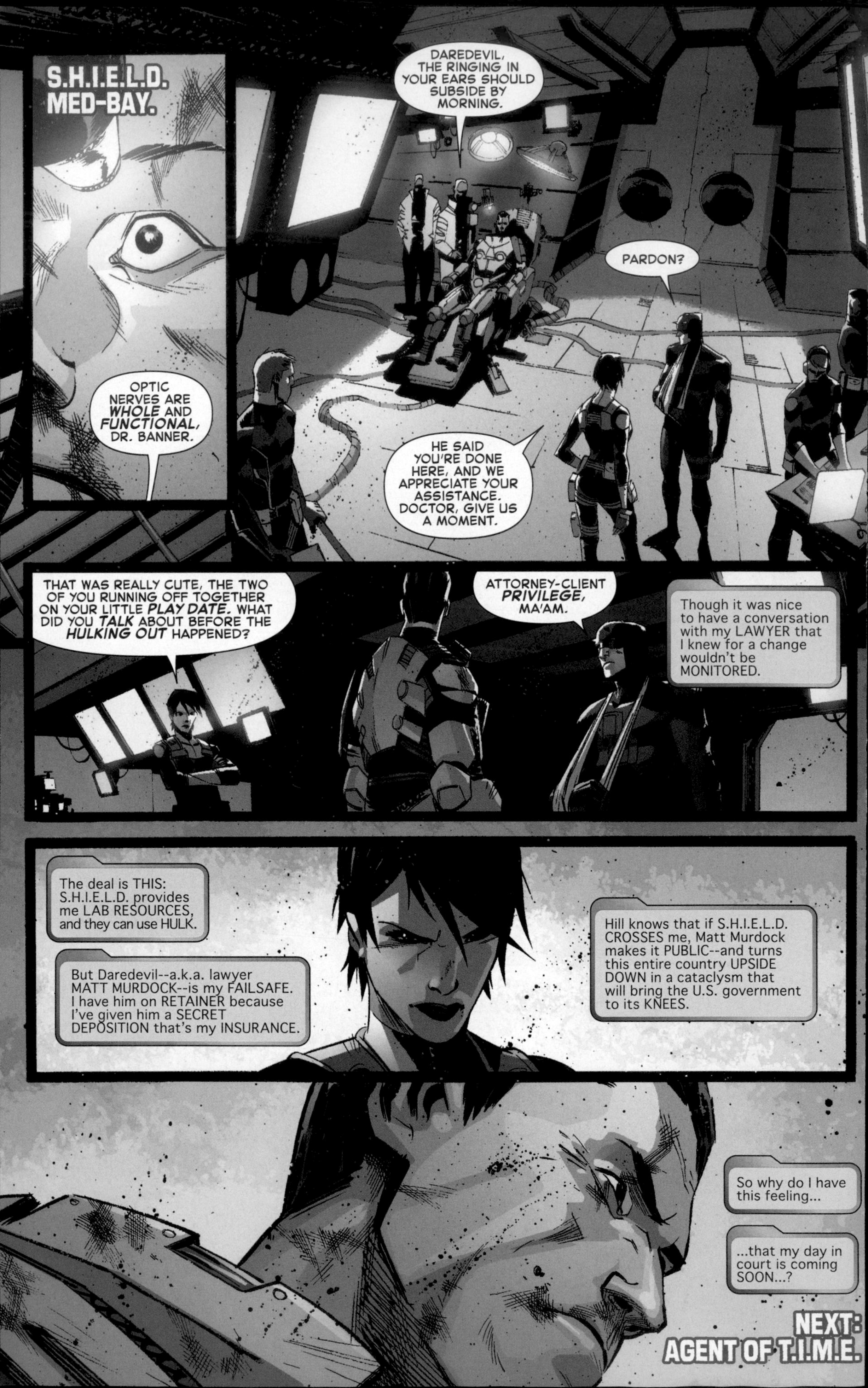
S.H.I.E.L.D. MED-BAY.
OPTIC NERVES ARE WHOLE AND FUNCTIONAL, DR. BANNER.
DAREDEVIL, THE RINGING IN YOUR EARS SHOULD SUBSIDE BY MORNING.
PARDON?
HE SAID YOU'RE DONE HERE, AND WE APPRECIATE YOUR ASSISTANCE. DOCTOR, GIVE US A MOMENT.
THAT WAS REALLY CUTE, THE TWO OF YOU RUNNING OFF TOGETHER ON YOUR LITTLE PLAY DATE. WHAT DID YOU TALK ABOUT BEFORE THE HULKING OUT HAPPENED?
ATTORNEY-CLIENT PRIVILEGE, MA'AM.
Though it was nice to have a conversation with my LAWYER that I knew for a change wouldn't be MONITORED.
The deal is THIS: S.H.I.E.L.D. provides me LAB RESOURCES, and they can use HULK.
But Daredevil--a.k.a. lawyer MATT MURDOCK--is my FAILSAFE. I have him on RETAINER because I've given him a SECRET DEPOSITION that's my INSURANCE.
Hill knows that if S.H.I.E.L.D. CROSSES me, Matt Murdock makes it PUBLIC--and turns this entire country UPSIDE DOWN in a cataclysm that will bring the U.S. government to its KNEES.
So why do I have this feeling...
...that my day in court is coming SOON...?
NEXT: AGENT OF T.I.M.E.

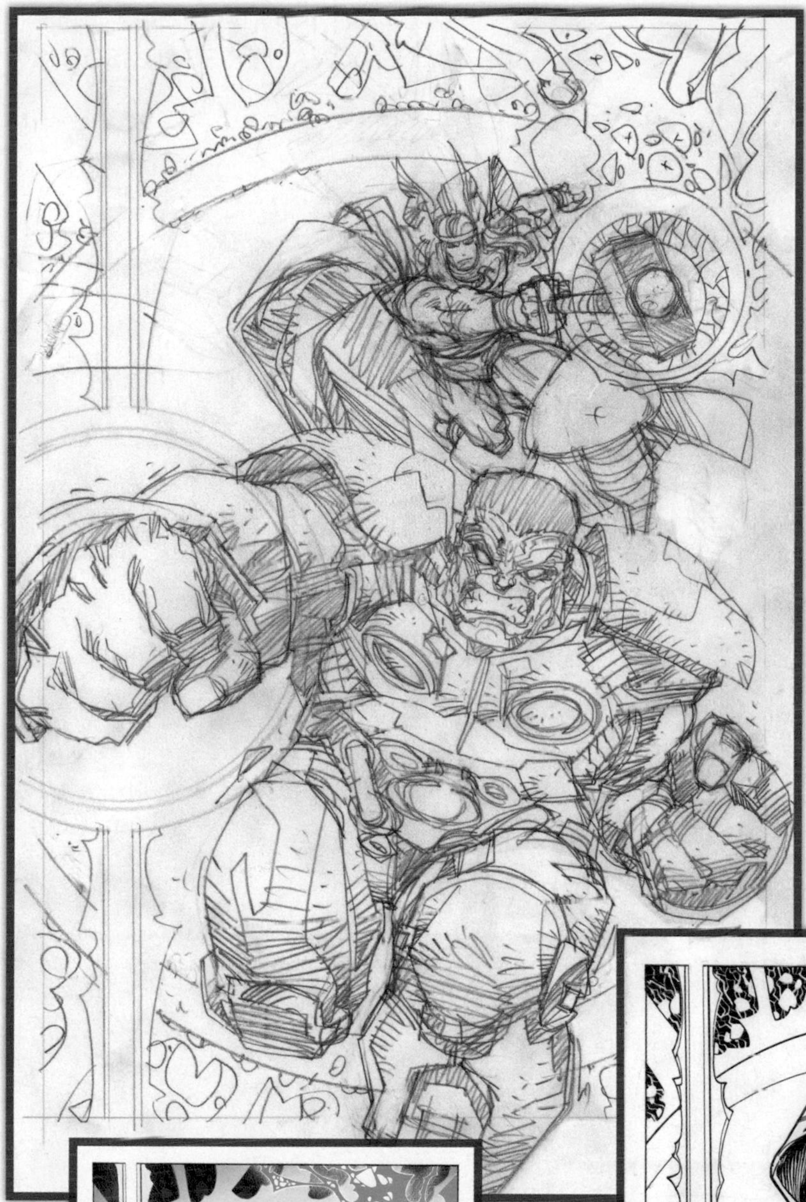

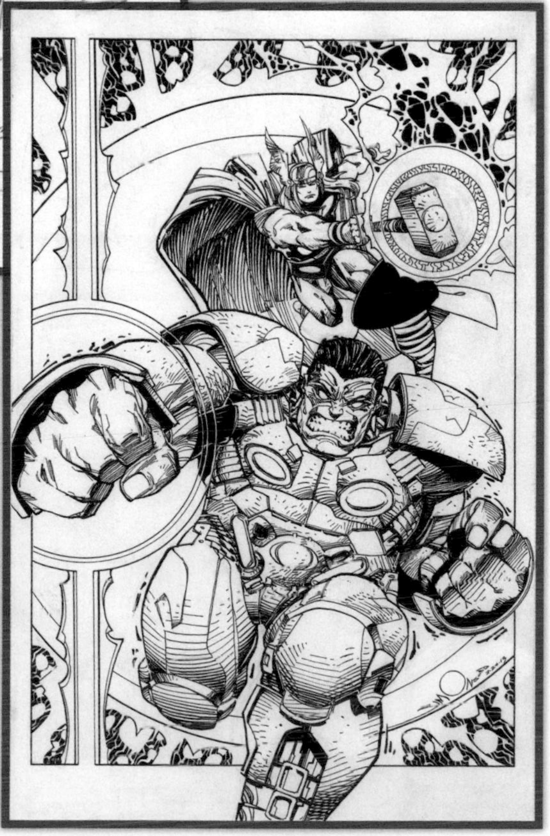

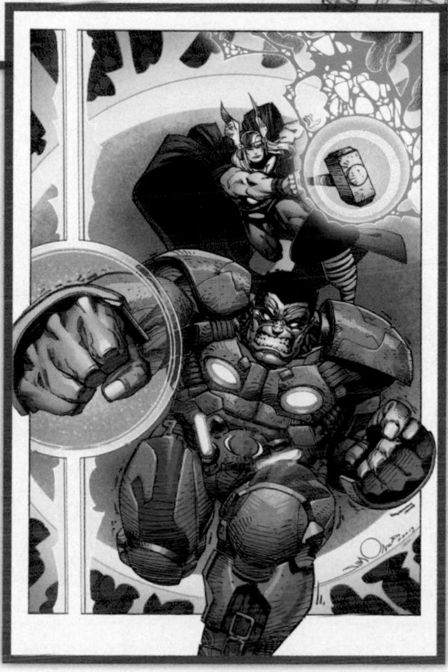

ISSUE #8 COVER PROCESS BY WALTER SIMONSON & LAURA MARTIN

ART PROCESS
BY WALTER SIMONSON

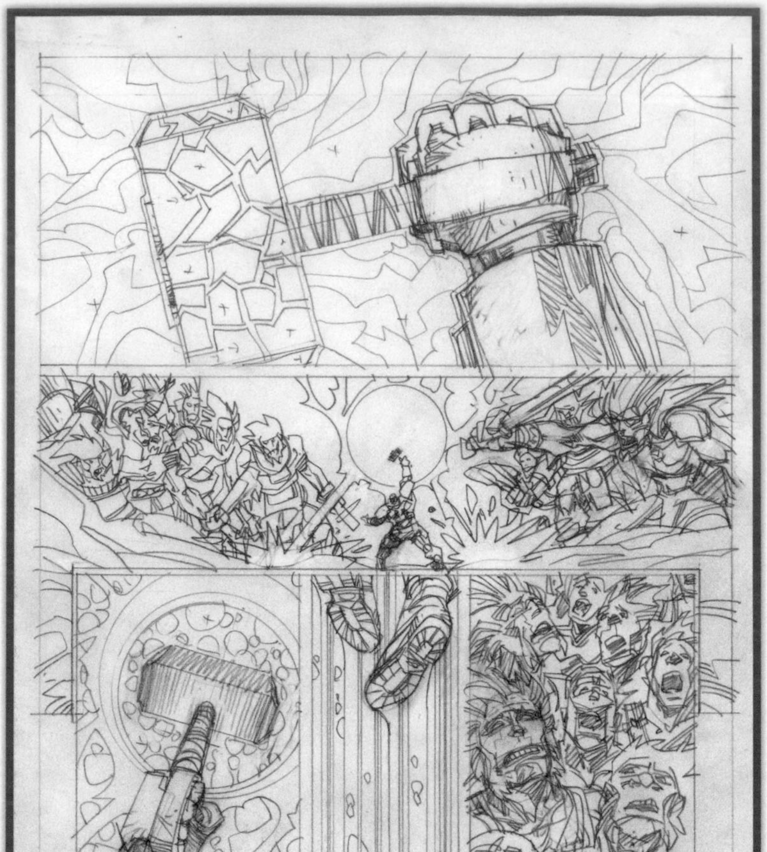

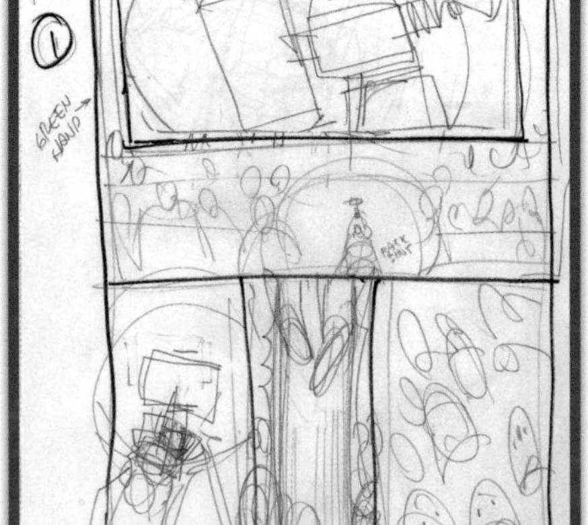
GREEN HAND
BACK SHOT
HULK LIFTS OFF

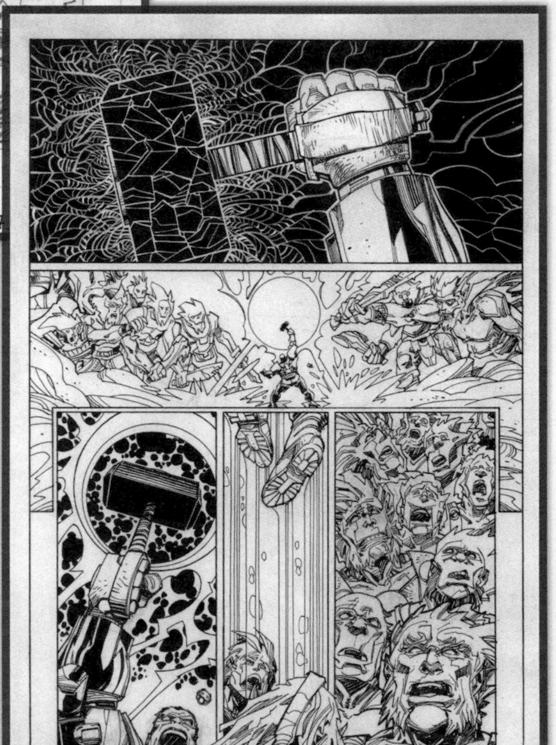
HULK 7/PG 1

#7, PAGE 1

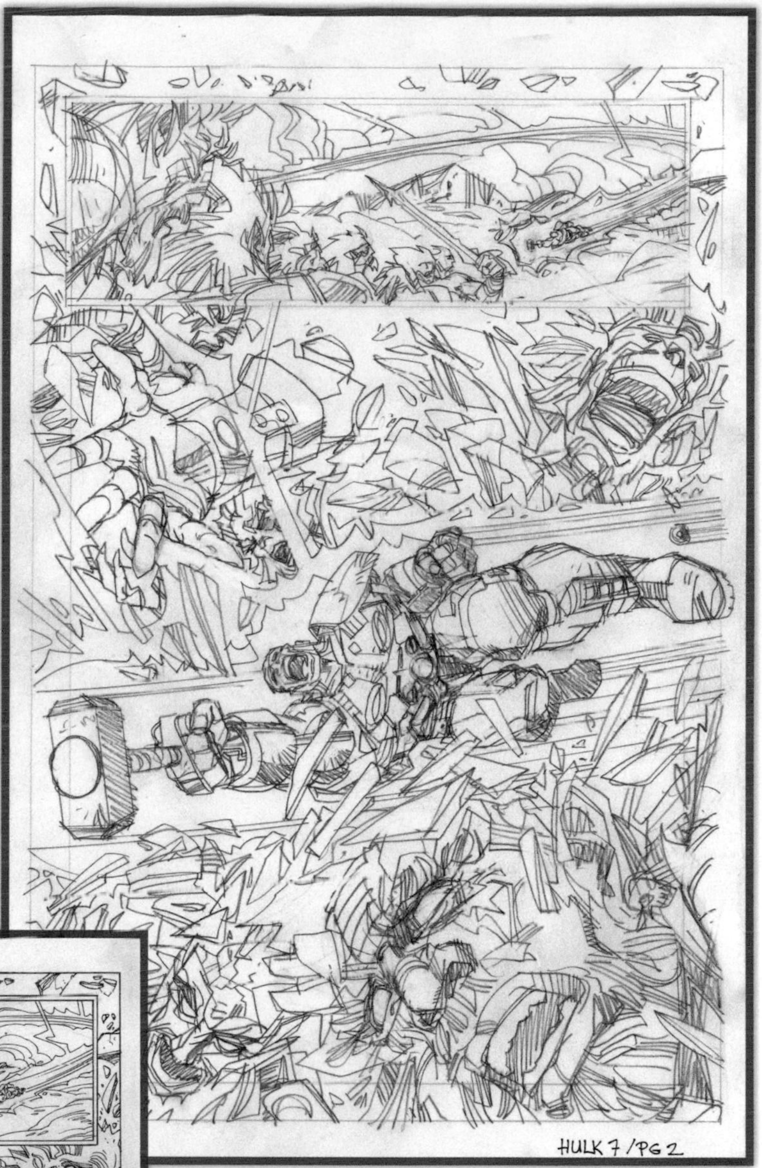
HULK 7 /PG 2

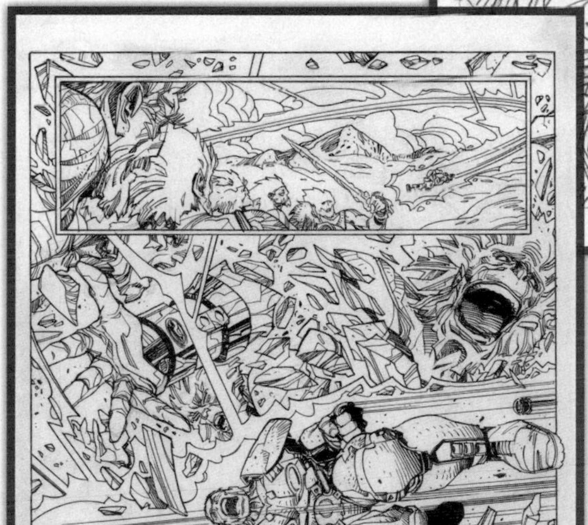
HULK 7 /PG 2

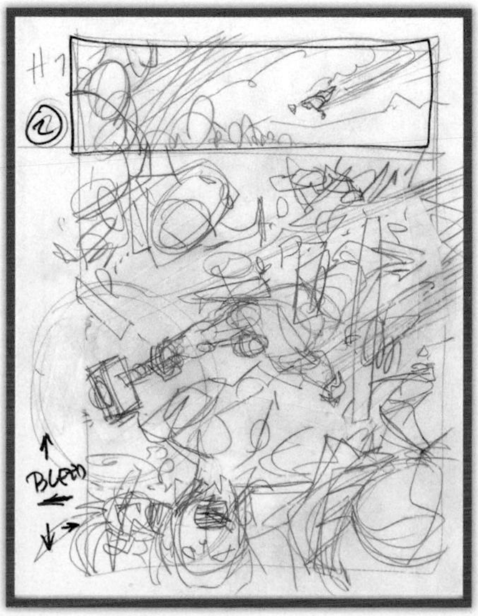

#7, PAGE 2

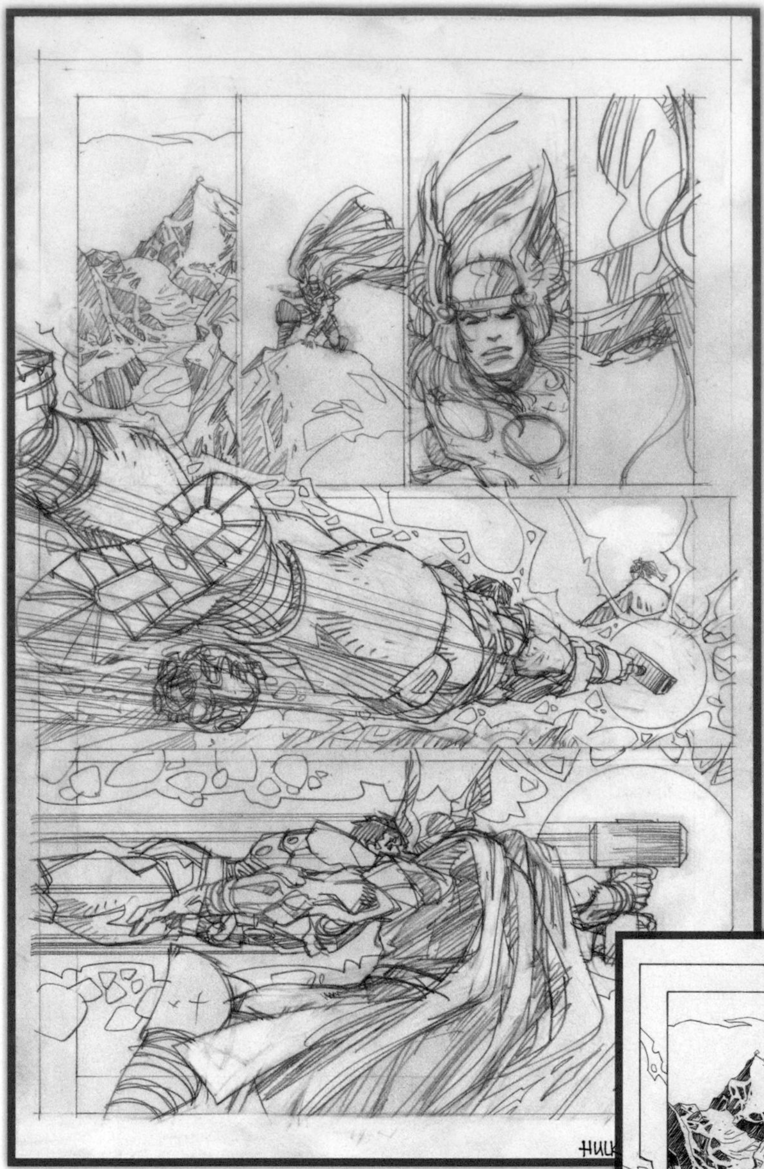
HULK

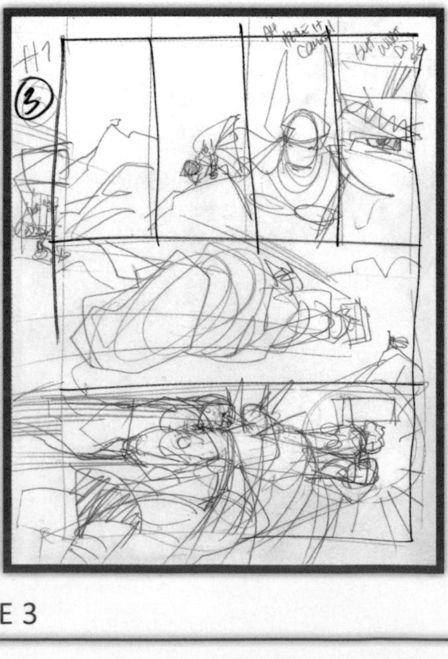
#7
3

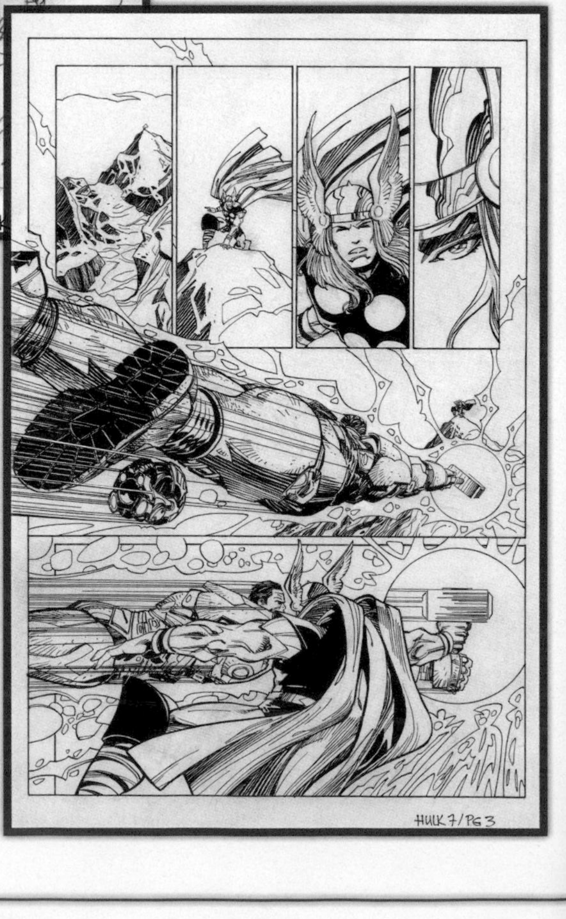
HULK 7/PG 3

#7, PAGE 3

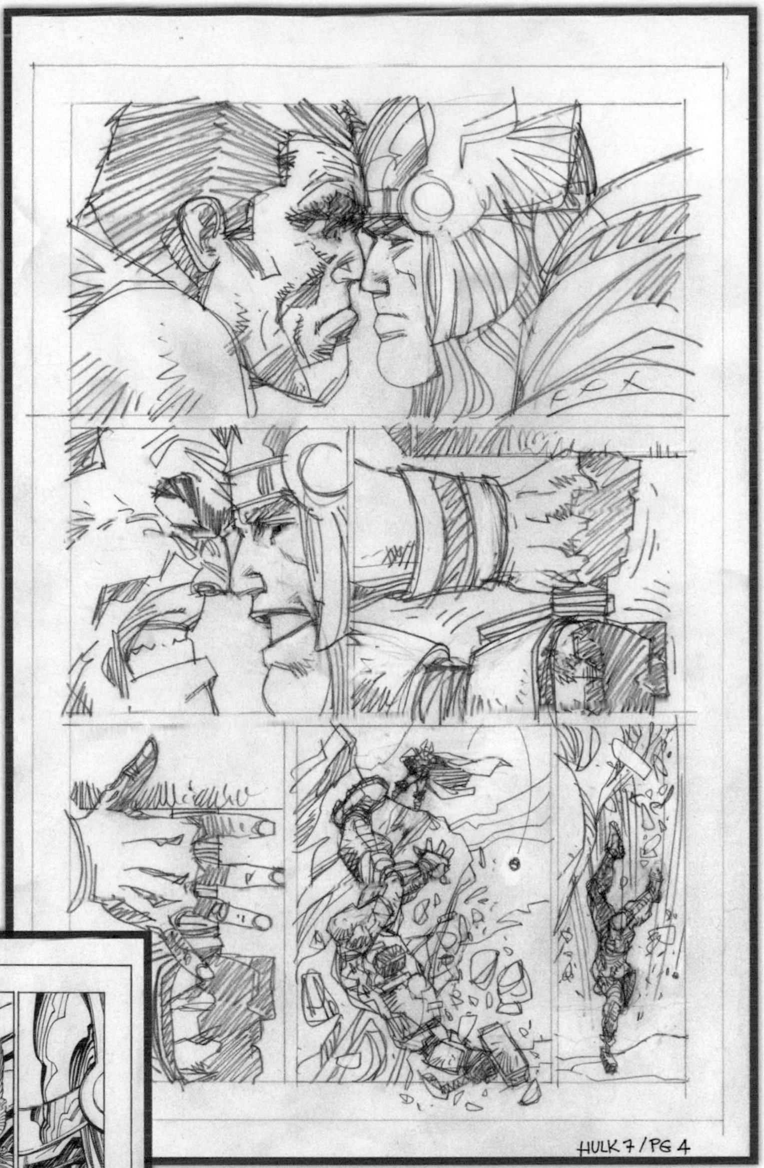
HULK 7/PG 4

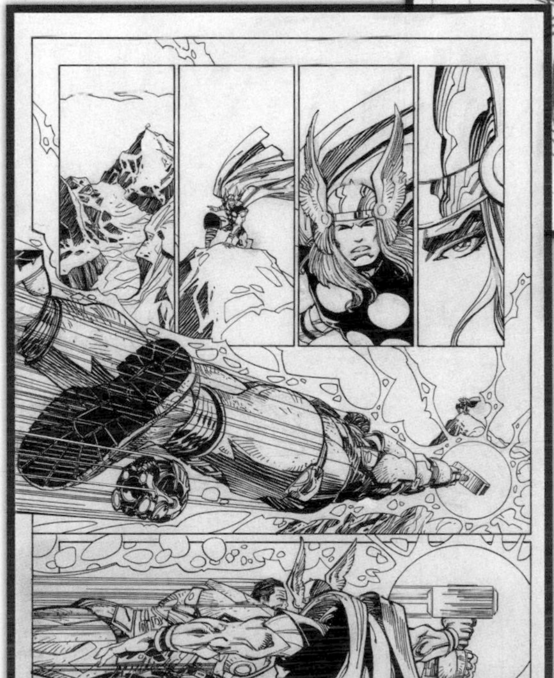
HULK 7/PG 3

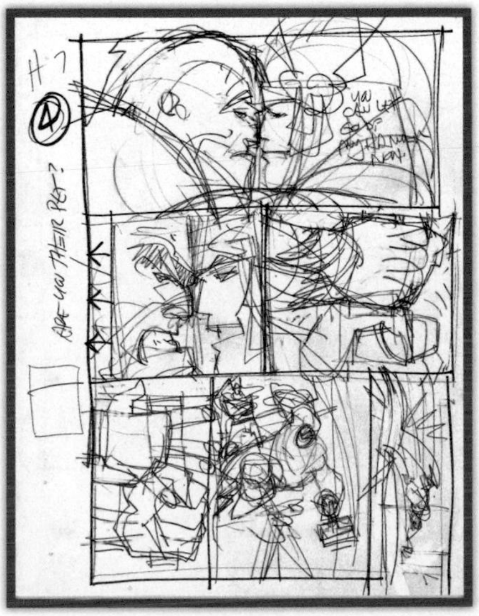
#7
ARE YOU THEIR PET?

#7, PAGE 4

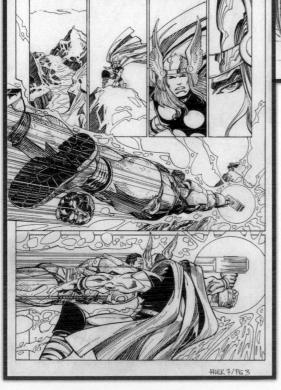

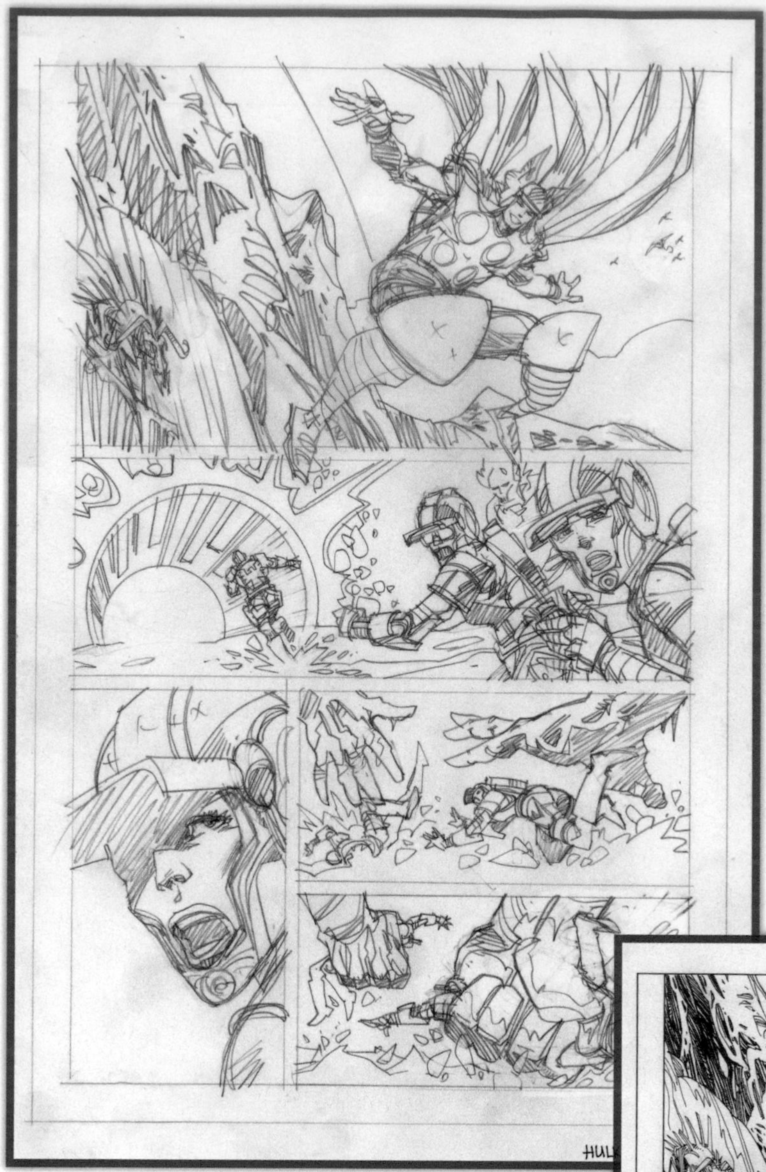
HULK

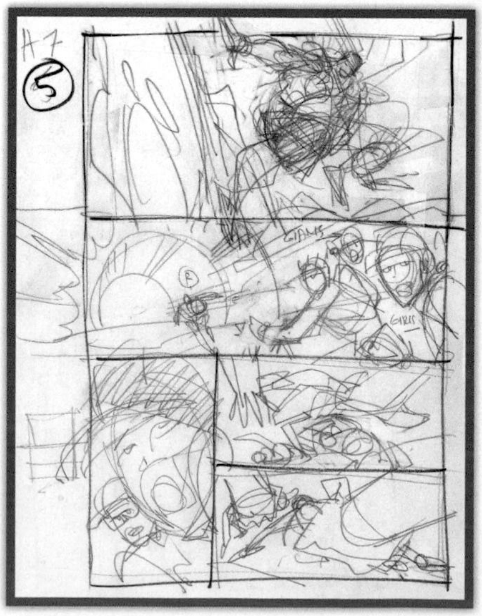
#7
5

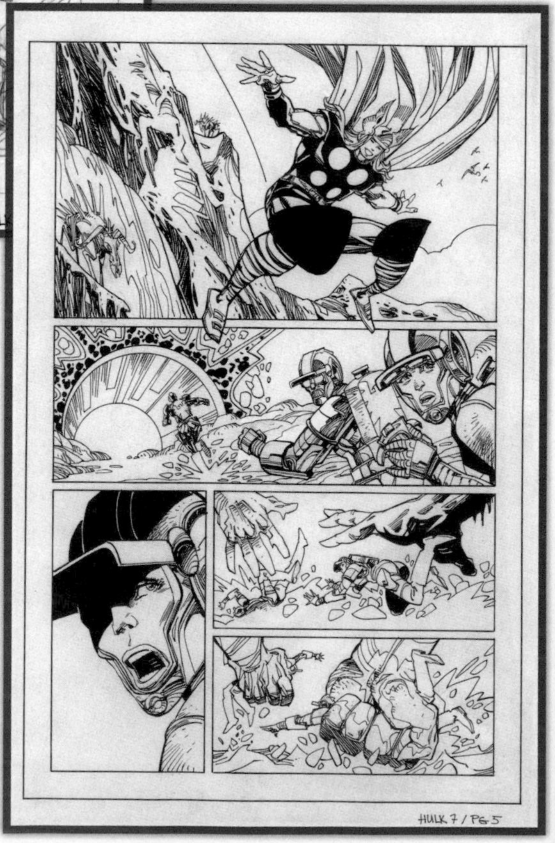
HULK 7 / PG 5

#7, PAGE 5

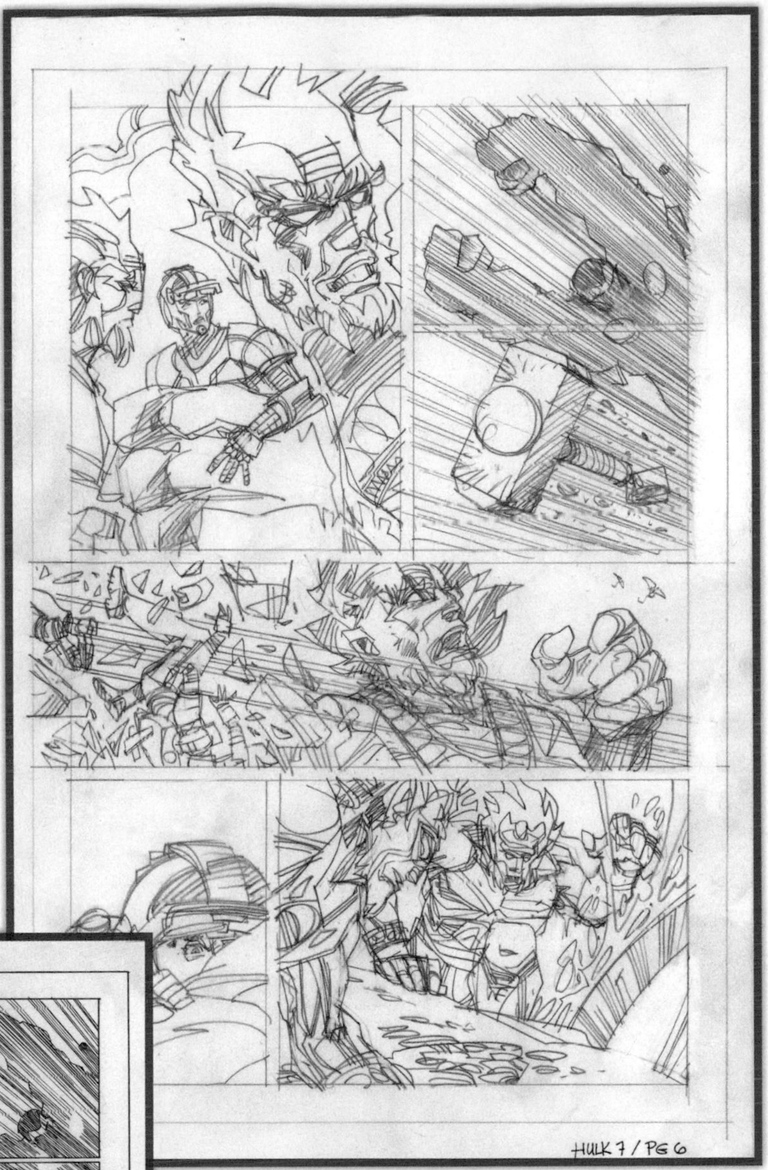
HULK 7 / PG 6

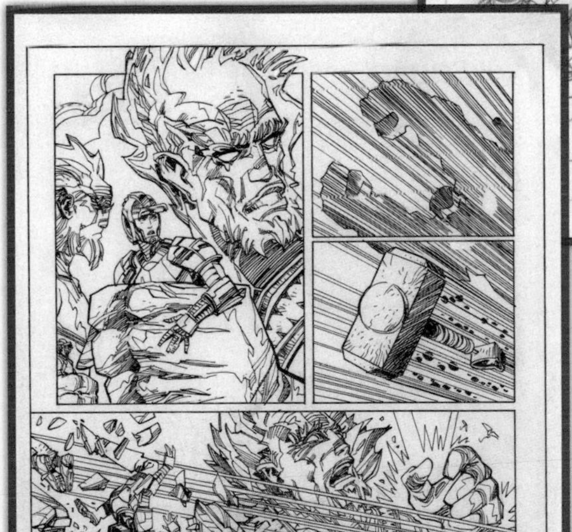
HULK 7 / PG 6

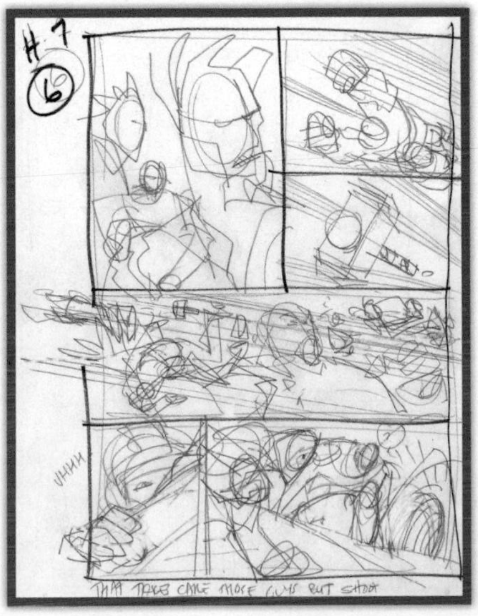
H 7
6

#7, PAGE 6

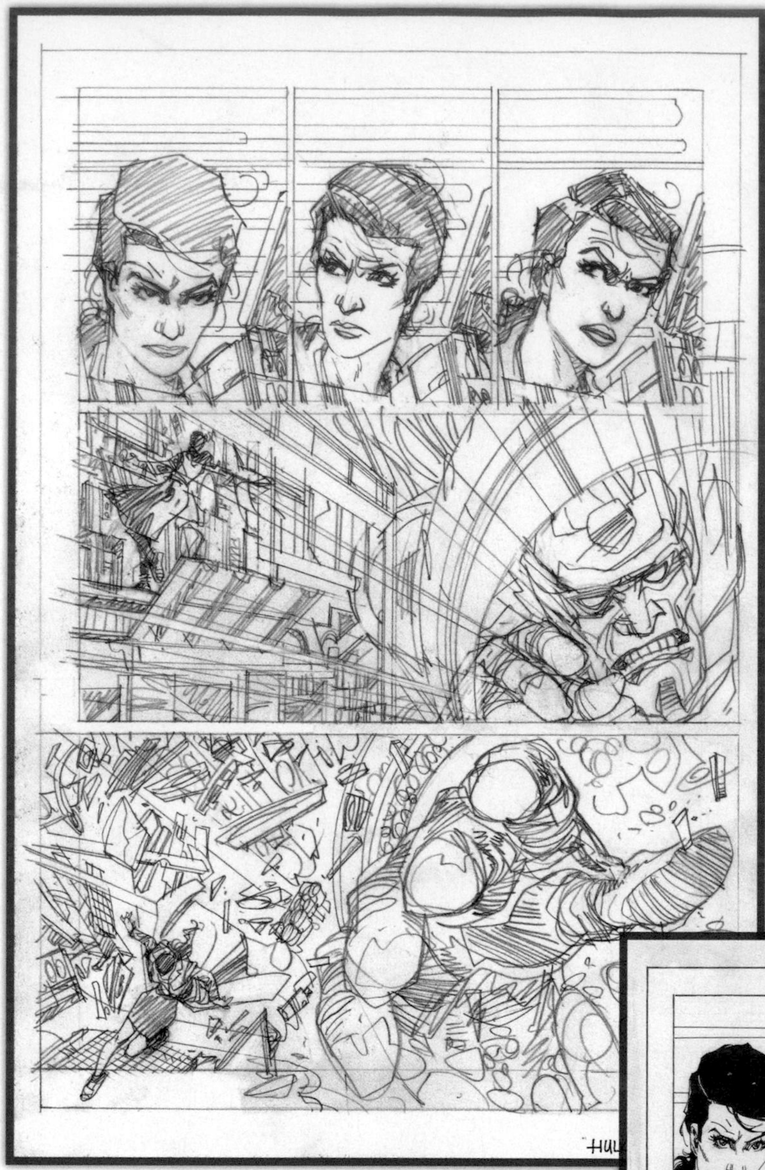

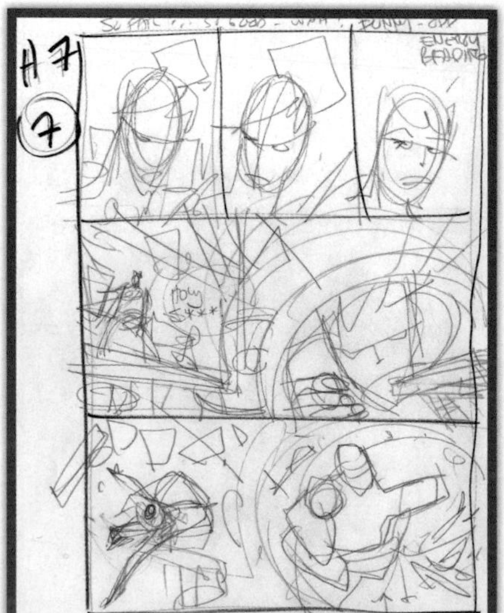

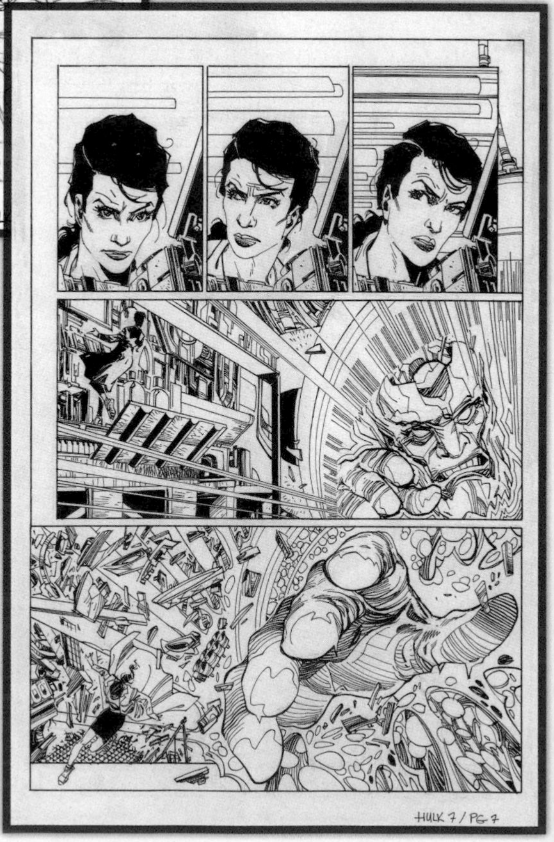
HULK 7 / PG 7

#7, PAGE 7

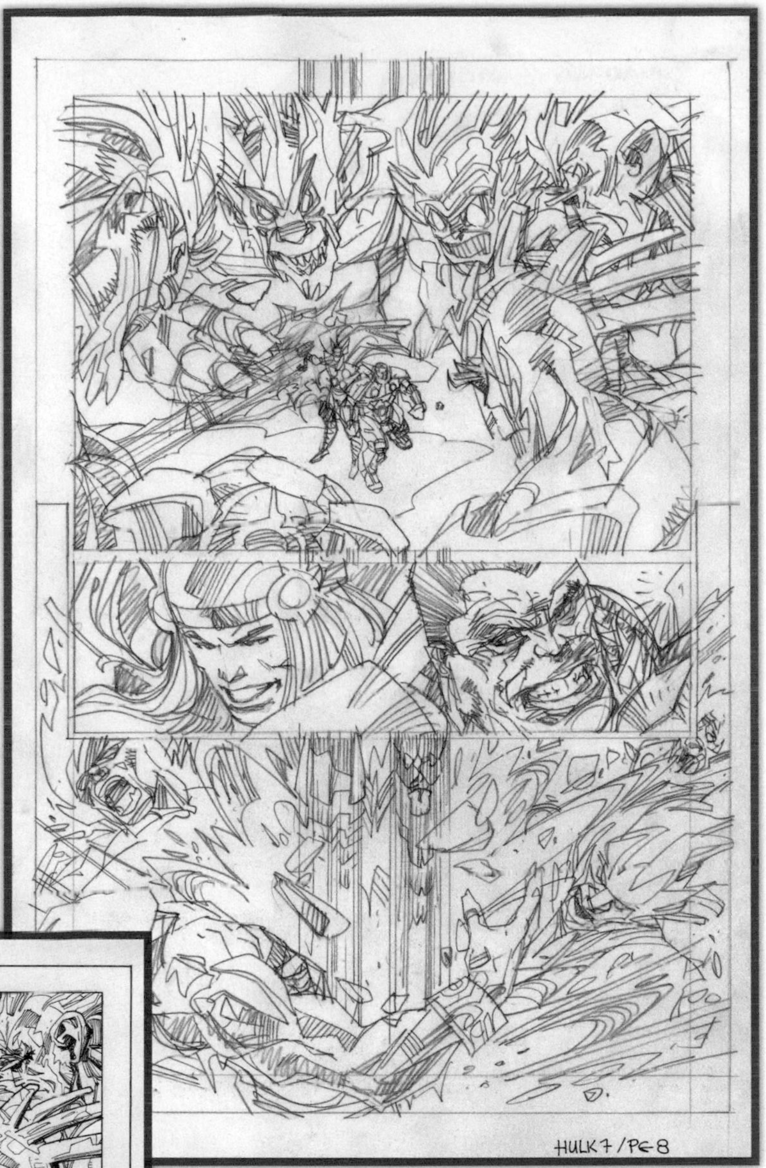
HULK7/PG-8

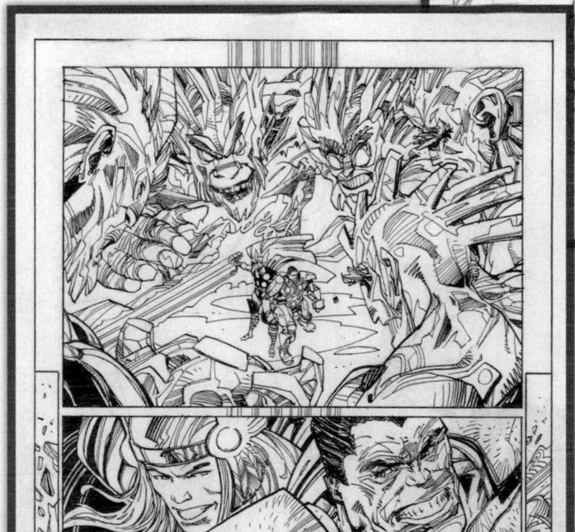
HULK7/PG-8

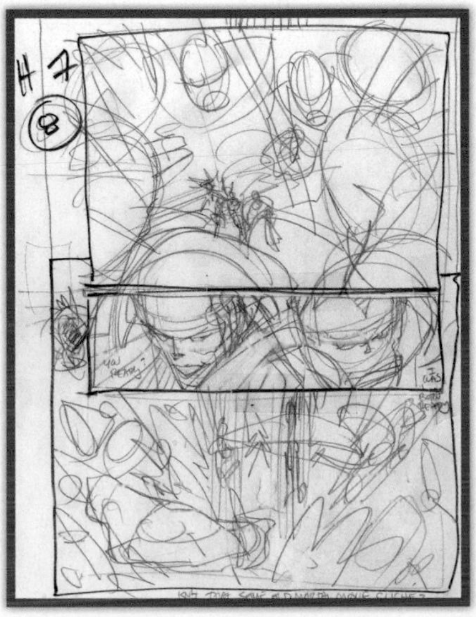
#7
8

#7, PAGE 8

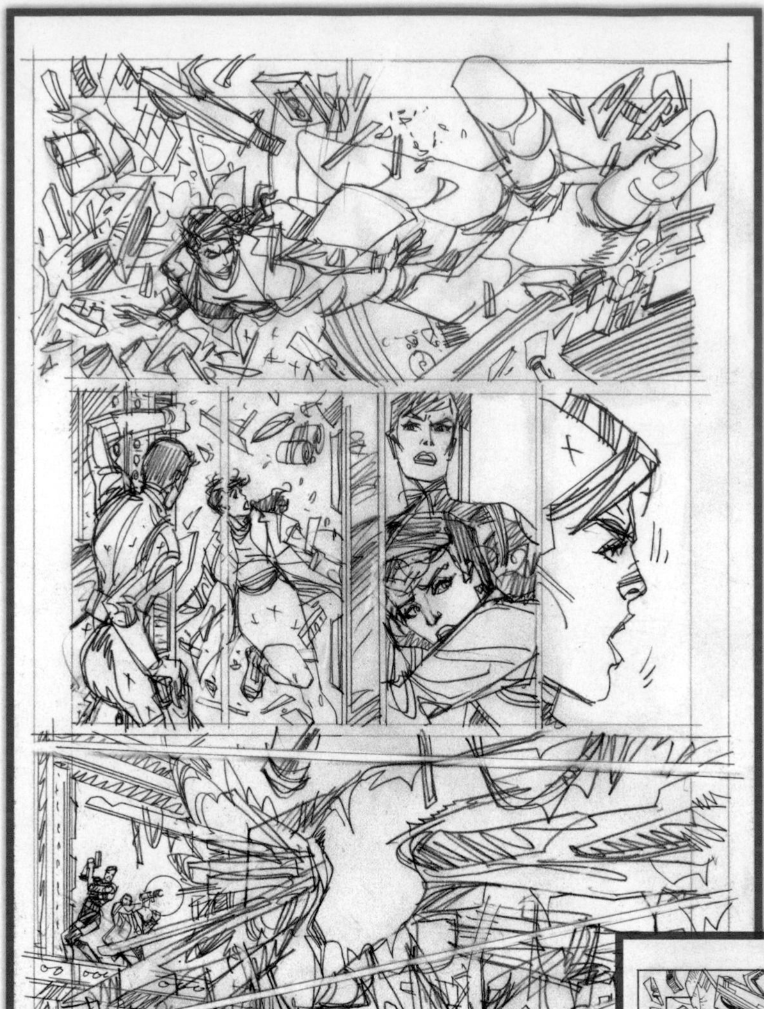
HULK

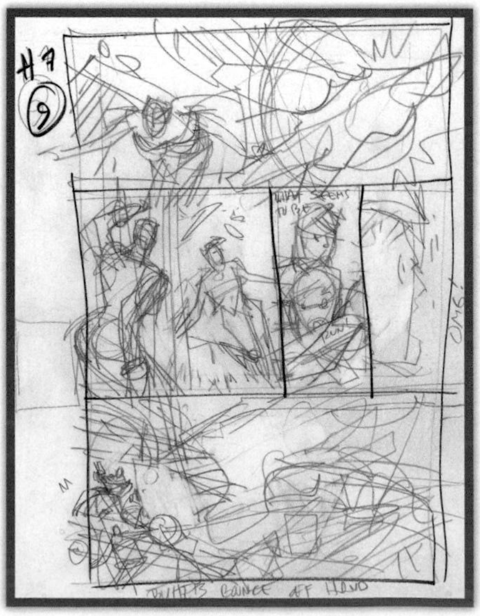
#7
9
RUN!
OMG!

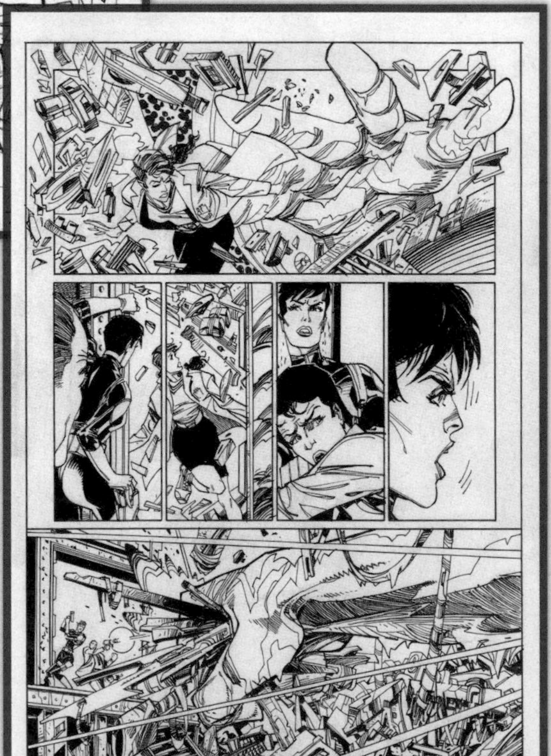
HULK 7/PG 9

#7, PAGE 9

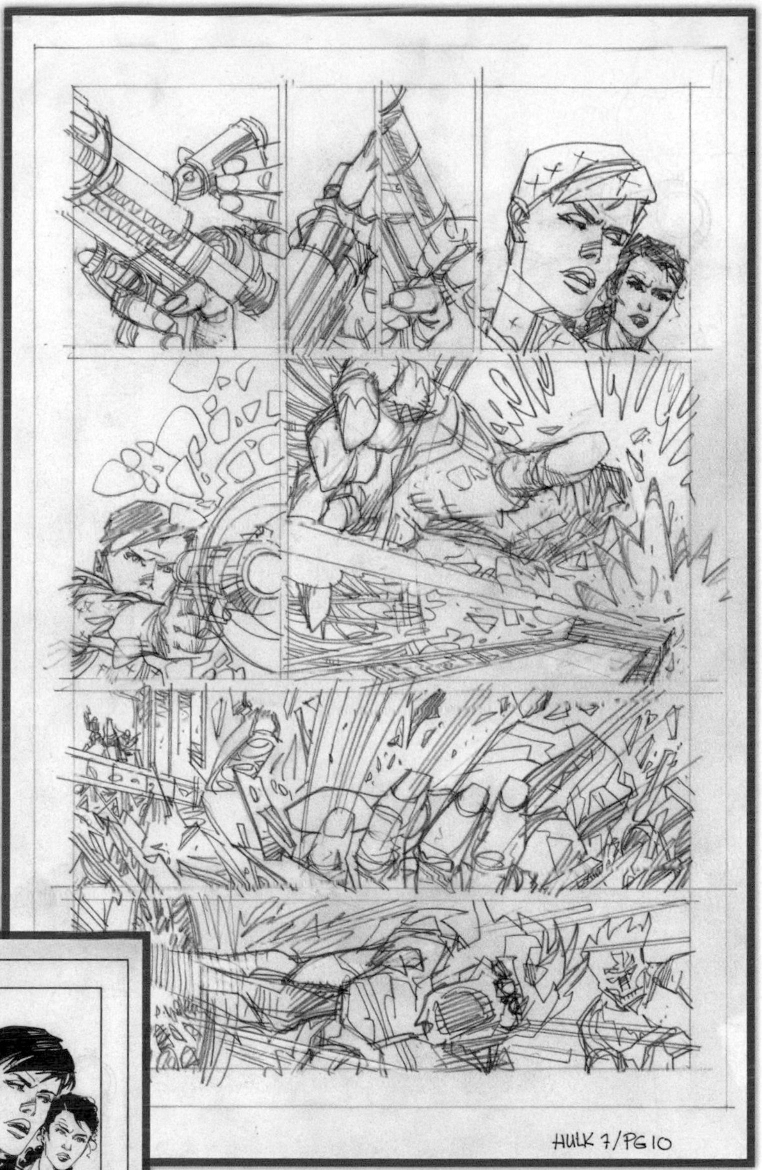
HULK 7/PG10

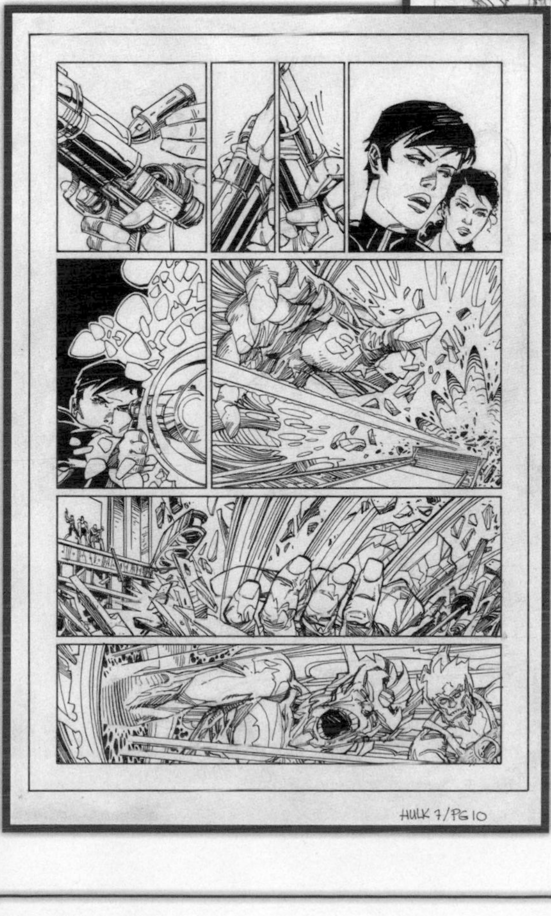
HULK 7/PG10

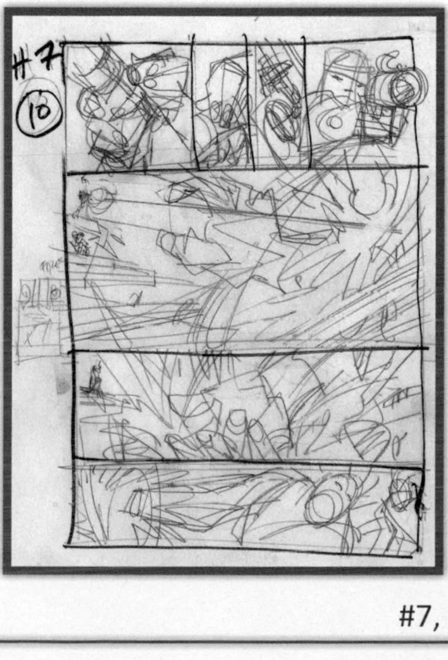
#7
10

#7, PAGE 10

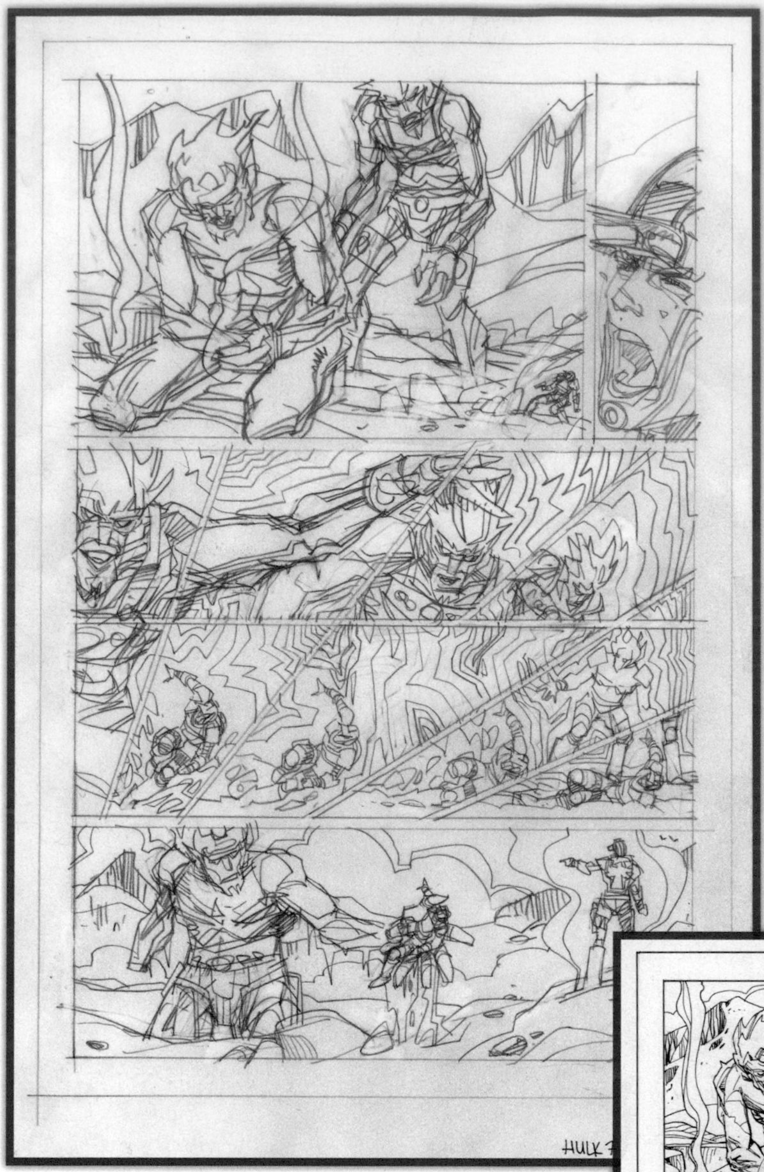
HULK

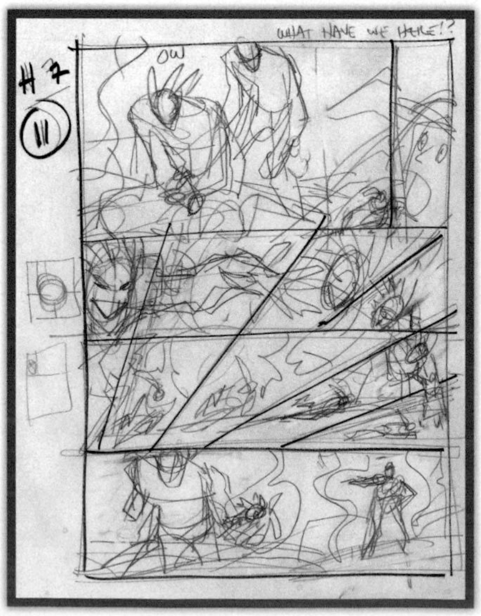
WHAT HAVE WE HERE!?
#7
11
OW

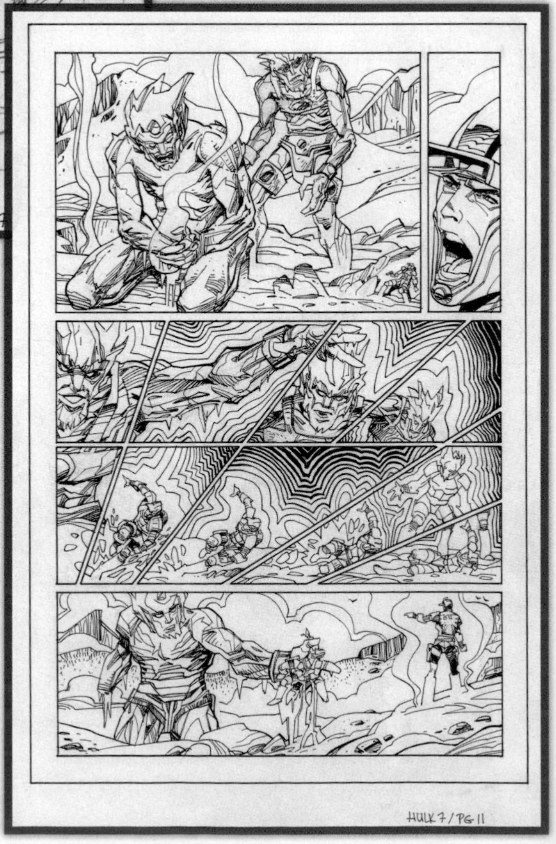
HULK 7/PG 11

#7, PAGE 11

ART PROCESS
BY MATTEO SCALERA

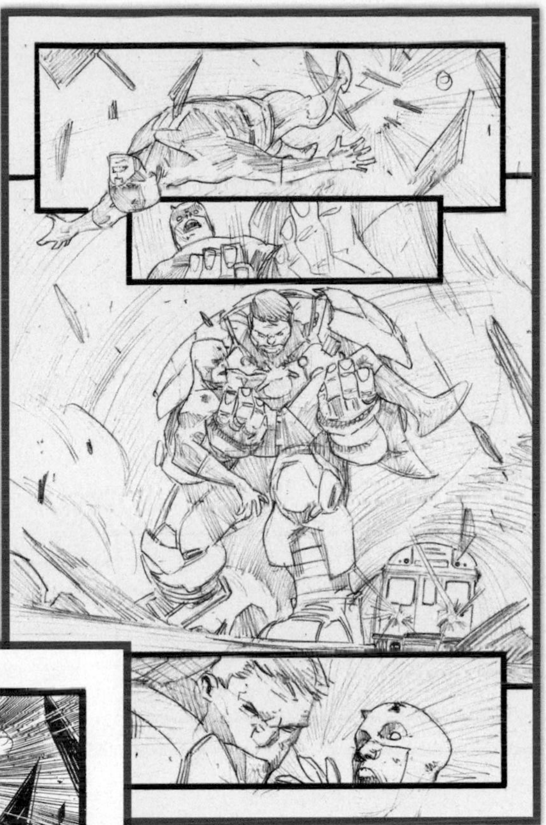

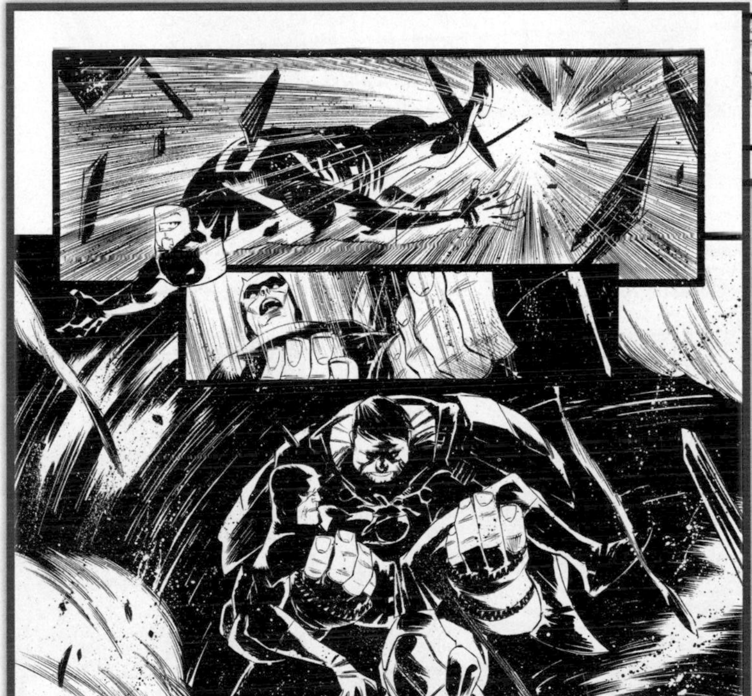

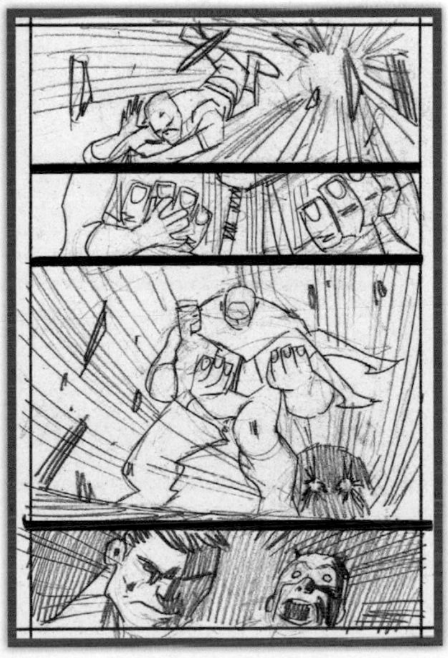

#10, PAGE 1

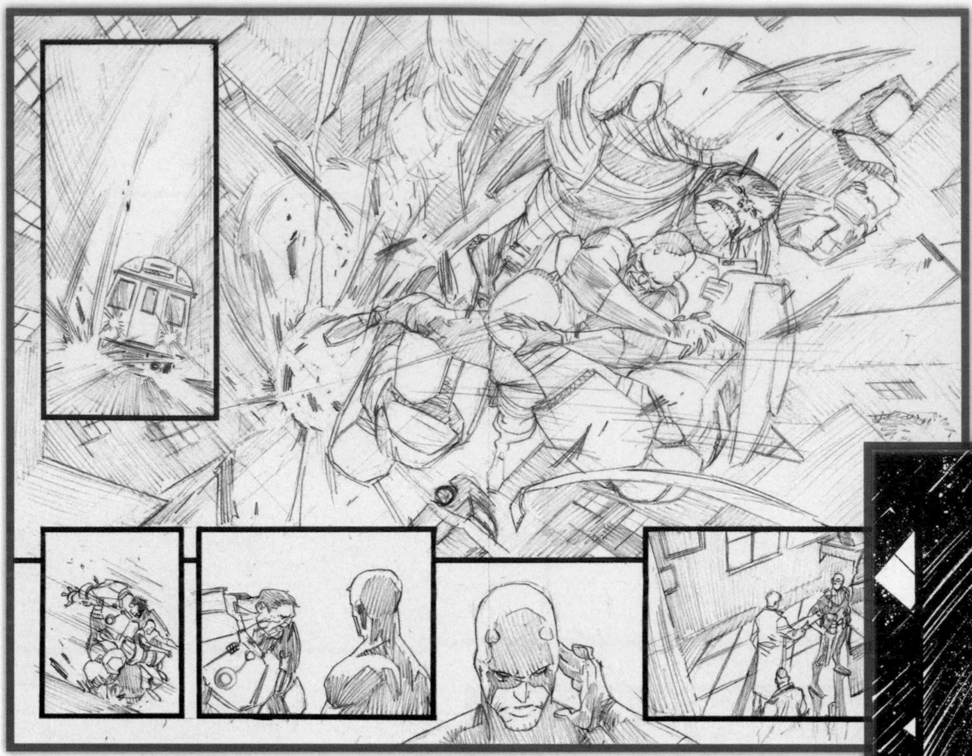

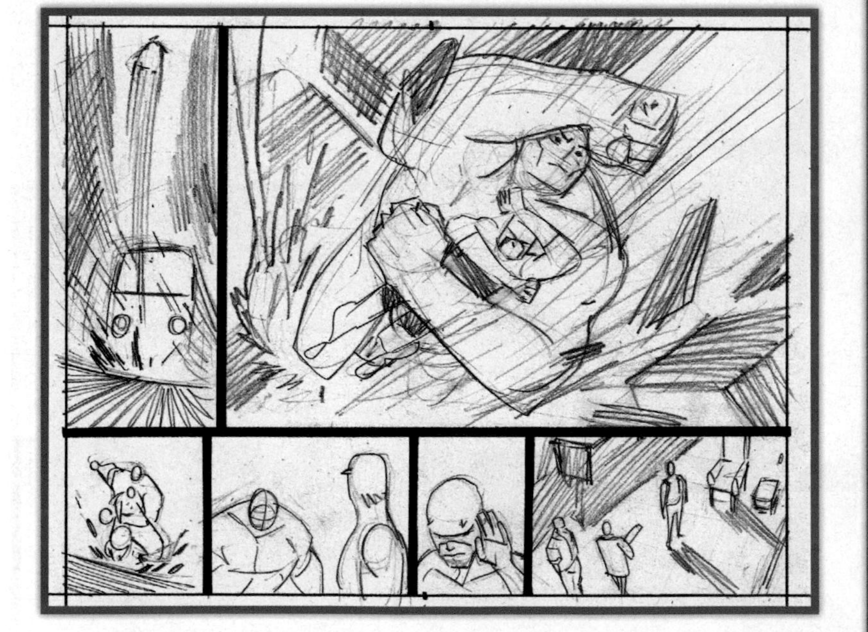

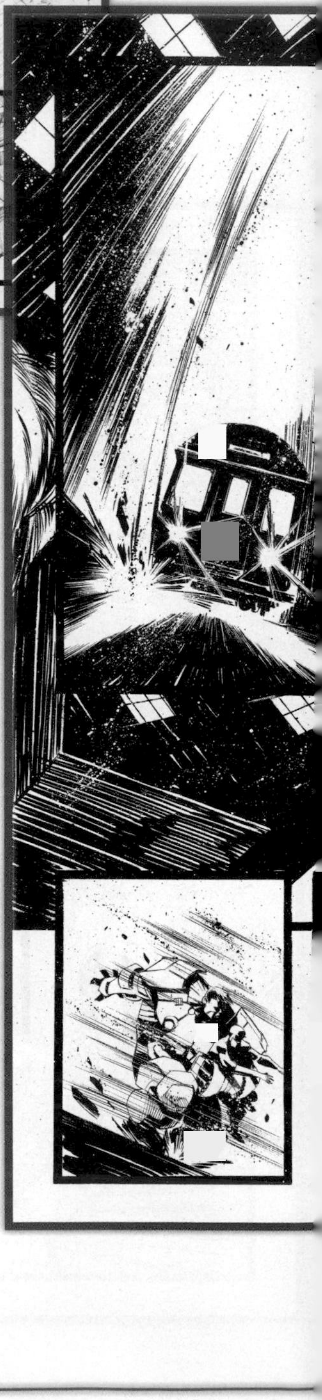

#10, PAGES 2-3

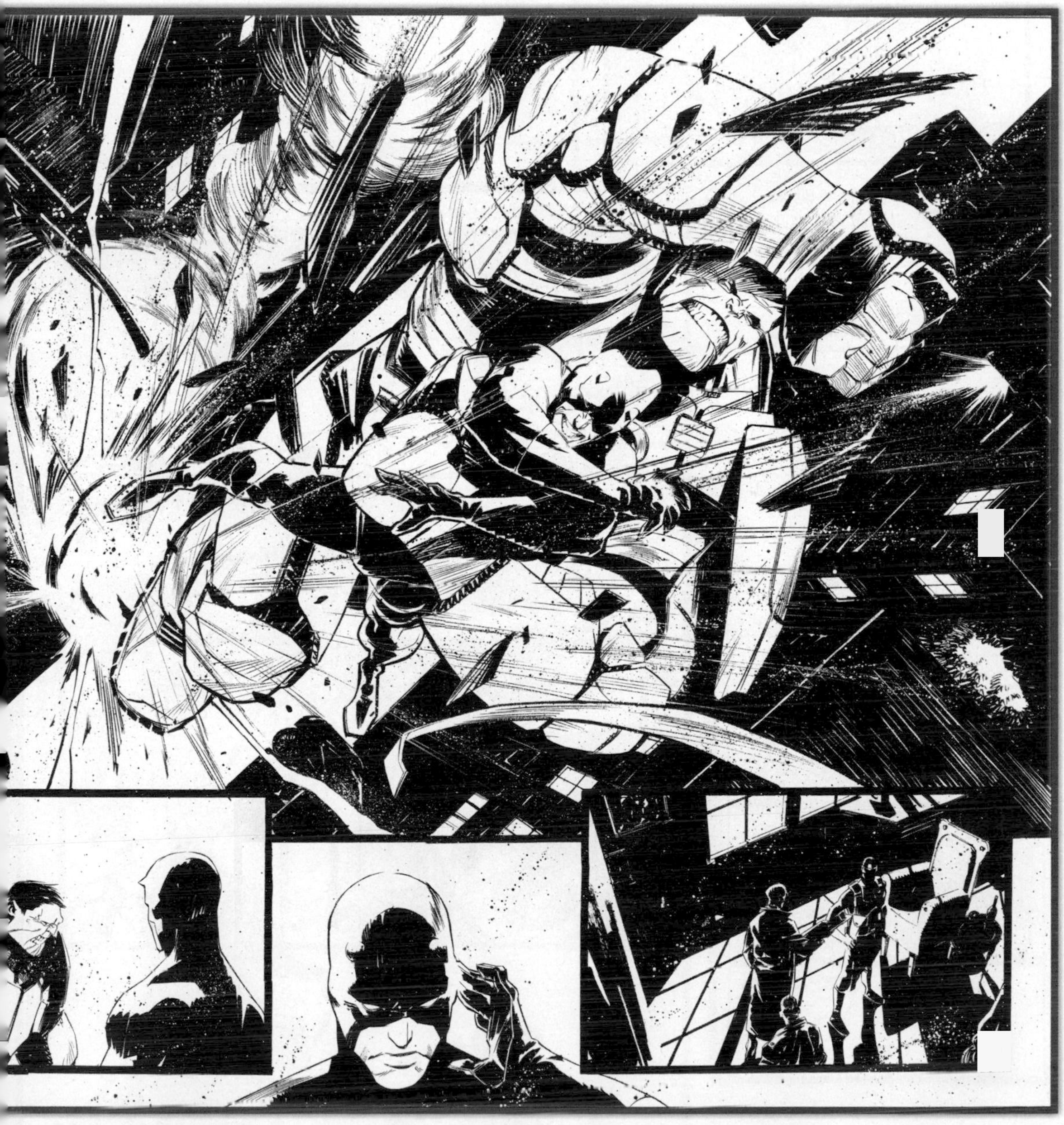

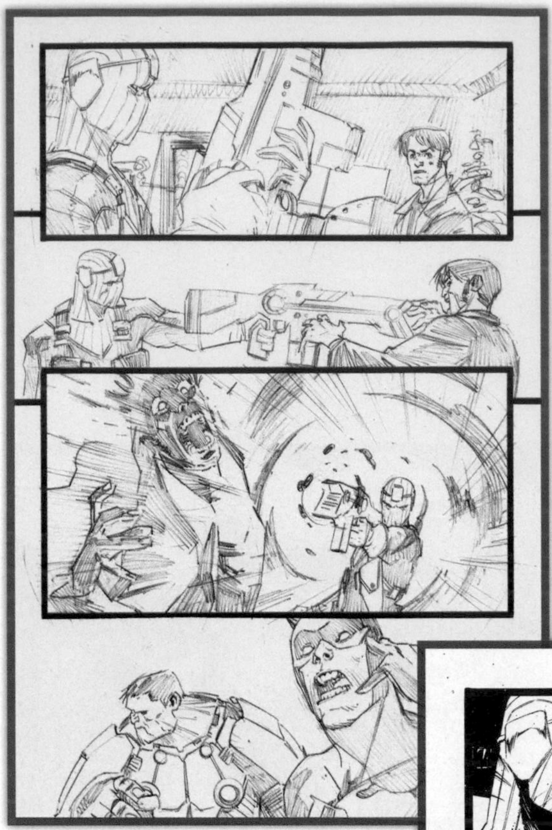

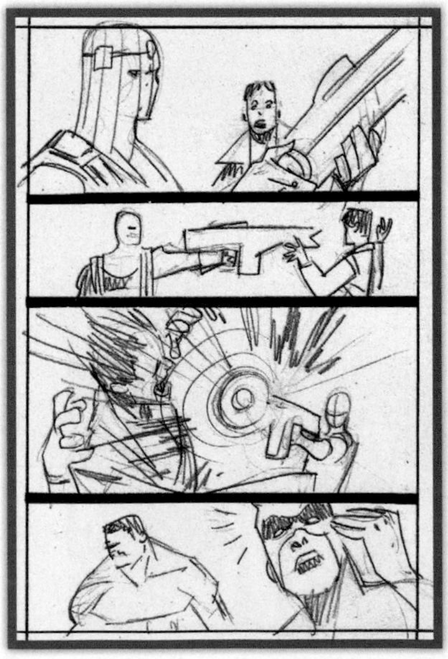

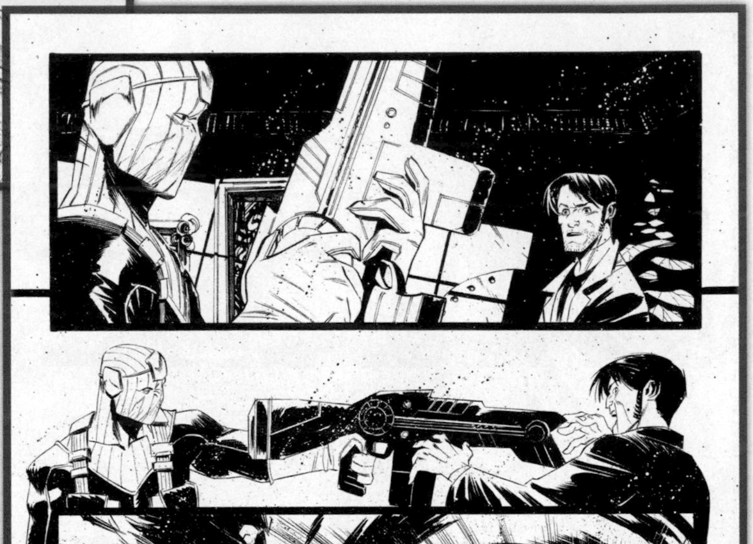

#10, PAGE 4

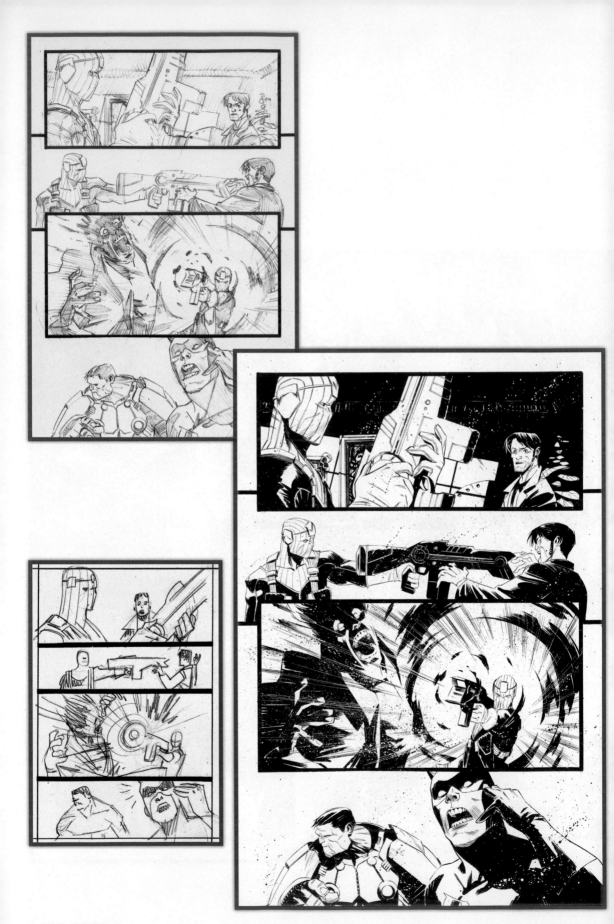

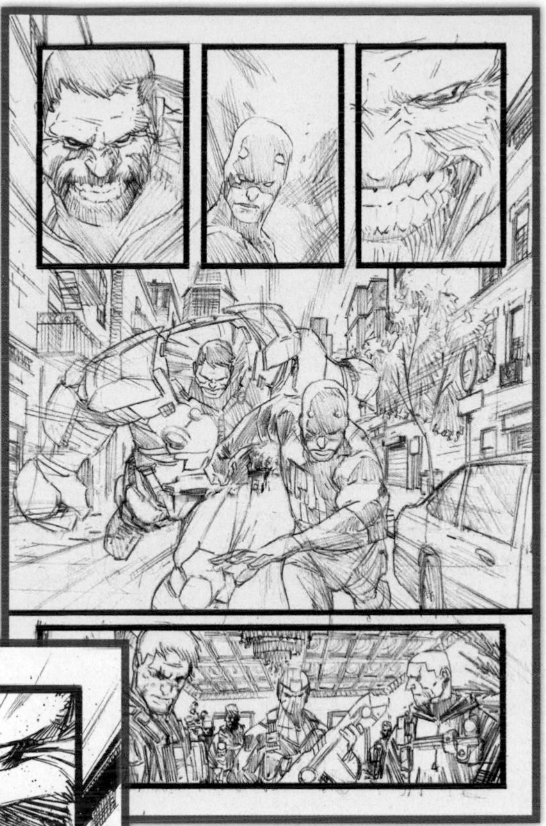

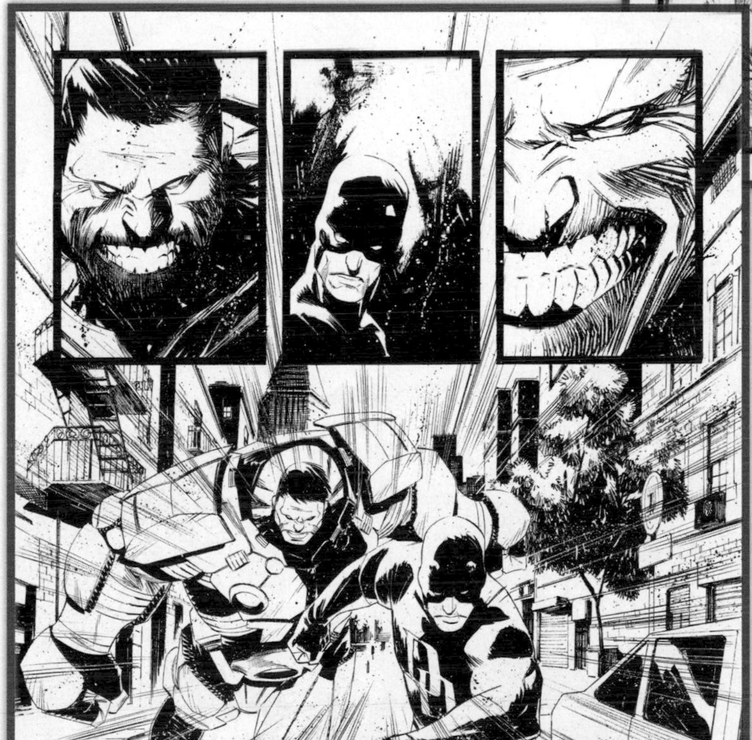

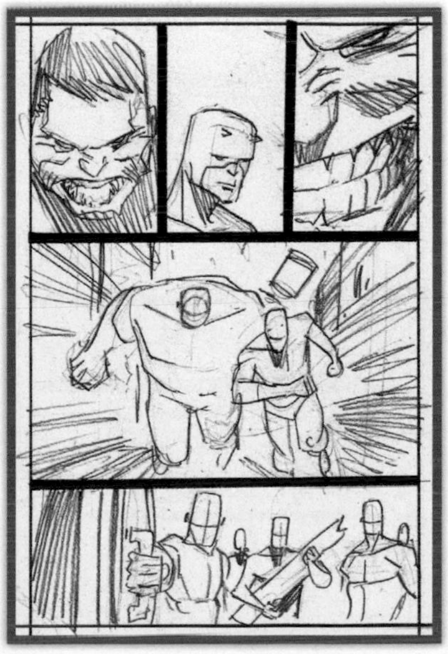

#10, PAGE 5

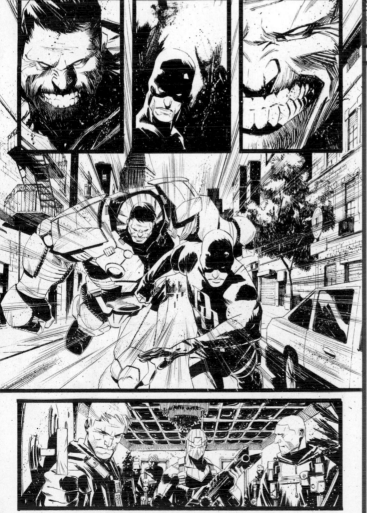

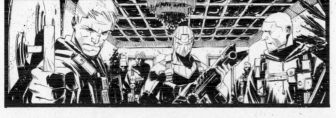

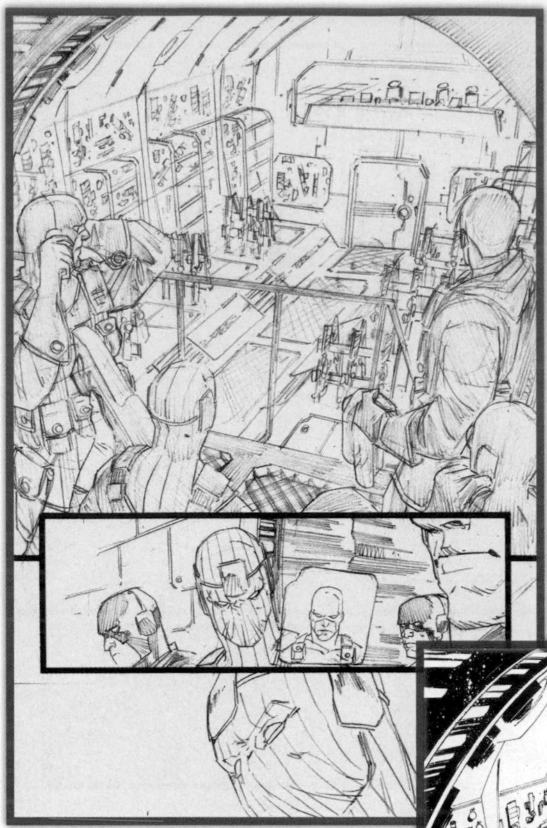

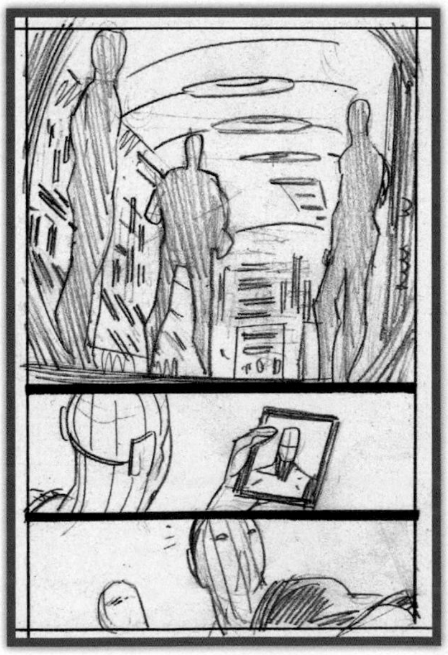

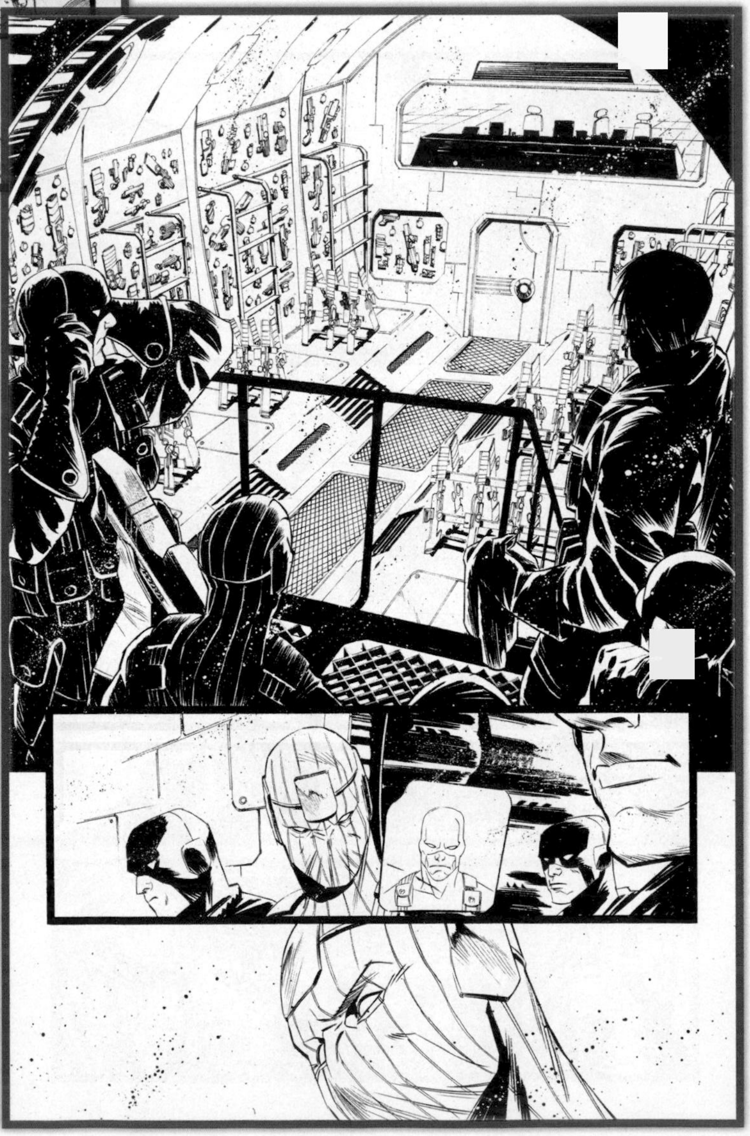

#10, PAGE 6

#10, PAGE 7

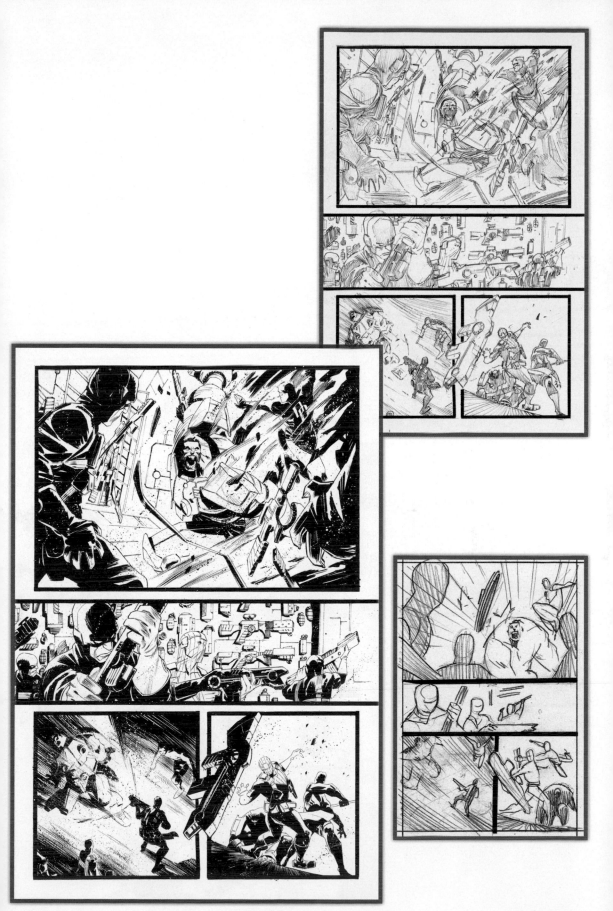

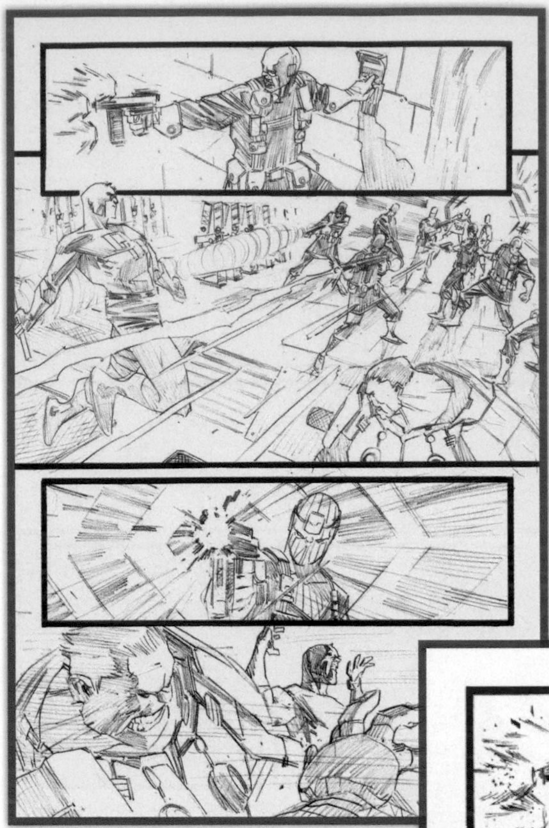

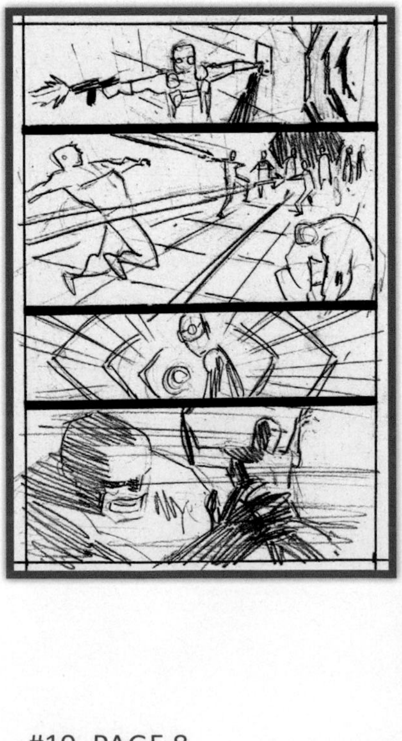

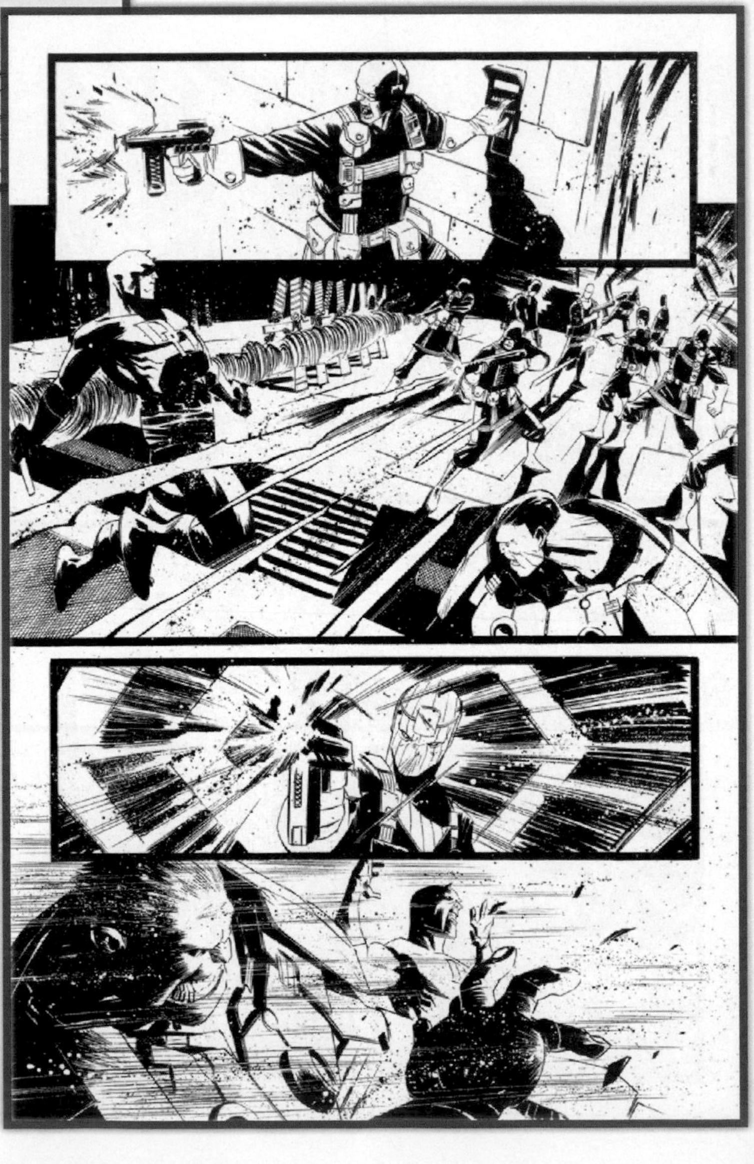

#10, PAGE 8

#10, PAGE 9

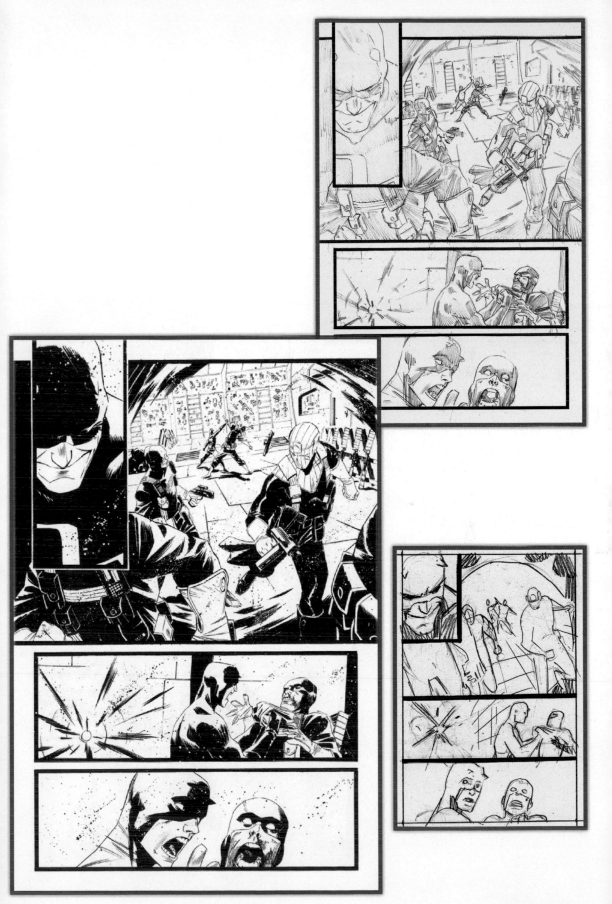

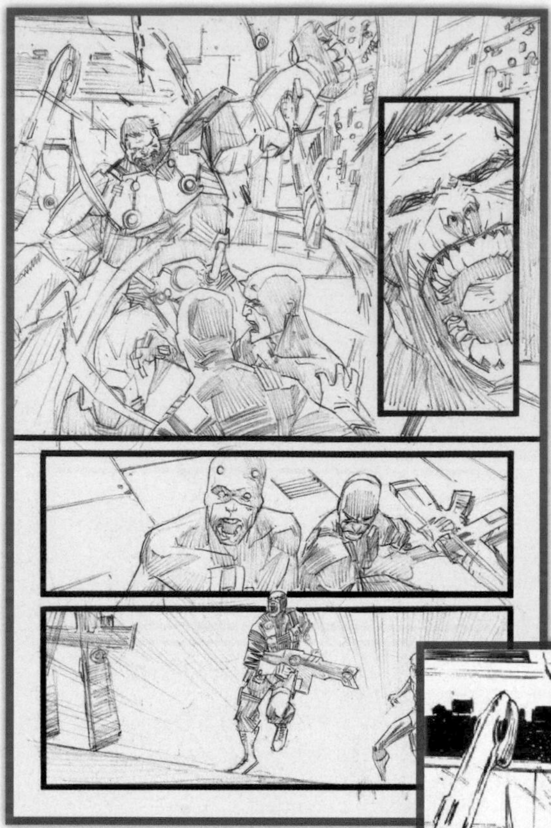

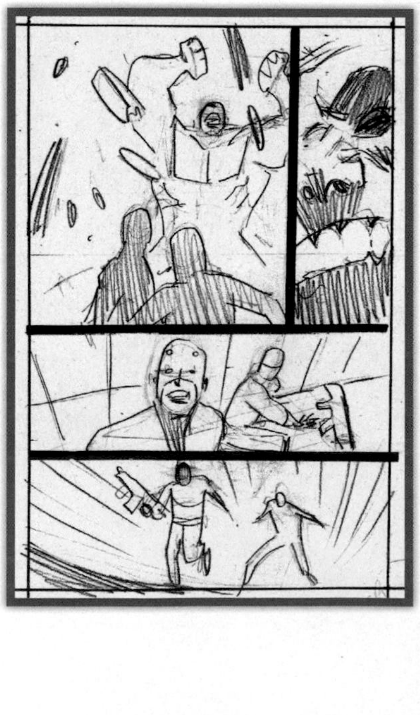

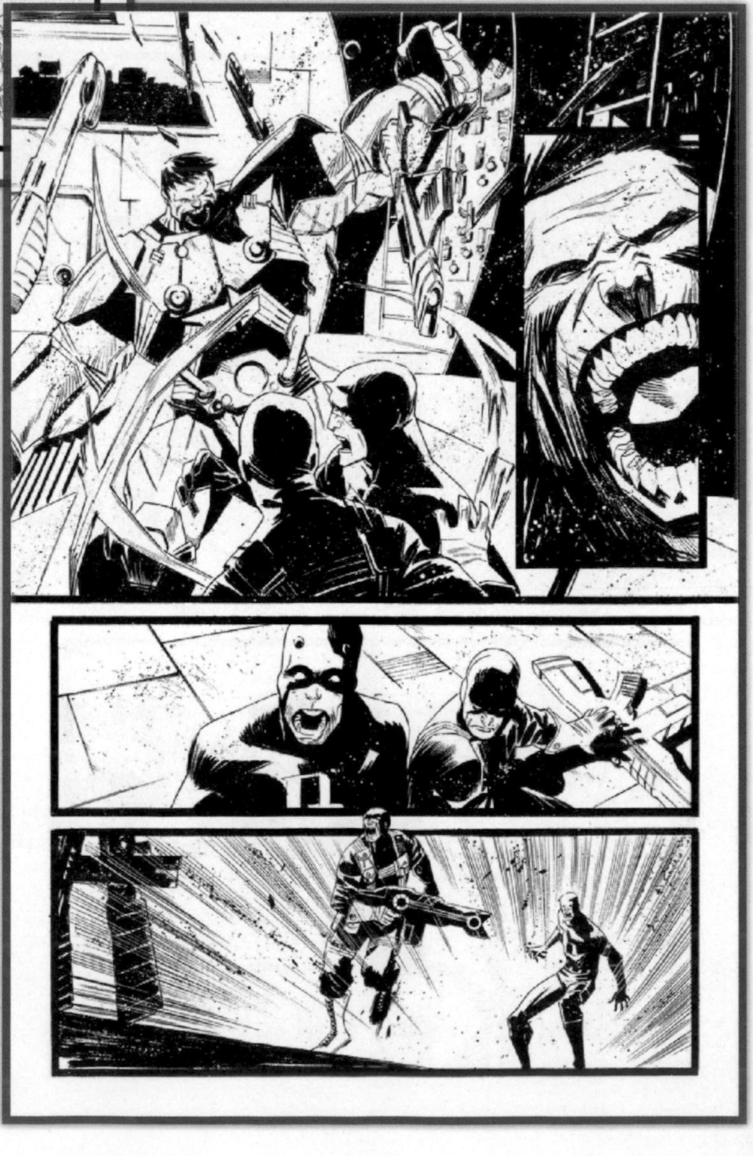

#10, PAGE 10

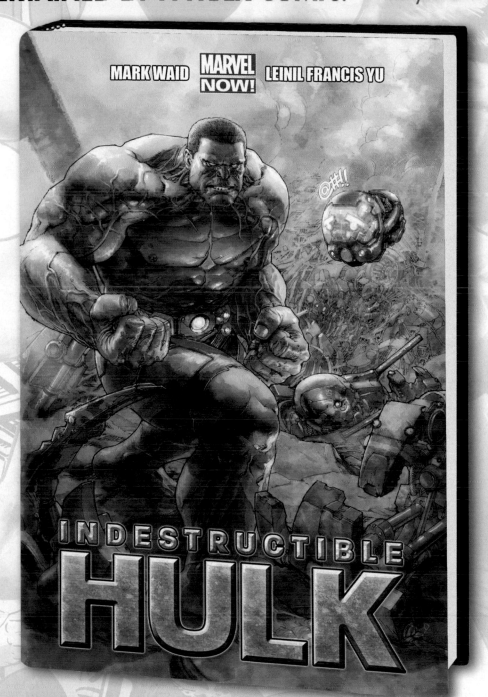

TO ACCESS THE FREE *MARVEL AUGMENTED REALITY APP* THAT ENHANCES AND CHANGES THE WAY YOU EXPERIENCE COMICS:

1. **Download the app for free via** marvel.com/ARapp
2. **Launch the app on your camera-enabled Apple iOS® or Android™ device***
3. **Hold your mobile device's camera over** any cover or panel with the **AR** graphic
4. **Sit back and see the future of comics in action!**

*Available on most camera-enabled Apple iOS® and Android™ devices. Content subject to change and availability.

INDESTRUCTIBLE HULK AR INDEX

TO REDEEM YOUR CODE FOR A FREE DIGITAL COPY:

1. GO TO MARVEL.COM/REDEEM. OFFER EXPIRES ON 9/11/15.
2. FOLLOW THE ON-SCREEN INSTRUCTIONS TO REDEEM YOUR DIGITAL COPY.
3. LAUNCH THE MARVEL COMICS APP TO READ YOUR COMIC NOW!
4. YOUR DIGITAL COPY WILL BE FOUND UNDER THE *MY COMICS* TAB.
5. READ & ENJOY!

YOUR FREE DIGITAL COPY WILL BE AVAILABLE ON:

MARVEL COMICS APP FOR APPLE® iOS DEVICES	MARVEL COMICS APP FOR ANDROID™ DEVICES